PW

WITHDRAWN

QUANTITATIVE
SOCIAL SCIENCE RESEARCH
ON LATIN AMERICA

CENTER FOR LATIN AMERICAN
AND CARIBBEAN STUDIES

Number 1

Published in conjunction with the

OFFICE OF INTERNATIONAL
PROGRAMS AND STUDIES

QUANTITATIVE
SOCIAL SCIENCE RESEARCH
ON LATIN AMERICA

Edited by
Robert S. Byars *and* Joseph L. Love

UNIVERSITY OF ILLINOIS PRESS
Urbana   Chicago   London

ACKNOWLEDGMENTS

The editors wish to thank the following persons for their criticism of individual manuscripts appearing in this volume: Stephen A. Douglas, Donald Drapeau, Jaime Litvak, Curtis C. Roseman, and Kenneth E. Southwood. We also thank Alejandro Portes and Karl F. Johnson for their technical advice on the papers. Of course, each author assumes responsibility for errors and weaknesses that still remain in his essay.

Carl W. Deal, Merlin H. Forster, and Robert E. Scott provided essential support throughout the writing and editing; the Center for Latin American Studies and the Center for International Comparative Studies, both of the University of Illinois, generously funded the project that resulted in this volume. Finally, the editors offer special thanks to Dorothy Osborne and Deborah Danby Augelli for their careful preparation of the manuscript's several stages.

Urbana, Illinois   R.S.B.
April, 1973   J.L.L.

Contents

INTRODUCTION   1
   Robert S. Byars and Joseph L. Love

HISTORY   14
   Peter H. Smith

SOCIAL ANTHROPOLOGY   62
   Robert C. Hunt

ARCHAEOLOGY   104
   George L. Cowgill

GEOGRAPHY   132
   Howard L. Gauthier

POLITICAL SCIENCE   162
   Clifford Kaufman

SOCIOLOGY AND THE USE OF SECONDARY DATA   208
   Alejandro Portes

DATA BANK APPENDIX   263

NOTES ON CONTRIBUTORS   271

INTRODUCTION

Robert S. Byars and Joseph L. Love

The essays in this volume constitute a guidebook for
quantitative social science research on Latin America.
Their collective implications extend beyond the hemisphere or the confines of specific disciplines, and they
should interest the experienced investigator as well as
the novice. They challenge present methods of training
regionally oriented social scientists, as well as question the performance of practicing academic professionals and the usefulness of their findings for regional
policy-makers. Whether one is statistically uninitiated
or a mature research methodologist, we believe the Latin
Americanist or other area specialist can profit from
these studies.

Today most practitioners of the disciplines treated
in this volume (history, anthropology, archaeology, geography, political science, and sociology) accept the
legitimacy and importance of quantitative analysis,
though in studying Latin America surprisingly few use
it well. Statistical sophistication in sociology and
political science usually surpasses that of geography,
history, and anthropology, and is currently approaching
that of economics. But a heuristic use of statistics
can be made at low levels of technical manipulation, as
demonstrated recently in Spanish history by Edward Male-

fakis (1970); furthermore, otherwise nonquantitative
studies in such traditionally qualitative fields as anthropology and history regularly employ simple statistical data in tabular form. Here, as in other disciplines, quantification helps eliminate conceptual ambiguities and affords opportunities for comparison and
generalization. Indeed, aided by the computer, more sophisticated applications have vastly expanded the hori-
zon for discovery of systematic relations among a bewil-
dering variety of quantifiable variables.

One major advantage of quantitative analysis seems to
be its potential for cross-disciplinary research. Too
often the artificial and arbitrary boundaries between
academic disciplines result in an intellectual particu-
larism almost as restrictive as the cultural parochial-
ism which researchers have consciously attempted to minimize. If we posit the interdependence of many measur-
able variables in human activity, it would appear impossible to achieve complex analysis of "hard" data in
disciplinary isolation. Fortunately, most of the social
sciences have by now developed sufficient theoretical
sophistication, buttressed by new techniques of quantitative analysis capable of manipulating vast numbers of
variables, to permit cross-disciplinary investigation
and interpretation.

Given the growing sophistication of statistical techniques and the availability of new data bank collections
of Latin American materials, the lag in using quantitative approaches should be cause for concern among social
scientists. To bring attention to this problem and to
assist in its resolution, the University of Illinois
Center for Latin American Studies and Center for International Comparative Studies cosponsored a faculty-grad-
uate student seminar, "Social Science Research in Latin
America: The Uses of Quantitative Data," during the

spring of 1971.

Individuals offering papers, revised for reproduction here, included Peter H. Smith (history, University of Wisconsin); Robert C. Hunt (anthropology, Brandeis University); George L. Cowgill (archaeology, Brandeis University); Howard L. Gauthier (geography, Ohio State University); Clifford Kaufman (political science, University of Pennsylvania, now at Wayne State); Alejandro Portes (sociology, University of Illinois, now at Texas). While the editors regret the absence of an essay on economics, the logic of priorities imposed by time and funds made this the obvious field to omit. Most economic literature on Latin America, as on other world regions, is already almost exclusively quantitative, so there seems little need to introduce economists to the joys and frustrations of such research.

In considering quantification problems of six disciplines, the substance of the papers clusters around four related issues--problems of operationalizing concepts; the quality of data concerning Latin America; the appropriateness and utility of Latin America as an analytical unit; and the achievements, opportunities, and perils of quantitative social science analysis in the Latin American area. A few remarks on each of these issues seem appropriate.

Difficulty in operationalizing social concepts is a problem by no means unique to Latin America, for general methodological issues are involved. Despite the appearance of concreteness that quantification provides, unless the researcher has a clear understanding about what is to be measured, the numbers may be more misleading than informative. Likewise, manipulating data with mathematical models or seeking correlations among groups of indicators presupposes not only the existence of reliable data but also a careful assessment of their mean-

ing. Several contributors discuss these problems in
detail; in general terms, they probably would agree
with Philippe Schmitter that "for a large number of
variables there exist only proximate indicators" (1969:
95). A striking example of such problems is the concept of economic growth. Everett Hagen suggests that
although virtually all economists discussing economic
growth initially acknowledge the importance of noneco-
nomic factors, their subsequent analysis too often ignores or underestimates such elements (1960:624-25).
This may occur because neither economists nor other social scientists have yet learned how to quantify such
elements effectively.

Not unexpectedly, all six essays discuss problems
growing out of the quality of data on Latin America--
for example, the enumeration of phenomona or the appropriateness of classification schemes. Yet Alejandro
Portes, for one, argues that reliability and validity
of Latin American survey data are *a priori* no lower
than for data from the United States or Europe. Schmitter also has made a case for reliability of aggregate
data from Latin America relative to those from other
less developed areas (1969:92-93).

Nonetheless, the writers represented here have emphasized the need to take into account inadequacies in
the collection of aggregate and survey data on Latin
America. One notorious example is related in anthropologist Richard Patch's report on "The La Paz Census
of 1970," which estimates an official undercount of
some two-sevenths in the population of Bolivia's capital (1970:1,4). The same article illustrates that data
are no better than the schemes and categories used to
order them. Patch, a North American, appears in the
1970 La Paz census as a Bolivian army veteran because
the census question on military service did not differ-

entiate by country. Similarly, only 5 of 164 questions
on the form were asked by the census-taker. Although
Patch asserts his experience is not typical, one wonders
whether field observations of census-taking would not
yield similar horror stories in other countries. Con-
flicting totals of presumably hard data from different
official sources certainly encourage such speculation.

While we should not overgeneralize from Carmelo Mesa-
Lago's warnings about inaccuracies in contemporary Cuban
data (1969:53-54), we must recognize that in any country
ideology and inconsistencies and irregularities in the
collection and publication of data can interact in complex ways to introduce distortion into social science
investigation. This caveat does not mean that good
quantitative analysis is impossible, or that it requires
more methodological sophistication than qualitative interpretation; it does mean that quantitative work requires multiple skills and that it is difficult to do
well.

One basic issue raised by the authors grows out of
the quantitative nature of their research interests.
Too few qualitative commentators have seriously debated
the question of whether Latin America as such is a valid
analytical unit. Of necessity, investigators trying to
match data cross-nationally must consider whether the
figures represent the same thing in one country as in
others--although some social scientists argue that, giv-
en similarities of language, historical evolution, religious and cultural values, and social structure, Latin
America is perhaps the best laboratory for comparative
analysis among the world's principal cultural regions
(for example, Wagley 1964:23-25).

Several of the essayists are theoretically agnostic
on this point, but most of them apparently assume the
existence of a contextual effect until contrary evidence

is adduced. That is, they operate on the assumption
that quantitatively as well as qualitatively Latin American societies have more in common with each other than
with other areas of the world and, therefore, that they
are more meaningful to compare. Nonetheless, Kaufman's
observations on the interaction of domestic factors and
foreign influences raises the possibility that the cross-
national correlations we find in our "Latin American"
research may be spurious. As he points out, diffusion
of external influences and dependency may produce effects which cannot be disregarded in aggregate regional
analysis.

The dominant theme of most of these essays is the
last issue: the possibilities and limitations of quantitative social science approaches in the Latin American context. Certainly there has been an increase in
quantitative analysis in the social sciences during the
last two decades; it has been prompted partly by recognition of the need for generating more precise data and
partly by the power of the computer. Latin American
studies have shared in this trend. During recent years
data banks in the United States have amassed large collections of Latin American statistical materials, a development offering opportunities which social scientists
can ignore only at their peril. If opportunities for
collecting data on location are likely to decrease in
coming years, as Portes argues, researchers should make
every effort to utilize existing statistical and survey
materials in new ways. At the same time, they should
make available, as promptly and efficiently as possible,
newly collected information; these goals are best facilitated through computerized storage. Furthermore, North
American researchers should recognize the urgency of
making these data available to Latin American depositor-
ies, to underscore their potential utility for analyzing

problems in the countries studied. For these reasons
we have included a list of the major banks and supporting details in an appendix to this volume. (For anno-
tated bibliographies of aggregate data, see Montenegro
1967 and Population Research Center 1965).

Problems in applying quantitative analysis are discussed in each essay. Sometimes perplexing questions
are raised; often new insights are provided. Most papers deal with the reliability and validity of data,
and the inferences which can (or cannot) be drawn there-
from. The contributors consider how investigators can
avoid pseudo-scientific and spurious findings. For example, although survey data can provide us with some
understanding of twentieth-century Latin America, we
must remind ourselves that such information has limited
temporal perspective. In treating such problems, this
volume suggests how quantitative findings from hitherto
underutilized disciplines can add strength to other
fields of investigation. Quantitative history and archaeology can add an important temporal dimension to
our vision of Latin America; quantitative geography can
supply a significant spatial input for the work of social anthropologists, sociologists, or political scientists.

Each essay discusses methodology, particularly the
appropriateness in a given discipline of applying specific quantitative strategies and techniques in Latin
American research situations. All discuss relevant mon-
ographic literature and the critical areas for new research. The six papers are presented in order of difficulty, in that they proceed from lesser to greater
demands on the reader's knowledge of quantitative techniques. This ordering reflects the general level of
quantitative development in the various disciplines,
with history, social anthropology, and archaeology at

one end of the continuum (not necessarily in the order given here), and political science and sociology at the other; geography seems to fall somewhere between. While all six papers treat the general topics indicated above, they naturally differ in emphasis. Gauthier's essay is oriented toward the solution of practical problems, while Kaufman's is concerned with basic epistemological issues. The first four essays (by Smith, Hunt, Cowgill, and Gauthier) plead the case for greater use of quantitative techniques to colleagues who are assumed to be somewhat skeptical and statistically inexperienced.

In the final two essays on political science and sociology, Kaufman and Portes assume implicitly that in their respective disciplines no case need be made for the utility of quantitative analysis. They go beyond the other contributors in discussing basic theoretical issues and coping strategies that, with modification, could be applied in the other social sciences as well, and to geographic regions other than Latin America. In the final article Alejandro Portes offers a salvage strategy for making better use of materials already available in data banks. Again, in broad outline his approach certainly is applicable to other fields of inquiry and to other regions of the world.

The application of systematic quantitative analysis to Latin American problems is a recent phenomenon in each discipline treated here. As the bibliographies for each essay attest, the great bulk of quantitatively oriented publications appeared after 1960. The still evolving and mutually ignored trends toward quantification in the various fields and geographic subregions, plus the potential for cross-fertilization, have led most of the writers to call for systematic research efforts or, at the very least, for systematic pooling of data for secondary and comparative analysis.

Although the essays deal with the whole of Latin
America in a general way, specific items in the bibliography are principally the product of the existing literature, with an uneven spread across the region, and
secondarily the product of each scholar's interests and
special knowledge. (The subdivisions of Latin America
best covered are Mexico and Central America, Argentina,
Chile, and Brazil.) Each contributor is a pioneer in
the quantitative analysis of Latin American data, so by
discussing his own work he often carries the reader to
the frontiers of knowledge.

It is evident from the essays that, for most social
sciences, systematic quantitative analysis hardly dom-
inates North American research projects or the relevant
North American academic literature. Yet some scholars
will feel that quantitative research reflects a North
American or Anglo-Saxon bias toward mechanistic or numerical norms which neglects human or moral values.
Ideally, this volume should be answered by Latin American scholars, as Wagley, ed., *Social Science Research
in Latin America* (1964) was by Diégues and Wood, eds.,
Social Science in Latin America (1967). While all contributors to the papers are North American-trained, they
do comment extensively upon the limitations of such approaches.

We believe that quantitative analysis offers construc-
tive and innovative perceptions of social reality, without producing millennial solutions. Quantification is
but one mode of science and should not be viewed as con-
flicting or competing with qualitative forms of analysis.
After all, when we measure, we measure qualities and provide them with numerical dimensions. If the qualities
we measure are of little theoretical or normative significance, the end results likewise will have little im-

portance, regardless of the level of sophistication we
can achieve through statistical manipulations. The ul-
timate value of quantitative analysis depends on its
contribution to the discovery and delineation of important concepts, and on the integration of such concepts
into the corpus of theoretical knowledge about Latin
American social phenomona.

It should be clear by now that this volume is far
from an unqualified plea for quantification. We agree
with Anthony Leeds that quantification which "occurs in
a theoretical, methodological, and empirical vacuum" is
"mindless," and that social scientists ought not to replace "fundamental thinking" with statistical "gimmicks"
(1968:79). Yet his criticism also could be directed at
many nonquantifiers; probably the most frequent perpe-
trators of mindless quantification are the casual users
of statistics who generalize unjustifiably from limited
data and who show little understanding of the difficulties of measuring the changes implied in such concepts
as "modernization." Nonetheless, we wish to stress that
neither the editors nor the essayists represented herein
seek to downgrade the usefulness of in-depth, nonquantitative studies which can clarify conceptual boundaries
and provide insights into areas of fruitful social research, including new forms of quantitative investigation.

Finally, the editors believe that quantitative research on Latin America should not be cloaked in an ideology of empirical conservatism (Easton 1969:1058; Marcuse 1964: Ch. IV). Far too often the description and
understanding of the way in which social realities *currently* operate translate somehow into the way things
ought to operate. Existing social structures are thereby provided with a stamp of normative legitimacy. Kenneth Dolbeare cautions political scientists doing empir-

ical research against becoming "mere technocratic instruments of the status quo" (1970:86). His warnings
should also be heeded by other social scientists, area
specialists and generalists alike.

REFERENCES

Diégues Júnior, Manuel, and Wood, Bryce
    1967   *Social science in Latin America: papers presented at
            the conference on Latin American studies held at Rio de
            Janeiro, March 29-31, 1965.* New York.

Dolbeare, Kenneth M.
    1970   Public policy analysis and the coming struggle for the
            soul of the postbehavioral revolution. In *Power and
            community: dissenting essays in political science,* Phil-
            ip Green and Sanford Levinson, eds. New York.

Easton, David
    1969   The new revolution in political science. *American Polit-
            ical Science Review* 63 (No. 4):1051-61.

Hagen, Everett
    1960   Turning parameters into variables in the theory of eco-
            nomic growth. *American Economic Review, Papers and Pro-
            ceedings* I (No. 2):624-25.

Leeds, Anthony
    1968   Commentary on Bwy's "Political instability in Latin
            America: the cross-cultural test of a causal model."
            Latin American Research Review 3 (No. 2):79-87.

Malefakis, Edward E.
    1970   *Agrarian reform and peasant revolution in Spain: origins
            of the civil war.* New Haven, Conn.

Marcuse, Herbert
    1964   *One-dimensional man.* Boston.

Mesa-Lago, Carmelo
    1969   Availability and reliability of statistics in socialist
            Cuba. *Latin American Research Review* 4 (No. 1):53-91;
            (No. 2):47-81.

Montenegro, Tulo Hostilio
    1967   Bibliografía anotada de las principales fuentes de esta-
            dísticas sobre América Latina. *Handbook of Latin Ameri-
            can Studies* 29:613-39.

Patch, Richard W.
    1970   The La Paz census of 1970. *American Universities Field
            Staff: Fieldstaff Reports, West Coast South America
            Series* 17 (12).

Population Research Center, University of Texas
    1965   *International population census bibliography: Latin
            America and the Caribbean.* Austin, Tex.

Schmitter, Philippe C.
　　1969　New strategies for the comparative analysis of Latin
　　　　　American politics. *Latin American Research Review* 4
　　　　　(No. 2):83–110.

Wagley, Charles
　　1964　*Social science research on Latin America: report and
　　　　　papers of a seminar on Latin American studies in the
　　　　　United States held at Stanford, Calif., July 8–August
　　　　　23, 1963.* New York.

HISTORY

Peter H. Smith

Quantitative techniques have gained many adherents
within the historical profession during the past ten
years. Students of politics have made statistical
studies of elite composition, legislative behavior,
and voting trends within electorates. Social historians have worked on class structure, social mobility,
and demographic change. Economists have devised methods for identifying causal links in historical processes of economic growth. Electronic computers have made
it possible to manipulate masses of data--and hence to
ask questions--that seemed unthinkable a generation ago.
The combined impact of these developments has led to
major innovations in the historiography of Europe, Asia,
and the United States (Price 1969).

Not so with Latin America, where quantitative history
is most conspicuous by its scarcity. Throughout the
hemisphere only a handful of scholars have made substantial use of statistical data. Anthologies and bibliographies on quantitative history hardly mention work
about Latin America (Rowney and Graham 1969; Swierenga
1970; Dollar and Jensen 1971:256-97; Shorter 1971:11-27;
Historical Methods Newsletter 1967-). To the best of
my knowledge no correlation coefficient of any kind had
ever appeared in the pages of the *Hispanic American His-*

torical Review prior to 1972.

I believe that the nonstatistical quality of historical research in this area stems from the generalized assumption that human behavior and capriciousness defy all rules of mathematics. In the words of Arthur Schlesinger, Jr., "Almost all important questions are important precisely because they are not susceptible to quantitative answers" (Fischer 1970:94). As sometimes applied to Latin America by North Americans, this notion has double appeal: it allows us to indulge romantic fancy and to dream of epic heroes, while at the same time maintaining an implicit (if unintentional) attitude of condescension toward the "irrational" behavior of the populace below the Rio Grande. Of course, there are other obstacles. Skeptics often say statistically manipulable material does not exist, but then again they have not looked. Basically, we have not written quantitative history because we have not wanted to.[1]

This posture strikes me as unfortunate because it is unnecessary. Quantification *per se* should not be the issue. Notwithstanding Schlesinger, many matters "important" by any definition are susceptible to quantitative techniques. The real issue is how to employ statistical methods in such a way as to enhance our knowledge of the past.[2]

With this problem in mind I shall propose some ways that Latin American historians might make productive use of quantitative techniques. Because of personal interests, and given previous statements by William Paul McGreevey (1968, 1972), James Lockhart (1972a), and John J. TePaske (1972), I shall focus on social and political rather than economic history, treating aspects of social history which specifically seem to bear close relationships to politics. To emphasize the utilities (and drawbacks) of historical statistics, I shall stress the prac-

tical feasibility and relevance of several approaches. I
shall discuss mainly topics, sources, and methods, rather
than theory and hypothesis construction. (On general
sources and data see Montenegro 1967; Ruddle and Hamour
1971; Ruddle 1972; on epistemology see Berkhofer 1969.)

Social Bases of Stability and Instability

Most scholars agree that social change exerts a crucial influence upon political order, but they cannot
agree on definitions for the basic concepts. "Social
change" is hopelessly elusive. "Political stability"
also has defied strict categorization. Definitions are
often elliptical--"instability" is identified by the absence of stability, and vice versa. At a minimum, stability and instability involve a relationship between
two groups: the rulers, who presumably want to maintain
their position; and the ruled, who can either accept or
deny their leaders' claims to authority.

Regardless of the definitions used, one aspect of
stability involves the elite's capacity to stay in power.
Quantitative measures of this ability are fairly simple
to design. Length of tenure in office, incidence of res-
ignations, ratio of cabinet ministers to number of port-
folios, and frequency of coups can all provide useful
indicators (Needler 1968a, 1968b; Russett 1969; Dean
1970).

Popular acceptance or rejection of authority presents
another problem. Perhaps the most common strategy is to
assume that violence equals rejection--if not by the populace at large, at least by a counter-elite with substantial support. Demonstrations, strikes, assassinations,
crime rates, revolts, and other such phenomena provide
an eminently usable notion of societal disequilibrium
(Johnson 1966:119-34; Bwy 1968). Most analytical procedures for quantifying violence are essentially straight-

forward. One strategy is to count up the number of outbreaks, select some criterion for weighting the gravity
of each occurrence, add up the scores for comparable
chronological units, and then trace trends through time
(Tilly and Rule 1965; Graham and Gurr 1969; Denton and
Phillips 1971). As an example, Figure 1 presents a noncompliance behavior index which Wayne A. Cornelius, Jr.,
has constructed for Mexico from 1929 to 1941. It shows
how the succession of power led to conflict--first in
the change from Callista to Cardenista supremacy in 1935,
and later, to a lesser degree, during the presidential
election of 1940.

Cornelius's index reveals the difficulty, as well as
the utility, of quantifying violence. The procedures
for constructing his curve are explicit, and its interpretive significance seems fairly clear. The problem
concerns some basic assumptions: that varying acts of
violence have an additive or cumulative impact, they all
relate to presidential politics, the assigned weights
are appropriate, and the weighting scheme is valid for
all years from 1929 to 1941, a time when Mexico was un-
dergoing drastic institutional and social change. Cornelius has raised considerably the level of scholarly
discourse on this subject, which has customarily involved
impressionistic views of more or less violence, but he
also has demonstrated the analytical frailty of aggregative indices.

In addition to such vexing methodological issues, the
historian of violence must further face a central conceptual question: what meaning does violence have in
each particular society? James Payne (1965) and others
(e.g., Needler 1968a:43-76) have argued that some types
of violence comprise integral parts of the political
process in Latin America. If this is true, then by definition some civil disturbances are not really disturb-

Figure 1.   Index of Noncompliance in Mexico, 1929–41

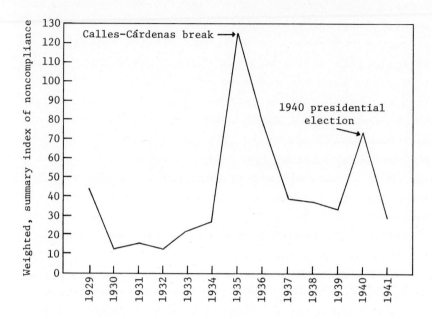

Data base: Frequency counts obtained through systematic search of Mexican dispatches to the *New York Times* (1929–41), *Christian Science Mon-
itor* (1929–41), daily issues of *Excelsior* (1929–41), and weekly issues
of *Mexican Labor News* (1936–41).   The total frequency counts employed in
construction of the index do not reflect the full range of noncompliance
behavior due to underenumeration of conflict events of low-to-medium intensity occurring outside major cities.   In constructing the index the
following weightings were employed: protest demonstrations (urban): 1.0;
protest demonstrations (rural): 1.5; acts of terrorism or sabotage: 1.5;
unspecified behavior resulting in mass arrests, imprisonment, or execu-
tions: 1.5; illegal land seizures or raids on haciendas: 2.0; anti-gov-
ernment plots or "pronouncements" (not involving armed rebellion): 2.0;
assassinations of politically significant persons (attempted or successful): 2.0; riots (urban, involving casualties or loss of life): 3.0; riots (rural) or peasant uprisings (involving casualties or loss of life):
3.5; armed clashes between government and opposition forces: 4.0; major
revolts (involving in excess of 1,000 insurgents): 5.0.   These intensity
weightings were obtained by asking 12 judges knowledgeable in Mexican
and Latin American history to sort the eleven types of noncompliance behavior along an 11-point scale ranging from 0.0 (denoting minimum intensity) to 5.0 (maximum intensity).   The level of agreement among judges
on the assigned weightings, as measured by Kendall's coefficient of con-
cordance, was 0.81.   Aggregate noncompliance intensity scores for each
year in the 1929–41 period were computed by multiplying the number of actions of each type by the intensity weighting assigned to that category
and summing the products across categories.

Source: Cornelius (1973:435).

ances at all; they indicate that the system is functioning as always--not breaking down! Also, nonviolence can
represent abject terror rather than popular compliance
with the prevailing regime. Both possibilities have extremely serious implications for the use of violence as
a sign of political instability.

By illustrating the dangers of quantification, this
discussion points up what I personally take to be the
most important contribution of statistical technique:
it forces historians to confront the assumptions which
they unavoidably bring to their work (Potter 1963; Aydelotte 1971). Quantification, rightly done, demands
the formulation of rules for inference and evaluation
in a standard and explicit form. This requirement en-
hances both the rigor and the logic of historical analysis.

At any rate, whatever the approach to political order, one kind of influential social change is undoubted-
ly demographic. Just as the transition from high birth
and death rates to low birth and death rates can stimulate economic development by expanding the number of
people at an economically productive age level, so may
a growing proportion of young adults affect politics by
weakening the credibility of tradition and providing
the conditions for generational conflict. As Woodrow W.
Borah (1951) has linked New Spain's "century of depres-
sion" to a precipitous decline in the size of the Indian
work force, it is also possible that consequently decreasing economic autonomy for Spanish settlers can help
account for political quiescence during the seventeenth
century.

Several classic problems in Latin American history
relate to demographic questions. Did Creoles acquire
economic power in the eighteenth century partly through
repopulation of American Indians? Were mestizos repro-

ducing more rapidly than whites or Indians? Did population pressures on the food supply help generate the move
toward independence, as Enrique Florescano (1969) suggests in the case of Mexico? What kind of populations
existed in the nineteenth century? Can demographic
change (or lack of it) help account for patterns of economic growth and the elitist structure of politics? Does
the population explosion, with its ominous political
overtones, have historical roots?

There are several sources for this kind of work.
National censuses offer rich and substantial amounts of
data. Reluctance to use them seems inexplicable: they
are fairly abundant (as shown in Table 1), thorough, and,
if used with caution, reasonably reliable (Collver 1965;
Arriaga 1968; Schmitter 1969). Colonial historians have
access to official reports which contain a great amount
of demographic data. Where censuses and reports are unavailable, one could turn to parish registers. The art
of family reconstitution, which seeks to determine at
what age people were getting married, having babies, and
dying (instead of producing vital rates for a whole population), has made substantial contributions in other
historical fields (Vann 1969). It has obvious applicability to Latin America.[3]

The changing socioeconomic structure of a society has
even more direct implications for political order than
have its birth and death rates. In the late 1950's John
J. Johnson (1958) attributed the rise of democratic re-
formism in Latin America to the emergence of the middle
sectors. Other scholars have recently challenged this
view by stressing the persistence of continuities within
social structures variously characterized as "dualism,"
"internal colonialism," and "neocolonialism" (Adams 1967;
Lambert 1967; Frank 1967, 1969; Stavenhagen 1969; Havens
and Flinn 1970; Stein and Stein 1970). In one way or

another, the revisionists see the nature and maintenance
of archaic social structures as principally responsible
for the concentration of political power in the hands of
an elite.

In my opinion the historical relationship between the
social structure and the political system remains an open
question, partly a matter of conjecture and ideological
preference, but one which stands to gain a great deal
from thorough and thoughtful use of census data. Information on changing patterns of occupational distribution
would be particularly relevant, although, as Otis Dudley
Duncan (1968) has warned, occupational differentiation
provides a dubious clue to social inequality or stratification. Nor would quantitative census data alone resolve the overriding qualitative issues about the character and definition of the social order, unless someone
can think of valid statistical tests for competing hypotheses.

Another approach to social structure entails the
study of individual and intergenerational mobility, as
distinct from aggregate census records, and work on mobility has led to significant breakthroughs in the historiography of the United States. Merle Curti (1959),
Stephan Thernstrom (1964), and Peter Knights (Thernstrom
and Knights [1970]), for example, have been able to use
manuscript census returns and city directories in order
to examine social strata in three nineteenth-century
communities--Trempealeau County (Wisconsin), Newburyport
(Massachusetts), and the city of Boston, respectively.
And fully two decades ago Natalie Rogoff (1953) utilized
marriage license applications in Marion County, Indiana,
to produce a brilliant work on trends in occupational
mobility. Data for similar investigations might or might
not exist in Latin America. Some manuscript censuses and
comparable sources for the colonial period have turned up

Table 1. General Censuses in Latin America since 1774

	Prior to 1900	1900–19	1920–39	1940–49	1950–59	1960–69	1970's
Argentina	1869, 1895	1914	---	1947	---	1960	1970
Bolivia	1831, 1835, 1845, 1854, 1882	1900	---	---	1950	1965	---
Brazil	1872, 1890	1900	1920	1940	1950	1960	1970
Chile	1835, 1843, 1854, 1865, 1875, 1885, 1895	1907	1920, 1930	1940	1952	1960	1970
Colombia	1825, 1835, 1843, 1851, 1864, 1870	1905, 1912, 1918	1928, 1938	---	1951	1964	---
Costa Rica	1864, 1883, 1892	---	1927	---	1950	1963	---
Cuba	1774, 1792, 1817, 1827, 1841, 1861, 1877, 1887, 1899	1907, 1919	1931	1943	1953	1967	1970
Dominican Republic	---	---	1920, 1935	---°	1950	1960	1970

Ecuador	---	---	---	---	1962	---
El Salvador	---	1901	1930	---	1961	---
Guatemala	1880, 1893	---	1921, 1930	1940	1964	---
Haiti	---	1918, 1919	---	---	1968	---
Honduras	1791, 1801, 1881, 1887	1901, 1905, 1910, 1916	1926, 1930, 1935	1940	1961	---
Mexico	1895	1900, 1910	1921, 1930	1940	1960	1970
Nicaragua	1778, 1867	1906	1920	1940	1963	---
Panama	---	1911	1920, 1930	1940	1960	1970
Paraguay	---	1917	1936	---	1950, 1956, 1958 / 1962	---
Peru	1836, 1850, 1862, 1876	---	1933	1940	1961	---
Uruguay	1852, 1860	1900, 1908	---	---	1963	---
Venezuela	1873, 1881, 1891	1910	1920, 1926, 1936	1941	1961	---

Sources: Schmitter (1969:86); Ruddle and Hamour (1971:57); also see Population Research Center (1965).

in scattered locations (Layne 1936; Cook 1968; Jowdy 1971).[4] For the modern period, governmental census archives will be the principal source.[5]

Political scientists have propounded several other hypotheses about social sources of political tension and change. It is often argued that urbanization has presented challenges to the "ruling oligarchy." Foreign immigration is said to disrupt tradition and stimulate modernization. Internal migration, especially from country to city, presumably creates a social base for populist mass movements. Education spawns defiance of sacrosanct orthodoxy. Such ideas seem persuasive enough for recent years (Deutsch 1961; Duff and McCamant 1968); the question is whether they hold true over time. Did urbanization bring discord during the colonial period? Was there much internal migration in the nineteenth century? Has education over the years tended to enforce the status quo? Such matters call for serious historical inquiry.

One of the most common explanations for political instability, particularly revolution, concerns the unequal distribution of political, social, or economic benefits. A standard premise, as Crane Brinton (1965) has suggested, is that people revolt when they feel underrepresented, underrated, undersold, or underpaid—even though their objective conditions might well be improving. To examine this notion, historians could make use of several simple measures. To get at the objective dimension, for example, they could examine the changing proportion of values controlled by the top 10 percent of the population or, depending upon the focus of research, the changing proportion allotted to the bottom half.

I call special attention to another measure—the Gini index. In relation to the Lorenz curve, which expresses the inequality of income distribution in a given popula-

tion (shown in Figure 2), this index expresses the area
between the line of perfect equality AC and the actual
distribution curve as a proportion of the total area in
the triangle ABC. Zero distance between the equality
line and actual distribution signifies perfect equality;
the higher the index, the greater the inequality. (For
computation and applications of the index, see Dollar
and Jensen 1971:121-26; Alker 1965:29-53; Bwy 1968; and
Russett 1969:356-67.) Since the Gini index by definition summarizes the cumulative distribution for the entire community, rather than for a specific segment, it
is more appropriate for some problems than for others.
One important practical advantage is that comparable
Gini indices can be constructed from differing types of
data. That is, the percentage intervals of people or
values can vary indiscriminately from one year to another or from one place to another. And, being a single
number, the index allows us to trace chronological tendencies in distribution which might in turn account for
political crisis (Figure 3). Furthermore, one need not
use the index on income alone; it can also be used for
land tenure or other sources of wealth.

Though few historians in any field have made extensive use of inequality measures, Latin Americanists
could learn much from use of these techniques. It would
be most instructive to discover how the rate and extent
of land concentration in nineteenth-century Mexico helped
stimulate the revolution; if political malapportionment
has generated tensions in Chile; whether racial or ethnic distribution patterns in Brazil (or any other country) reveal de facto segregation. The approach is applicable to local as well as national, and colonial as
well as modern history. Furthermore, it can employ
sources ranging from notarial records and tax levies
(Jowdy 1971) to published census data.

Figure 2.   Illustration of the Gini Index

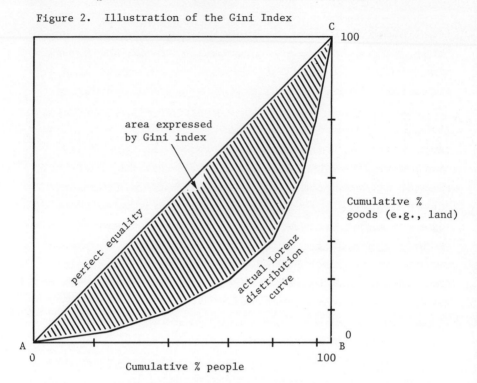

Figure 3.   Some Possible Patterns of Change

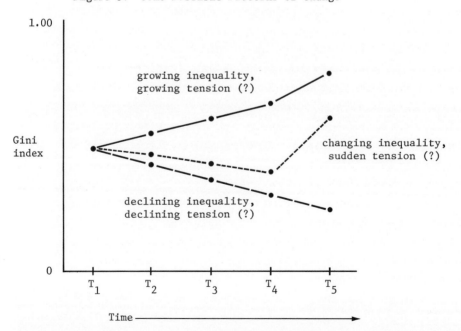

Careful studies of inequality at a single point in
time can yield insight on regional disparities. Despite
the revolution, the total distribution of non-*ejido* land
in Mexico has remained extremely unequal (from data in
Tello [1968] I have computed Gini indices of .945 or
more since 1930). Table 2 reveals curious variations
among the country's regions in 1960. States in the central valley tend to have relatively equal land distribution, with Gini scores below the national median, while
states in the Gulf and South Pacific tend to cluster
above the median. As different crops involve different
economies of scale, one reason for this pattern might
be ecological. Another cause could be political--that
is, some states (or land-owning groups in some states)
might have been able to resist the central government's
land reform program better than others. The question
merits exploration.

Still another frequently cited source of political
instability in Latin America consists of commercial dependence upon foreign markets and trade. Area specialists have long invoked this theory to explain the rash
of coups in 1930. Export prices fell with the Depres-
sion, and governments came tumbling after. (For a more
subtle analysis, see Dean 1970.) Some analysts have
argued also that economic dependence places satellite
political systems at the mercy of imperial powers, which
can use commercial strength to political advantage. To
examine such ideas or to evaluate governmental efficacy
in gaining economic autonomy, historians might employ
the import coefficient, a measure well known to economists as the ratio of imports to gross domestic product.
Seeking to estimate the extent of concentration in trade
(and, hence, commercial vulnerability to outside influence), Albert O. Hirschman has devised the indices in
Table 3, which presents some figures for selected coun-

Table 2. Gini Indices of Non-*Ejido* Land Concentration for Mexican States and Regions, 1960

Pacific North		North		Center		Gulf		South Pacific	
Baja California Territory	79.7	Chihuahua	79.8	Michoacán	81.6	Campeche	88.3	Colima	71.5
Nayarit	87.4	Durango	73.0	Querétaro	71.4	Quintana Roo	98.1	Guerrero	91.6
Sinaloa	77.7	San Luis Potosí	99.6	Tlaxcala	79.9	Veracruz	85.9	Oaxaca	80.2
						Yucatán	85.7		
Median 71.3									
Baja California	49.4	Coahuila	71.2	Aguascalientes	67.7	Tabasco	68.0	Chiapas	70.8
Sonora	65.7	Nuevo León	71.9	Distrito Federal	38.5				
		Tamaulipas	66.3	Guanajuato	68.0				
		Zacatecas	56.5	Hidalgo	55.5				
				Jalisco	51.8				
				México	50.0				
				Morelos	46.4				
				Puebla	57.4				

Sources: México. Secretaría de Industria y Comercio (1965: Cuadro 4); and Tello (1968: Cuadro 14).

Note: Gini indices have been converted to percentages.

tries in 1913 and 1938. According to these data Argentina, Brazil, and Uruguay seem to have been the least dependent countries in Latin America, while the index for Mexico remained fairly high despite the revolution. The implications of such inquiry are obvious. How have trends developed over time, both before 1913 and since 1938? Have Latin polities become more or less dependent upon the vagaries of international trade? Which countries have suffered most?

While Hirschman's index permits direct comparisons between countries throughout the world, it may have limited relevance to Latin American history. First, it measures only commercial concentration, omitting the direct investment and government loans which have become so important in the years since World War II. Second, it does not identify the direction of commercial relationships, or show who is dependent on whom. Historians might learn what they need to know from simpler measures (for example, by computing a given country's trade with Britain, Germany, or the United States as a percentage of total trade), but they should keep the Hirschman index in mind.

Although instability has been characteristic of Latin American politics, an exclusive emphasis on this subject would be both fallacious and misleading. Latin American societies have undergone periods of immense stress since the Conquest, yet they retain a remarkable degree of continuity and cohesiveness. With governments coming and going, institutions such as *compadrazgo* have played a major role in ordering social and political relations. To examine the strength of these arrangements, it should be possible for historians to follow *compadre* relationships through baptismal records and to use them to identify extended kinship networks. Stephanie Blank (1971) has used this technique to discover a network in seven-

Table 3. Indices of Trade Concentration for Selected Countries, 1913 and 1938[a]

Country	1913		1938	
	Imports	Exports	Imports	Exports
United Kingdom	27.7	22.0	21.8	19.6
Canada	67.6	62.7	65.3	53.5
Argentina	40.7	--[b]	30.6	37.6
Bolivia	45.1	81.5	37.3	66.5
Brazil	37.1	40.9	39.0	41.8
Chile	43.4	49.5	40.6	--[b]
Colombia	42.1	59.0	55.8	61.5
Cuba	56.2	80.8	71.3	77.3
Ecuador	47.6	46.6	44.3	44.0
Mexico	55.0	78.2	61.1	68.7
Peru	43.9	52.4	42.2	37.7
Uruguay	36.9	35.8	29.1	38.3

[a]For either exports or imports, the trade concentration index is computed from the formula

$$TCI_A = \sqrt{P_1{}^2 + P_2{}^2 \ldots + P_k{}^2}$$

where P_1 through P_k stand for the respective percentages of A's total trade held by countries 1 through k.

[b]No data available.

Source: Hirschman (1945): Table 2, 102-5.

teenth-century Caracas which cuts across socioeconomic
lines and helps account for social stability; conversely, the existence of two or more major clusters in a
city or village could throw light on patterns of conflict.

Marital networks provide another possible clue to social cohesion amidst change. It is said that in Latin
America most aspiring politicians are married to daugh-
ters of important men. Upper-class land-owning groups
are endogamous; so are rural village populations. For
analyzing such propositions, historians could employ
the intermarriage index which Charles Tilly (1964:94-98)
has proposed and used:

$$\text{Intermarriage} = \frac{(100) \; (M_{x,y}) \; (N_m)}{(N_x) \; (N_y)}$$

where $M_{x,y}$ is the number of marriages between people of
group X and group Y, N_m is the total number of all marriages in the community, N_x is the total number of people in the marital sample from group X, and N_y is the
total number from group Y. With this equation, an index of 50 would represent the statistically expected
rate of intermarriage between the two groups; a higher
score would show a disproportionately high rate of intermarriage; a lower score would show a disproportionately low rate. By relating each group in the sample
to every other group, this measure would go far beyond
Edgar Love's finding (1971) that some racial intermarriage took place in colonial Mexico City. It provides
a statistically meaningful way of placing interracial
unions within the marriage pattern of the whole society.
It can apply to other transactions as well.

Of course, connections by *compadrazgo* and marriage
are formalistic relationships which do not reveal pos-

sible informal ties between social groups or categories
(concubinage, illegitimate parenthood, etc.). Research
on social networks consumes a great deal of time and
energy and is much more feasible for local than for national history. For the study of trends over time, one
might focus on people who stay within a given community,
leaving out the emigrants. But with these caveats in
mind one must recognize the potential value in this sort
of investigation and its implications for exploring the
social basis of political conflict and consensus.

The Study of Elites

The question of social grouping brings us to one of
the central issues for historical analysis of any society. Who have been the rulers? From what social strata
have they come? In whose interest do they rule? In his
remarkable work on eighteenth-century England, Sir Lewis
Namier (1957) shows how the social composition of political elites can provide vital information about channels
for social mobility, access to power, the relative open-
ness or exclusiveness of the political system, and patterns of conflict and change.

Some observers have viewed the concentration of political, economic, and social influence in a single elite
as a source of instability because outsiders must resort
to revolution, or at least violence, in order to share
power. Others have seen the separation of political and
economic elites as a cause of instability, since the two
groups tend to acquire diverging interests: conflict
and instability then result. Wilfredo Pareto has suggested that a blockage in the circulation of elites can
build up pre-revolutionary tensions. And, with specific
reference to Latin America, Merle Kling (1962) has hypothesized that limitations on economic opportunity have
turned ambitious young men toward politics, where chances

for advancement seem greater. The consequent scramble
for status, which is a scarce commodity, takes the form
of political instability.

In an effort to deal with such propositions, my own
research on twentieth-century Mexico has involved the
accumulation of biographical data on approximately 6,000
national political figures from 1900 to 1971. Key variables include date and place of birth, education, occupation, career patterns, and father's education and occupation. Information has been difficult but not impossible to find. I have tapped a wide range of sources:
biographical dictionaries, newspapers, periodicals, ar-
chival records, personal informants, and responses to a
mailed questionnaire. To identify political leaders and
establish career patterns on the national level, I have
recorded the name of every incumbent in every major office for every year since 1900. This process has allowed
me to create complete dossiers on upper-level interposi-
tional mobility for every individual. While the technique is time-consuming, it should produce useful analytical results.

This approach can throw considerable light upon the
structure of elites at almost any time in Latin American
history. Several scholars have made intensive investigation of the social origins of conquerors and other
Spaniards in the New World (Góngora 1962; Boyd-Bowman
1964, 1968; Lockhart 1972b). Stuart Schwartz (1970)
uses biographical data on members of the High Court at
Bahia to demonstrate the emergence of a professional
bureaucracy in colonial Brazil. Contrary to what others
have argued, Schwartz finds that the separation of political and socioeconomic leadership tended to increase stability. One would like to know if this generalization
applies in Mexico, Peru, and elsewhere (see Brading 1971;
Barbier 1972; Burkholder 1972). Glen Dealy (1968) offers

insightful observations about leaders of the independence movement in northern South America; we could learn
a great deal by extending the analysis to New Spain and
the River Plate (with an important new source in Editorial Porrúa 1969).

Standard interpretations concerning nineteenth-century
oligarchies should become another subject for empirical
research. Such studies would enhance our understanding
of the liberal-conservative split in many countries. David Fleischer's work on legislators in Brazil's Old Republic (1971) invites comparison with studies of political leadership during the Empire and subsequent periods.
Darío Cantón (1966a) and José Luis de Imaz (1970) have
pioneered in the study of political recruitment in modern Argentina.[6] Their findings can aid in the formulation of hypotheses for the investigation of elites in
other countries. The possibilities for this kind of research are virtually endless,[7] and the results can be
extremely rewarding. To be sure, the analysis of elites
involves delicate conceptual and methodological problems.
Fortunately there is a good deal of literature on the
subject (Rustow 1966; Welsh 1970, 1971), and Frederick
Frey has constructed an outstanding model for analysis
in *The Turkish Political Elite* (1965).

Aside from exploring the socioeconomic composition
of elites, we would like to explore their attitudes and
behavior. One quantitative indicator of policy preference among ruling groups can come from budgetary expenditures. Money is a reliable guide to action--merely
authorizing programs is one thing; funding them is another. In his well-known work on Mexico, James W. Wilkie (1967) makes considerable use of budgetary accounts
to examine governmental spending priorities since 1910.
However, I think he abuses the data in fundamental ways
(Skidmore and Smith 1970; Wilkie 1970b; Barkin 1972).

By omitting government payments to decentralized agencies and state-supported enterprises, he leaves out a
sizeable share of expenditures. His categorization of
spending as "social," "economic," or "political" is exceedingly vague. His implicit conclusion about the causal impact of budgetary expenditure on the standard of
living is totally unwarranted, and I harbor doubts about
his measurement of poverty. Yet Wilkie has written an
important book, illustrating both the problems and possibilities of using public expenditures as behavioral
indicators of policy preferences.

Data on budgets are widely available. Paul E. Hoffman (1970) reports that the Spanish royal treasury accounts are intact and accessible in the Archivo General
de Indias. He has even presented a plan for putting
them into machine-readable form for computer analysis.[8]
Moreover, national governments have kept budget records,
though discrepancies between proposed and actual expenditures indicate the need for cautious use.

The statistical analysis of written and oral expression, known as content analysis, offers still another
instrument for understanding elite behavior (North *et al.*
1963; Holsti 1969). In the same way that government
spending reveals practical preferences, the frequency
and intensity of references to certain themes (e.g., social justice, economic growth, national autonomy) can
provide another clue to functional priorities. A study
of political symbols might specify the conditions under
which leaders resort to various types of nationalism.
Or one might want to correlate trends in budgetary expenditure and official statements in search of patterns
of congruence and disparity.

Moreover, content analysis can shed light upon the
determinants of policy-making. A quantitative treatment
of reports to the Spanish Crown could yield an image of

the New World as seen from Madrid and illuminate crucial
imperial decisions. A similar approach to diplomatic
communiques regarding the Venezuelan dispute of 1903 or
the Panamanian controversy that same year could help explain the actions of participants in those unseemly quar-
rels.

One major advantage of content analysis is that it
does not require a special kind of data. All we need is
good old-fashioned documents. In a sense this method is
no different from traditional modes of research, which
usually entail the detection of more or less important
themes according to intensity and frequency. Quantification in content analysis merely seeks to impose systematic rules for inferential interpretation. It often
yields startling results in the process (Merritt 1970).

Roll-call analysis, a technique widely applied in
U.S. history (Anderson *et al.* 1966; MacRae 1970), provides another approach to the study of political leadership. Area specialists have neglected this method, partly because Latin American legislatures generally have
not played a paramount role in governmental decision-
making. Nonetheless, one could make profitable use of
roll-call measurement to study patterns of cleavage and
consensus within a sample of a political elite, if not
among the uppermost echelons. The fact is that some
Latin American legislatures have taken *votaciones nomi-
nales*, albeit unevenly, and they offer an important historical source. For example, I have gathered data on
about 1,700 roll calls in the Argentine Chamber of Deputies from 1904 to 1955, along with biographical information on the 1,569 people who served in the Chamber
during those years. My plans are first to explore group
behavior within this elite, and then to relate the findings to broad political trends and developments.[9] Figure
4 displays preliminary results on the intensification of

Figure 4. Party Voting Index for the Argentine Chamber of Deputies,
1916-30[a]

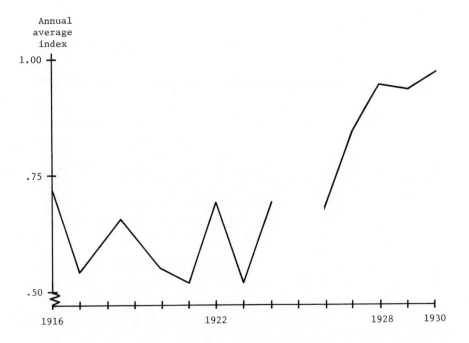

[a]The index derives basically from the percentage of deputies voting
with the majority in their respective parties on selected roll calls.
Since this figure can not go below .50, the index is standardized to
1.0 by the formula

$$PVI = 2(\frac{m}{N} - .50)$$

where m is the number of deputies in party majorities and N represents
the total number of deputies voting. Since annual average indices
have been computed only for three or more roll calls, votes for 1918
and 1919 were combined to meet this minimum; no average has been obtained for 1925. Selected roll calls refer to substantive issues; the
elections of Chamber presidents have been excluded because they were
usually pre-arranged votes along strict party lines.

Source: Smith (1970).

party discipline from 1916 to 1930. The growth of partisan intransigence provides a clue to the source of tensions which culminated in the coup of 1930 (Smith 1970).

Historians can use roll-call methods wherever roll calls exist. Colonial *cabildos*, such as that of Caracas, took some votes by name. National and state legislatures have kept track of some divisions in the house since independence. Transcripts of constitutional congresses often contain roll calls (see Sinkin 1973; Smith 1971 and 1972b). Newspaper articles and memoirs sometimes carry lists of opposing sides on various issues. And where all else fails, it remains possible to detect alignments by searching for cleavages through a careful reading of debates (Smith 1969).

Approaching Non-Elites

Partly in reaction to long-standing emphasis upon elites, a growing number of historians and social scientists have turned to the study of popular masses or, in more familiar language, "common men." Irving Louis Horowitz (1970:3) proclaims the basic assumption: "To understand the processes that go under the rubric of social development it is necessary to study masses as well as elites, nameless peasants and urban slum dwellers no less than military manipulators and political celebrities." The point is valid; the problem lies in execution. How can we analyze mass groups, about which so little is written? Censuses and related sources might offer general ideas about the size and shape of the lower class, but how can we proceed to study patterns in popular behavior?

One strategy for resolving this problem involves the correlation of social characteristics of geographical units with election results. This technique already

has helped elucidate several basic issues in European
and U.S. history (e.g., O'Lessker 1968; Kleppner 1970).
The same technique can be applied to Latin America.
Darío Cantón (1966b) and Ezequiel Gallo and Silvia Sigal
(1965) have made important voting behavior studies on
early twentieth-century Argentina; Glaucio Soares and
Robert Hamblin (1967) have studied the Chilean election
of 1952; Barry Ames (1970) has worked on Mexico; and I have
written a paper on socioeconomic correlates of the Peron-
ist vote in 1946 (Smith 1972a). Note that such relationships are ecological. They refer to proportional votes
in aggregate communities, not within a sample of human
individuals. Consequently, the relationships do not
provide a definitive guide to group voting. In view of
the absence of survey data and barring the excellent
luck of Cantón (1968a), historians have little choice
but to accept this limitation and draw their conclusions
with caution (Dogan and Rokkan 1969).

To illustrate, Table 4 presents regression equations
and correlation coefficients (Blalock 1960, 1964; Draper
and Smith 1966) for associations between the Mexican government party vote in 1964 and selected variables for
the country's thirty-two "federal entities."[10] Though
the correlations are not strong, it is revealing that
the PRI vote tends to show positive relationships with
indicators of underdevelopment--specifically, illiteracy
and rurality. Questions come quickly to mind. Why is
the PRI able to cultivate stronger followings in rural
rather than urban states? Even voter turnout has a positive correlation with the rural population. It does
not appear that land reform has much to do with loyalty
among the peasantry, since the proportion of land in
ejidos yields virtually no correlation, and the Gini index for non-*ejido* land distribution has a positive association with the party vote. What are the mechanisms of

Table 4. Relationships between Selected Variables and PRI Vote[a]
for Federal Entities in Mexico, 1964

Variables	Regression equations	Correlations (r)
% illiterates, 1960[b]	PRI = 84.0 + .19 ILLITERACY	.37
% rural population, 1960[b]	PRI = 79.6 + .21 RURAL	.55
% land in *ejidos*, 1960[c]	PRI = 90.9 + .0003 *EJIDOS*	.01
Gini index of land concentration, 1960[d]	PRI = 79.6 + .16 GINI	.35
% voter turnout[e]	PRI = 71.5 + .34 TURNOUT	.46
	in addition	
	TURNOUT = 47.5 + .18 RURAL	.34

Sources:

[a]Wilkie (1969).

[b]Wilkie (1967: Tables 9-1 and 9-4). Rural communities are defined as those with less than 2,500 inhabitants.

[c]México. Secretaría de Industria y Comercio (1965: Cuadro 7).

[d]See Table 2.

[e]González Casanova (1967: Cuadro LXIII-b).

control? What are the political implications of urbanization and industrial growth in post-revolutionary Mexico? Although the equations in Table 4 cannot resolve
such difficult issues, they plainly illustrate the heuristic function which ecological election analysis can
perform by defining crucial questions.

In addition to voting, one conspicuous form of mass
political participation is rioting. It is easy enough
to establish the occurrence, duration, and intensity of
such upheavals. But how can we find out who took part?
How are we to examine the social composition of mobs?
Investigations by European historians, particularly specialists on France (Rudé 1959; Soboul 1964), have uncov-
ered two major sources of data. One consists of police
arrest records, which usually contain names, addresses,
ages, and occupations of people apprehended during riots.
Another is hospital admissions records, which give similar data for wounded individuals. Such information refers to only a sample of riot participants--perhaps the
most daring, the most active, or the slowest of foot--
but it is not clear whether this bias would prevent the
sample from being representative. One can only wonder
how this sort of research might illuminate such critical
events in Latin American history as the Colombian *bogo-
tazo* of 1948.

Other species of internal war could provide valuable
evidence about mass politics. Military suppression of
armed insurrection might have generated prisoner-of-war
records. Regional revolts permit the use of aggregate
socioeconomic statistics for identifying differences between the area of rebellion and the rest of the country.
In this way we can begin to discern why an outbreak oc-
curred in a particular place at a particular time. Charles Tilly (1964) employs this strategy in his masterly
work on *The Vendée*. He offers a fine model for histor-

ical approaches to Canudos, *La Violencia*, and the Cristero revolt in Mexico.[11]

Content analysis can provide considerable insight into the attitudes and values of the non-elites as well as elites. Instead of dealing with public pronouncements, the researcher might focus on expressions of mass culture: popular songs (Simmons 1957; Cantón 1968b), inexpensive novels, comic books, and oral traditions (Vansina 1971). Such applications of content analysis demand painstaking care and superb knowledge of the language, but they can yield rich results.

Testing for Reliability and Significance

All these proposals seem fine, a critic might say, but they begin with the preposterous assumption that historical statistics are accurate. In Latin America! Such disbelief of course has no bearing on collective biography and content analysis, where historians assemble their own data, but it clearly relates to official statistics. We never can *know* if the numbers are right, just as we never can tell if a man has told the truth in his diary. We can, however, assess the reliability of data in several ways.

One means is to check for elementary consistency. In census records, for example, the population figure for County A in Table X should be the same as in Table Y. The number of children in school should not exceed the number of school-age children. Percentages should add up to 100. Such exercises do not really test reliability, but a source which meets these basic requirements is probably usable for many purposes--at least as usable as personal papers in a private archive. It would be difficult for officials to tamper with census results in clairvoyant anticipation of subsequent historical analysis and still retain consistency.[12]

If possible, we should seek the same information from more than one source. Agreement among two or three genuinely separate sources tends to confirm the credibility of data. In cases of discrepancy we can simply correlate the different statistical series. If the product-moment correlation is high (+.8 or so), it would seem legitimate to use either series for dealing with relative change over time. Alternatively, we could use the arithmetic mean for both.

Rough measures provide another means for resolving intuitive doubts about data. For instance, many historians harbor suspicions about the numerical accuracy of Mexican voting results. But if the researcher has reasonable confidence in the rank order of statewide election returns, Spearman's rho provides an appropriate measure for relating party strength to percent rural population. A true skeptic might prefer ordered categories of high-medium-low and use gamma. As a last resort, one could put the data in dichotomous high-low categories and employ a statistic like phi. In so doing, one must remember that the arbitrary thresholds between high and low are just as unreal as distortions in the original interval scale, and it would be only fair to say so in writing up the study.

To illustrate these statistical alternatives, Table 5 shows how various measures express the relationship between the Mexican government-party vote and percent rural population in 1940 and 1964. All indicate the same basic result: in both years the national party did better in rural areas than in urban ones, but the relationship was not as strong in 1964 as in 1940. Perhaps the PRI is slowly losing its grip on the countryside.

Finally, we can make some tests to establish the statistical significance of any particular association to assess the probability that a random selection of data

Table 5. Various Correlation Measures for Relationships between
PRI Vote and Rural Population, 1940 and 1964[a]

Measures	Scales	Strength of Relationships	
		1940 (N=31)	1964 (N=32)
Yule's Q	Dichotomous	.54	.47
Phi	Dichotomous	.29	.25
Lambda-b	Nominal[b]	.25	.25
Contingency coefficient C	Nominal[b]	.43	.33
Gamma	Ordered nominal[b]	.54	.47
Spearman's rho	Ordinal	.55	.53
Product-moment correlation	Interval	.73	.55

[a]The PRI was known as the *Partido de la Revolución Mexicana* (PRM) in 1940.

[b]Computed from 2x2 table because of small N, though these coefficients can also handle complex tables.

Sources: See Table 4.

would have produced the same result. Significance at the
.05 level, for instance, means that a random set of numbers would yield the association in question no more than
five times out of a hundred. When dealing with a sample
of the entire population under study, as in generalizing
about the composition of entire mobs from the biographies
of people who happened to be injured or arrested, historians can use this device to estimate confidence in the
representativeness of the findings (assuming that the sample is a random one). But even when working with whole
populations, as with all thirty-two states in Mexico, significance tests can help determine the interpretive value
of statistical relationships, though it is customary to
focus on the strength (not the significance) of associations in such situations.

Conclusions

Quantitative methods can strengthen historical research
on Latin American politics in many ways. Statistical analysis of demographic patterns and social relationships can
throw light on the social bases of political change, though
it probably cannot resolve questions about the quality and
definition of social structures. Documentation for this
sort of work, including marriage records and manuscript
censuses, is perhaps more frequently available for the colonial than for the modern period.

Quantification can also furnish information on the composition and behavior of political elites, a traditional
concern of historians. Data on the social background and
career patterns of political leaders are fairly abundant,
they are becoming more plentiful, and they offer one of the
most promising avenues for research in the entire field.
Attitudes and behavior present a more difficult problem.
In a few instances legislative roll-call techniques can be

helpful. Content analysis and the study of budgetary expenditures are probably the most usable instruments for this kind of inquiry.

Finally, statistical research can reveal knowledge about the structure and action of non-elites. For some countries, mainly in the twentieth century, it is possible to correlate socioeconomic patterns with election results. Where mass disturbances or revolts have led to arrests or injuries, police and hospital records can provide excellent sources. Regional outbreaks can be feasibly studied along the lines of Tilly's work (1964). Content analysis of popular media can reveal much about prevailing attitudes. For the most part non-elite groups are extremely difficult to investigate, since they have usually left few documents. The problem remains acute for historians of every methodological persuasion.

In sum, quantification can substantially improve our knowledge of Latin American history, but the obstacles to such research are formidable. Historians will have to make a determined effort to reap its manifold rewards.

First, we must take time to learn statistical techniques. This exhortation might seem onerous to scholars who have spent years conquering various languages, poring over lengthy bibliographies, and finding their way through musty archives, but it is unavoidable. A good portion of the scanty quantitative literature in history actually consists of simple tabulations, in which little or no awareness of statistical methods is evident. The result is often quantification, poorly done. To overcome this problem, historians will have to pay particular attention to the intricate and difficult task of time-series analysis.

Second, and more important, we must cultivate an abiding concern with matters of theory and epistemology.

Historians have the habit of defining specializations according to categories of data: intellectual history, political history, economic history. Instead, we must turn our concern (and self-definition) to the type, relevance, and soundness of the questions that we ask. Then we can try to devise quantitative and other means of answering them.

Third, we must develop flexible strategies for linking data with research questions. Unlike other social scientists, historians do not usually spend much time designing operational tests for detailed hypotheses prior to investigation in the field. We frame a question, try to get some data, probably find different data, revise the original question, and start anew (for ingenious tips on data-gathering, see Webb *et al.* 1966). There are advantages to this eclectic process, and we need not lose flexibility or serendipity, as Robert Hunt warns in his paper on social anthropology. But we must take care to learn what our data really measure.

Fourth, we must establish data banks. Sadly enough, there are no major Latin American history data banks anywhere that have significant amounts of information antedating World War II.[13] The need is immediate and imperative for at least three types of repositories.

We need a central census bank. The University of Florida and the University of Wisconsin have collected a few censuses from the 1940's to the present. Philippe Schmitter has gathered aggregate data for all Latin American countries on a year-by-year basis since approximately 1950 (Schmitter 1969). The political science department at the University of Minas Gerais has begun collecting data from Brazilian censuses since 1872 (*Historical Methods Newsletter* 4 [No. 1]:21). We must try to find a way to integrate such data banks, if only by establishing a central clearing house for information; and we must broaden and deepen their historical dimension.[14]

We need a collective biography bank containing machine-readable data on the social composition of elites and non-elites. T. K. Rabb has already started to establish a Historical Data Center for Collective Biography at Princeton University. Latin Americanists could either place their data there or establish a separate bank. But we ought to start somewhere.

We also need a budget bank, housing all available budgetary accounts from the Conquest to the present.

Fifth, for any or all of these banks, we should agree upon standard procedures for gathering and coding data. In all instances we ought to store the data in their original, elemental form, rather than according to categories which might be suitable for some research tasks but not for others. It would be highly desirable, as David Herlihy (1971) has suggested in regard to European documents, to set up uniform codes.

Aside from their function as libraries, these collections could lend a comparative dimension to historical generalizations about Latin America. With access to data banks, a given researcher would compare his findings on occupational structure in Venezuela with another's findings for Peru. A student of the Cuban Revolution could compare the Fidelista elite to the Maderistas or the Carrancistas in Mexico. Such opportunities would provide an exceedingly valuable check on interpretations of specific phenomena. Ultimately, it should become feasible to build a solid empirical base for the cross-national testing of hypotheses and the writing of comparative history.

Having done all these things, we must at times be willing *not* to quantify. It will prove impossible to obtain statistical data for some research projects, but this is no reason to drop them. Ideas and insight, not

method, provide the basic key to learning. As David
Landes and Charles Tilly (1971:2) have affirmed, "The
growing sophistication of social scientific techniques
makes it all the more important for practitioners of
these techniques to know and appreciate the humanistic
approach to historical knowledge. We cannot afford to
gain a world of numbers and models, only to lose our
historical souls in the process."

NOTES

[1] This comment applies to scholars from North, Middle, and South
America, though it is only fair to recognize that Latin American
colleagues are handicapped by the relative inaccessibility of computers.

[2] The accusation that quantitative historians give an illusory
sense of finality to their conclusions through statistical manipulation is a common one, and brings up complicated matters of epistemology. I personally regard all historical analysis as a condi-
tional enterprise. If we use certain concepts, certain methods,
and certain data, then we can draw certain inferences. And since
the inferences by definition are tentative, I do not see much foundation to the charge.

[3] On the use of computers in such research see Winchester (1970).

[4] In a private communication David Sweet (1971) has told me of
an annual series of extensive manuscript census returns for "virtually every settlement in the Portuguese Amazon, c. 1750-95," located in the Biblioteca Pública do Pará (Belém).

[5] Notebooks for the Argentine national censuses of 1869 and 1895
have been found in the Archivo General de la Nación (Buenos Aires);
Thomas H. Holloway has also located the manuscript returns for an
agricultural census of the state of São Paulo, taken in 1905.

[6] Julio Fernández (1970) also has covered the 1958-66 period, but
his analysis is disappointingly weak.

[7] Demonstrating the feasibility of studying lower-level elites,
Paul Vanderwood is preparing biographical data on approximately
2,000 Mexican *rurales* for computer analysis. For an important
guide to basic sources, see del Toro (1971).

[8] In his opening paragraph Hoffman states that "quantifiable
data are to be found in most of the 1,953 *legajos* of the Contaduría

section, and in perhaps a fourth of the 5,873 *legajos* of the Contratación section. Scattered throughout other sections are numerous reports on population, volume of trade, prices and other statistically treatable aspects of colonial life."

[9]Lee C. Fennell has produced a paper on voting patterns in the Argentine legislature (1970) and is currently working on historical dimensions of the subject.

[10]One would prefer to have data at the *municipio* level because the smaller the unit, the stronger the analysis; but I am simply trying to demonstrate the use of ecological data for exploratory purposes, not to draw conclusive inferences about individual voting behavior. For some other equations see Ames (1970).

[11]Jean Meyer, a French historian and sociologist, has made some use of this approach in his recent work on the Cristeros.

[12]For numerous and detailed statements on methods of dealing with census data, consult the *Historical Methods Newsletter*.

[13]See the list of "Social Science Machine Readable Data Archives in the United States" in Dollar and Jensen (1971:254-55).

[14]The Di Tella Institute in Buenos Aires has announced plans for a census repository.

REFERENCES

The following bibliography includes a few items not specifically cited in the text, but it in no way constitutes an exhaustive catalog to literature on quantitative history (for the best guide, see Dollar and Jensen 1971:236-97). Journal articles subsequently appearing in anthologies are usually cited as chapters in the anthologies, which might also be of special interest.

Adams, Richard Newbold
 1967   *The second sowing: power and secondary development in Latin America.* San Francisco.

Alker, Hayward R., Jr.
 1965   *Mathematics and politics.* New York.

Ames, Barry
 1970   Bases of support for Mexico's dominant party. *American Political Science Review* 64 (No. 1):153-67.

Anderson, Lee F., *et al.*
 1966   *Legislative roll-call analysis.* Evanston, Ill.

Arriaga, Eduardo E.
 1968   *New life tables for Latin American populations in the nineteenth and twentieth centuries.* Berkeley, Calif.

Aydelotte, William O.
 1971   *Quantification in history.* Reading, Mass.

Barbier, Jacques A.
 1972   Elites and cadres in Bourbon Chile. *Hispanic American Historical Review* 52 (No. 3):416-35.

Barkin, David
 1972   Public expenditures and social change in Mexico: a methodological critique. *Journal of Latin American Studies* 4 (No. 2:105-12).

Berkhofer, Robert F., Jr.
 1969   *A behavioral approach to historical analysis.* New York.

Blalock, Hubert M., Jr.
 1960   *Social statistics.* New York.
 1964   *Causal inferences in nonexperimental research.* Chapel Hill, N.C.

Blank, Stephanie
    1971   Social integration and social stability in a colonial
            Spanish American city: Caracas (1595-1627). Ph.D. dis-
            sertation, University of Wisconsin.

Borah, Woodrow W.
    1951   *New Spain's century of depression*. Berkeley, Calif.

_____, and Cook, Sherburne F.
    1960a   *The Indian population of central Mexico, 1531-1610*. Ber-
            keley, Calif.
    1960b   *The population of central Mexico in 1548: an analysis
            of the suma de visitas de pueblos*. Berkeley, Calif.
    1963   *The aboriginal population of central Mexico on the eve
            of the Spanish conquest*. Berkeley, Calif.
    1968   *The population of the Mixteca Alta, 1520-1960*. Berkeley,
            Calif.
    1971   *Essays in population history: Mexico and the Caribbean*.
            Vol. 1. Berkeley, Calif.

Boyd-Bowman, Peter
    1964,   *Indice geobiográfico de cuarenta mil pobladores españoles
    1968   en América en el siglo XVI*. Vols. 1 (Bogotá, 1964) and
            2 (México, 1968).

Brading, D. A.
    1971   *Miners and merchants in Bourbon Mexico, 1763-1810*.
            Cambridge, England.

Brinton, Crane
    1965   *The anatomy of revolution*. Rev. ed. New York.

Burkholder, Mark A.
    1972   From Creole to *Peninsular*: the transformation of the
            audiencia of Lima. *Hispanic American Historical Review*
            52 (No. 3):395-415.

Bwy, D. P.
    1968   Political instability in Latin America: the cross-
            cultural test of a causal model. *Latin American Research
            Review* 3 (No. 2):17-66.

Cantón, Darío
    1966a   *El parlamento argentino en épocas de cambio: 1889, 1916
            y 1946*. Buenos Aires.
    1966b   Universal suffrage as an agent of mobilization. Paper
            presented at the Sixth World Congress of Sociology,
            Evian, France.
    1968a   La primera encuesta política argentina (1911). *Revista
            latinoamericana de sociología* 4 (No. 1):90-108.

1968b El mundo de los tangos de Gardel. *Revista latinoameri-cana de sociología* 4 (No. 3):341-62.

Collver, O. Andrew
    1965 *Birth rates in Latin America: new estimates of histori-cal trends and fluctuations.* Berkeley, Calif.

Cook, Noble David
    1968 *Padrón de los indios de Lima en 1613.* Lima.

Cornelius, Wayne A., Jr.
    1973 Nation-building, participation, and distribution: the politics of social reform under Cárdenas. In *Crisis, choice, and change: historical studies of political de-velopment.* Gabriel A. Almond *et al.*, eds. Boston.

Curti, Merle
    1959 *The making of an American community: a case study of democracy in a frontier county.* Stanford, Calif.

Curtin, Philip D.
    1969 *The Atlantic slave trade: a census.* Madison, Wis.

Dealy, Glen
    1968 Prolegomena on the Spanish American political tradition. *Hispanic American Historical Review* 48 (No. 1):37-58.

Dean, Warren
    1970 Latin American golpes and economic fluctuations, 1823-1966. *Social Science Quarterly* 51 (No. 1):70-80.

Denton, Frank H., and Phillips, Warren
    1971 Some patterns in the history of violence. In *Conflict and violence in Latin American politics: a book of readings,* Francisco José Moreno and Barbara Mitrani, eds. New York.

Deutsch, Karl W.
    1961 Social mobilization and political development. *American Political Science Review* 55 (No. 3):493-514.

Dogan, Mattei, and Rokkan, Stein (eds.)
    1969 *Quantitative ecological analysis in the social sciences.* Cambridge, Mass.

Dollar, Charles M., and Jensen, Richard J.
    1971 *Historian's guide to statistics: quantitative analysis and historical research.* New York.

Draper, N. R., and Smith, H.
    1966 *Applied regression analysis.* New York.

Duff, Ernest A., and McCamant, John F.
　　1968　Measuring social and political requirements for system
　　　　　stability in Latin America. *American Political Science
　　　　　Review* 62 (No. 4):1125-43.

Duncan, Otis Dudley
　　1968　Social stratification and mobility:　problems in the
　　　　　measurement of trend.　In *Indicators of social change:
　　　　　concepts and measurements*, Eleanor Bernert Sheldon and
　　　　　Wilbert E. Moore, eds.　New York.

Editorial Porrúa
　　1969　*Diccionario de insurgentes*.　México.

Feinberg, Stephen E.
　　1971　A statistical technique for historians:　standardizing
　　　　　tables of counts.　*Journal of Interdisciplinary History*
　　　　　1 (No. 2):305-15.

Fennell, Lee C.
　　1970　Legislative polarization and political cleavage in Argen-
　　　　　tina.　Paper presented at the annual meeting of the Amer-
　　　　　ican Political Science Association, Los Angeles.

Fernández, Julio
　　1970　*The political elite in Argentina*.　New York.

Fischer, David Hackett
　　1970　*Historian's fallacies:　toward a logic of historical
　　　　　thought*.　New York.

Fleischer, David V.
　　1971　O recrutamento político em Minas 1890/1918.　*Revista
　　　　　Brasileira de Estudos Políticos* (Estudos Sociais e Po-
　　　　　líticos, 30).

Florescano, Enrique
　　1969　*Precios del maíz y crisis agrícolas en México (1708-
　　　　　1810)*.　México.

Frank, André Gunder
　　1967　*Capitalism and underdevelopment in Latin America:　his-
　　　　　torical studies of Chile and Brazil*.　New York.
　　1969　*Latin America:　underdevelopment or revolution:　essays
　　　　　on the development of underdevelopment and the immediate
　　　　　enemy*.　New York.

Frey, Frederick W.
　　1965　*The Turkish political elite*.　Cambridge, Mass.

Gallo, Ezequiel (h.), and Sigal, Silvia
    1965   La formación de los partidos políticos contemporáneos:
            la U.C.R. (1890-1916). In *Argentina, sociedad de masas,*
            Torcuato di Tella *et al.*, eds. Buenos Aires.

Góngora, Mario
    1962   *Los grupos de conquistadores en Tierra Firme, 1509-1530:*
            fisonomía histórico-social de un tipo de conquista. San-
            tiago.

González Casanova, Pablo
    1967   *La democracia en México.* 2nd ed. México.

Graham, Hugh Davis, and Gurr, Ted Robert
    1969   *Violence in America: historical and comparative perspec-*
            tives. New York.

Havens, A. Eugene, and Flinn, William (eds.)
    1970   *Internal colonialism and structural change in Colombia.*
            New York.

Herlihy, David
    1971   Editing for the computer: the Florentine catasto of
            1427. *ACLS Newsletter* 22 (No. 2):1-7.

Hirschman, Albert O.
    1945   *National power and the structure of foreign trade.* Ber-
            keley, Calif.

Historical Methods Newsletter: Quantitative Analysis of Social,
Economic, and Political Development
    1967-   Published by the University of Pittsburgh.

Hoffman, Paul E.
    1970   The computer and colonial treasury accounts: a proposal
            for a methodology. *Hispanic American Historical Review*
            50 (No. 4):731-40.

Holsti, Ole R.
    1969   *Content analysis for the social sciences and humanities.*
            Reading, Mass.

Horowitz, Irving Louis (ed.)
    1970   *Masses in Latin America.* New York.

Imaz, José Luis de
    1970   *Los que mandan (Those who rule),* trans. and introd. by
            Carlos A. Astiz with Mary F. McCarthy. Albany, N.Y.
            First published, 1964.

Johnson, Chalmers
    1966   *Revolutionary change.* Boston, Mass.

Johnson, John J.
    1958   *Political change in Latin America: the emergence of the
            middle sectors*. Stanford, Calif.

Jowdy, E. William
    1971   Archival note: Archivo del Duque del Infantado. *His-
            panic American Historical Review* 51 (No. 1):128-29.

Kleppner, Paul
    1970   *The cross of culture: a social analysis of midwestern
            politics, 1850-1900*. New York.

Kling, Merle
    1962   Towards a theory of power and political instability in
            Latin America. In *Political change in underdeveloped
            countries: nationalism and communism*, John H. Kautsky,
            ed. New York.

Kreigel, A.; Gossez, R.; and Rougerie, J.
    1962   Sources et méthodes pour une histoire sociale de la
            classe ouvrière. *Le Mouvement Social* 40 (juillet-
            septembre):1-5.

Lambert, Jacques
    1967   *Latin America: social structures and political institu-
            tions*, trans. Helen Katel. Berkeley, Calif.

Landes, David S., and Tilly, Charles (eds.)
    1971   *History as social science*. Englewood Cliffs, N.J.

Layne, J. Gregg (ed.)
    1936   Padrón de la Ciudad de Los Angeles y su Jurisdicción.
            Historical Society of Southern California Quarterly 18
            (No. 3):81ff.

Lipset, Seymour Martin, and Hofstadter, Richard (eds.)
    1968   *Sociology and history: methods*. New York.

Lipset, Seymour Martin, and Solari, Aldo (eds.)
    1967   *Elites in Latin America*. New York.

Lockhart, James
    1972a   The social history of colonial Spanish America: evolu-
            tion and potential. *Latin American Research Review* 7
            (No. 1):6-45.
    1972b   *Men of Cajamarca: a social and biographical study of the
            first conquerors of Peru*. Austin, Tex.

Love, Edgar F.
    1971   Marriage patterns of persons of African descent in a
            colonial Mexico City parish. *Hispanic American Histor-
            ical Review* 51 (No. 1):79-91.

Love, Joseph L.
    1970   Political participation in Brazil, 1881-1969. *Luso-
            Brazilian Review* 7 (No. 2):3-24.

MacRae, Duncan, Jr.
    1970   *Issues and parties in legislative voting: methods of
            statistical analysis.* New York.

Mauro, Frédéric
    1969   La historia cuantitativa de Iberoamérica. *Atlántida* 7
            (No. 42):592-604.

McGreevey, William Paul
    1968   Recent research on the economic history of Latin America.
            Latin American Research Review 3 (No. 2):89-117.
    1972   Quantitative research in Latin American history of the
            nineteenth and twentieth centuries. In *The dimensions
            of the past: materials, problems, and opportunities for
            quantitative work in history,* Val R. Lorwin and Jacob M.
            Price, eds. New Haven, Conn.

Merritt, Richard L.
    1970   The emergence of American nationalism: a quantitative
            approach. In Swierenga, ed., cited below.

Mexico
    1965   Secretaría de Industria y Comercio, Dirección General de
            Estadística. *IV censo agrícola-ganadero y ejidal, 1960.
            Resumen general.* México.

Montenegro, Tulo H.
    1967   Bibliografía anotada de las principales fuentes de esta-
            dísticas sobre América Latina. In *Handbook of Latin
            American Studies,* No. 29. Gainesville, Fla.

Namier, Lewis
    1957   *The structure of politics at the accession of George III.*
            2nd ed. London.

Needler, Martin C.
    1968a   *Political development in Latin America: instability,
            violence, and evolutionary change.* New York.
    1968b   Political development and socioeconomic development: the
            case of Latin America. *American Political Science Review*
            62 (No. 3):889-97.

North, Robert C., *et al.*
    1963   *Content analysis: a handbook with applications for the
            study of international crisis.* Evanston, Ill.

O'Lessker, Karl
    1968   Who voted for Hitler? a new look at the class basis of
            Naziism. *American Journal of Sociology* 74 (No. 1):63-69.

Payne, James L.
   1965   *Labor and politics in Peru: the system of political
          bargaining.* New Haven, Conn.

Population Research Center, University of Texas
   1965   *International population census bibliography: Latin
          America and the Caribbean.* Austin, Tex.

Potter, David M.
   1963   Explicit data and implicit assumptions in historical
          study. In *Generalization in the writing of history,*
          Louis Gottschalk, ed. Chicago.

Price, Jacob M.
   1969   Recent quantitative work in history: a survey of the
          main trends. *History and Theory,* Beiheft 9 (Studies in
          quantitative history and the logic of the social sci-
          ences):1-13.

Rogoff, Natalie
   1953   *Recent trends in occupational mobility.* Glencoe, Ill.

Rowney, Don Karl, and Graham, James Q. (eds.)
   1969   *Quantitative history: selected readings in the quantita-
          tive analysis of historical data.* Homewood, Ill.

Ruddle, Kenneth (ed.)
   1972   *Latin American political statistics.* Los Angeles.

_____, and Hamour, Mukhtar (eds.)
   1971   *Statistical abstract of Latin America: 1970.* Los
          Angeles.

Rudé, George
   1959   *The crowd in the French revolution.* Oxford.

Russett, Bruce M.
   1969   Inequality and instability: the relation of land tenure
          to politics. In Rowney and Graham, eds., cited above.

Rustow, Dankwart A.
   1966   The study of elites: who's who, when, and how. *World
          Politics* 18 (No. 4):690-717.

Schmitter, Philippe C.
   1969   New strategies for the comparative analysis of Latin
          American politics. *Latin American Research Review* 4
          (No. 2):83-110.

Schwartz, Stuart B.
   1970   Magistracy and society in colonial Brazil. *Hispanic
          American Historical Review* 50 (No. 4):715-30.

Shorter, Edward
  1971   *The historian and the computer: a practical guide.*
          Englewood Cliffs, N.J.

Simmons, Merle E.
  1957   *The Mexican corrido as a source for interpretive study
          of modern Mexico, 1870-1950.* Indiana University Publi-
          cations, Humanities Series (No. 38). Bloomington.

Sinkin, Richard N.
  1973   The Mexican Constitutional Congress, 1856-1857: a sta-
          tistical analysis. *Hispanic American Historical Review*
          53 (No. 1):1-26.

Skidmore, Thomas E., and Smith, Peter H.
  1970   Notes on quantitative history: federal expenditure and
          social change in Mexico since 1910. *Latin American Re-
          search Review* 5 (No. 1):71-85.

Smith, Peter H.
  1969   *Politics and beef in Argentina: patterns of conflict
          and change.* New York.
  1970   The breakdown of democracy in Argentina, 1916-1930.
          Paper presented at the Seventh World Congress of Sociol-
          ogy, Varna, Bulgaria.
  1971   Politics within the [Mexican] revolution: the constitu-
          tional convention of 1916-1917. Paper presented at the
          annual convention of the American Historical Association,
          New York.
  1972a   The social base of Peronism. *Hispanic American Histor-
          ical Review* 52 (No. 1):55-73.
  1972b   The making of the Mexican constitution. Paper presented
          at a conference on the uses of quantitative methods for
          the analysis of legislative behavior in history, Iowa
          City.

Soares, Gláucio, and Hamblin, Robert L.
  1967   Socio-economic variables and voting for the radical left:
          Chile, 1952. *American Political Science Review* 61 (No.
          4):1053-65.

Soboul, Albert
  1964   *The Parisian sans-culottes and the French revolution
          1793-94.* Trans. Gwynne Lewis. Oxford.

Stavenhagen, Rodolfo
  1969   Seven erroneous theses about Latin America. In *Latin
          American radicalism: a documentary report on left and
          nationalist movements.* Irving Louis Horowitz, Josué de
          Castro, and John Gerassi, eds. New York.

Stein, Stanley J., and Stein, Barbara H.
  1970   *The colonial heritage of Latin America: essays on economic dependence in perspective.*   New York.

Swierenga, Robert P.
  1970   *Quantification in American history: theory and research.*
          New York.

Tello, Carlos
  1968   *La tenencia de la tierra en México.*   México.

TePaske, John J.
  1972   Quantification in Latin American colonial history.   In
          *The dimensions of the past: materials, problems, and
          opportunities for quantitative work in history,* Val R.
          Lorwin and Jacob M. Price, eds.   New Haven, Conn.

Thernstrom, Stephan
  1964   *Poverty and progress: social mobility in a nineteenth-
          century city.*   Cambridge, Mass.

_____, and Knights, Peter K.
  1970   Men in motion: some data and speculations about urban
          population mobility in nineteenth-century America.
          Journal of Interdisciplinary History 1 (No. 1):7-35.

Tilly, Charles
  1964   *The vendée.*   Cambridge, Mass.

_____, and Rule, James
  1965   *Measuring political upheaval.*   Research Monograph No. 19,
          Center of International Studies, Princeton University.

Toro, Josefina del
  1971   *Bibliography of the collective biography of Spanish
          America.*   Detroit.   First published, 1938.

Vann, Richard T.
  1969   History and demography.   *History and Theory,* Beiheft 9
          (Studies in quantitative history and the logic of the
          social sciences):64-78.

Vansina, Jan
  1971   Once upon a time: oral traditions as history in Africa.
          Daedalus (The historian and the world of the twentieth
          century):442-68.

Webb, Eugene J., *et al.*
  1966   *Unobtrusive measures: nonreactive research in the social
          sciences.*   Chicago.

Welsh, William A.
   1970   Methodological problems in the study of political leadership in Latin America. *Latin American Research Review* 5
(No. 3):3-33.
   1971   Toward effective typology construction in the study of
Latin American political leadership. *Comparative Politics* 3 (No. 2):271-80.

Wilkie, James W.
   1967   *The Mexican revolution: federal expenditure and social
change since 1910.* Berkeley, Calif.
   1969a *The Bolivian revolution and U.S. aid since 1952: financial background and context of political decisions.* Los
Angeles.
   1969b New approaches in contemporary Mexican historical research. Paper presented at the third meeting of Historians of Mexico and the United States, Oaxtepec, Mexico.
   1970a Statistical indicators of the impact of national revolution on the Catholic church in Mexico, 1910-1967. *Church
and State* 12 (No. 1):89-106.
   1970b On methodology and the use of historical statistics.
Latin American Research Review 5 (No. 1):87-91.
   1971   New hypotheses for statistical research in recent Mexican
history. *Latin American Research Review* 6 (No. 2):3-17.

Winchester, Ian
   1970   The linkage of historical records by man and computer:
techniques and problems. *Journal of Interdisciplinary
History* 1 (No. 1):107-24.

SOCIAL ANTHROPOLOGY

Robert C. Hunt

This paper is concerned with the uses of quantitative
data in Latin America from the perspective of sociocultural anthropology; my major purpose is to review the
types of approaches that have been used to generate and
utilize such data.[1] First, it should be pointed out
that there is very little research in social anthropology on Latin America as such. Latin America is not a
unified subject for most anthropologists; rather, it
represents a geographical cluster within which indivi-
uals specialize in some region or topic (e.g., central
Brazilian tribes). In this paper, then, I shall refer
to many studies which have been conducted wholly or
partly *in* Latin America, but few if any which are *on*
Latin America as a whole.

By Latin America I mean the mainland south of the
Rio Grande. Studies on various Spanish Caribbean and
other islands will not be covered, nor will I refer to
studies of those Latin American peoples and cultures
found outside the defined territory (e.g., studies of
Mexican-Americans). Another excluded category is the
enclave communities of foreigners in Latin America,
such as the Mennonites in Mexico and elsewhere, the
Japanese in Brazil and Peru, the Jews in various capi-
tals, the East Indians of the Caribbean rim, etc.

While these populations belong to the geographic universe of Latin America, in a cultural sense they clearly must be set apart. We take Latin America to mean a
cultural and social entity as well as a geographic one,
and the populations of primary interest are those which
are either aboriginal, in the sense of having a language
and a culture which is descended from populations present on the land mass in 1492, or Iberianized, in the
sense of speaking Spanish or Portuguese and having in-
tegrated institutions which derive from the Iberian pen-
insula throughout the colonial period. I wish to define
these latter two categories of culture carriers within
the geographic boundary as my ethnic universe.

A further point concerns the kind of territorial and
social units which anthropologists usually choose for
organizing research. While many disciplines focus on
the nation-state or on groups of nations, anthropology
typically focuses upon more restricted units, namely,
tribes (for aborigines) and communities (for people usually called peasants). There is some discussion of
these units in the literature (Arensberg 1961; Helm 1967;
R. Hunt 1969), but suffice it to say here that only recently has the injunction to study larger units in Latin
America received a hearing among anthropologists. A few
regional studies are now appearing (Pi-Sunyer 1964; Colby and Van den Berghe 1969; Adams 1970), but the regions
in question are usually small and relatively homogeneous
in terms of ecology and populations. The vast bulk of
the studies referred to here will utilize standard anthropological units, the tribe and the peasant community.

Turning to what we mean by anthropological, at least
five possibilities come to mind: studies done by professional anthropologists, studies of social and territorial units which are usually chosen by anthropologists
(tribes, communities, Indians, peasants), studies using
reports by professional anthropologists, studies of in-

terest to at least some social anthropologists who specialize in Latin America, and studies of anthropological
problems. The fourth and fifth criteria above are in-
adequate--the fourth because it hardly excludes anything,
and the fifth because there are very few problems which
are of interest to anthropologists alone. Our sample,
then, includes studies by professional anthropologists,
along with studies of social and territorial units usually studied by anthropologists but conducted by persons
in other professions (e.g., Belshaw 1967). However, I
will sometimes refer to comparative studies which do not
meet the first and second criteria. The exceptions utilize, in a significant way, insights or studies produced
by anthropologists.

By sociocultural anthropology I mean that part of the
discipline which deals primarily with cultural and social
variables. I exclude linguistic or biological anthropology, archaeology, and historical treatments.

Finally, this paper does not attempt an exhaustive
survey of all anthropological studies using quantitative
techniques and data. Rather, I intend to cover all major types of these studies, offering criticisms and evaluations of the investigators' efforts in the process.
Since most quantitative work in Latin America has been
done in Middle America, most of our examples will be
drawn from research there.

The Structure of Quantification

Measurement and measurement scales. The nature of quantification itself presents a major problem for social
anthropologists. Quantitative data are the numerically
expressed results of observations. The process of converting observations into numbers is a tricky one at
best for the anthropologist. One obvious way of accom-
plishing this is simply to count the frequency of items

of a class. A second method involves conceptualizing
the attributes of an observed phenomenon in terms of
numbers built into the observational technique. There
are entity attributes which can thus be measured easily:
the surface area of a community, the distance between
communities, the amount of time it takes to plow a field
of a given size. More difficult to measure attributes,
such as energy inputs and outputs, seem beyond most of
us at this time, although a thorough search of other
disciplines (e.g., physiology) might yield useful techniques.[2]

By far the most common form of quantitative data
found in sociocultural anthropology is the frequency
count of items of a class. National or local bureaucracies gather some of these data (census, school atten-
dance), and occasionally make special purpose surveys
(e.g., a regional economic summary--Attolini 1949, 1950).
Many anthropological studies report at least some of the
information gathered, processed, and presented by bureau-
cratic agencies. Judging the validity of this information is difficult, especially in countries where census-
takers are not professionally trained.

The social anthropologist also conducts his own frequency counts. Virtually all of the studies considered
in this paper rely upon data gathered by the investigator. In this process, a series of observations is summarized to provide a set of numbers. The operations
that may be legitimately applied to these numbers, as
well as the conclusions drawn from them, depend largely
on which measurement scales are appropriate. Converting
anthropological observations into numbers is a complex
operation and requires a working knowledge of the premises of measurement scales.[3]

Nominal scales. Although the properties ascribable to

numbers and to measurement scales are related, they are
separable. The first property of numbers is uniqueness.
Consider the set of numbers 1, 2, 3, . . . n.   Uniqueness means that any entity represented by one number of
this set cannot be represented by any other number in
the set (i.e., no entity can be represented by more than
one symbol). Moreover, any two or more identical entities can be represented by only one symbol.

The simplest (and least powerful) measurement scale,
the nominal scale, is based on this property of numbers.
This scale is composed of two or more categories of a
class, each of which is unique: any entity can be assigned to only one category of the class measured by
the scale. The construction of such a scale can be illustrated by the example of sex. All human beings can,
without major significant exceptions, be classified as
male or female, but not both. The scale may not involve
numbers per se at all.

Another property of the nominal scale is the law of
the excluded middle. No instance can be neither or both,
if a twofold dichotomy is used. A further assumption
which normally applies is that all categories on the
scale form a class; they are unitary or of the same kind
for at least one variable. Moreover, the class must be
divisible into at least two categories along another variable. With a nominal scale, then, measurement requires
deciding which of two or more categories of a class best
describes a particular observation.

By sampling and summing the number of instances in
each category, one can convert data generated in a nominal scale into quantitative terms. The summations give
frequencies which can be manipulated mathematically by
comparing, taking ratios, or testing for differences in
percentage of occurrence.

Ordinal scales. A second relevant mathematical property of numbers is order (i.e., the symbols can be arranged
in predictable sequences). The order may involve occurrence in time, relative size, or any other sequential
property.

The measurement scale derived from this property of
numbers is only ordinal. The ordinal scale does not
permit judgments about the absolute distance between
two or more adjacent pairs. For example, one might
measure the degree of social complexity of the Onas,
Nuers, Trobrianders, and Aztecs. We could assign a rank
of 1 to the Onas, 2 to the Nuers, 3 to the Trobriand
Islanders, and 4 to the Aztecs. Since 3 follows 1 and
2, we conclude that the Trobrianders are further than
the Nuers from the Onas. But we cannot conclude that
the difference between 3 and 2 is the same as the difference between 2 and 1 or 4 and 3. Historically, in
social anthropology, positions on ordinal scales of complexity were determined only for general empirical types
with a few categories (e.g., savagery, barbarism, civil-
ization; bands, tribes, chiefdoms, states). The procedure was to determine the ranks from a small arbitrary
sample, formulate theoretical definitions, and measure
other samples against the scale so constructed. But
quantitative anthropologists today are more sophisticated (Naroll 1956). A more common procedure recently has
been to collect an unbiased sample by any one of a variety of means, and then to rank all the items within the
sample. In this case, the number of positions on the
scale is not predetermined, and theoretically it may be
as numerous as the members of the sample. The ordering
is relativistic and particularistic with respect to a
given sample. Stages isolated by the researcher as a
result of scaling one sample are not necessarily significant for a different sample.

Whether a scale is nominal or ordinal is not always obvious. Ordinal scales can be dichotomized and thus may appear to be nominal scales (e.g., when societies in a modernization-level ordinal scale are divided between those which have and those which have not reached the takeoff point). One must decide what scale to use for every property of a society being measured. This decision is necessary because the statistical manipulations which one may perform on the resultant scores are determined by the properties of the measurement scale.

Ordinal scales permit more powerful statistics than nominal ones. The temptation is to use the most powerful scale, and in anthropology and other social sciences analysts frequently violate ground rules in order to use a more powerful test. The research design must take these pitfalls into account.

Interval and ratio scales. The next two scales are parametric, as opposed to the nonparametric nominal and ordinal types. For parametric scales the distance between any two positions can be measured in an absolute sense (equal intervals). For example, if societies are measured for size of settlement and one finds that settlement A has 10,000, B has 20,000, and C has 30,000, the difference between A and B is obviously the same as the difference between B and C. On scales of this kind, addition and subtraction can be performed, as well as the mathematical operations dependent upon them. Scales with all the previous properties and equal intervals between steps are known as interval scales. They are rarely usable in social anthropology.

The next property of scales is an absolute zero point. Interval scales do not have this property. Consider, for example, the scale of intelligence. The norm has been arbitrarily set at an IQ of 100, a mean value. The

amount that individuals differ from this score can be
measured. It is assumed that an IQ of 105 is as far
from 100 as an IQ of 95, but there is no absolute zero.
In measuring height or weight, on the other hand, there
is an absolute zero. Scales with this property, in addition to the previous ones, are called ratio scales,
and operations involving multiplication and division
are appropriate. More sophisticated mathematics is possible with ratio than with interval scales. For my purpose the difference between the two is not very relevant,
because neither is used often in sociocultural anthropology. Virtually all sample studies contain only nominal or ordinal scales and utilize nonparametric statistics.

Sampling. Sampling is a useful strategy in anthropology
because limited resources prevent one from gathering
data on the whole population. The ideal sample contains
all relevant characteristics of the parent population,
and in the same proportions. But without empirically
studying the parent population, there is no way to be
sure of such correspondence. Therefore, the strategy
best followed is to select the instances in the sample
randomly, and to select as many of them as resources
allow. Since any statement based on an examination of
less than the whole of the population is based on a sample, it is important to understand the relationship between the sample and the population.

Sampling involves several operations. First, the
universe or population from which the sample is drawn
should be highly specified. Second, the method of draw-
ing the sample should be specified. Since the objective
of analyzing a sample is to generalize the findings to
the population, uncertainty in either operation severely
hinders confidence in generalizing. In the literature

under review, sampling has received the least attention
of all the factors in research design and reporting; consequently, the generality of the results is uncertain.
Moreover, anthropologists seldom use random sampling
techniques. Most sociocultural anthropologists use what
they usually refer to as diagnostic samples in their
field work and analysis. Owing to technical limitations
on data gathering in the field, the samples often are
selected intuitively.

Empirical Studies[4]

There are two major purposes for conducting quantitative research. One is purely descriptive; for example,
one might attempt to describe an ethnic unit in terms of
a single variable or a set of variables (age distribution, income, residence patterns, numbers of people growing given kinds of crops, Rorschach responses). These
descriptions are commonly called distributions. Normally, two measures can be determined for every distribution. One is a measure of central tendency (mean, mode,
median). The other is a measure of disperson or variation (standard deviation for interval and ratio scales).
Such descriptions are not necessarily constructed to
bolster an argument, nor are they necessarily conceived
as something which must be explained. They may simply
be presented as facts. When they are used for more complex goals, however, the strictures on sampling must be
applied, or the results will be of little value.

The other purpose of quantitative research (and the
major one) is to test hypotheses. The scientist suspects
that something is true (i.e., a hypothesis is formulated),
and he sets out deliberately to gather and analyze quantitative data in such a way that he can make a clear decision about the validity of his insight. Thus one can
inquire only about the quantitative characteristics of a

phenomenon, and the relationship between two or more
phenomena.

Tabulations. A survey of the presence of quantitative
data in works of social anthropology of Latin America
reveals that, for most of the period under consideration
(1928-70), the most common quantitative technique has
been tabulation. Most field studies of a community or
small region present at least some demographic data in
numerical form. Other kinds of census materials may include information on amounts of crops planted (and by
whom), years of schooling by age cohort, number of trips
made outside the community, or kinds of material possessions in the household (see Redfield and Villa Rojas
1934:53). Data of this sort appear in almost every
study. Usually this material is presented as fact and
is neither explained nor utilized to explain something
else. The mode of gathering the data, the sampling procedures involved, and the accuracy of the materials are
almost never published with the study. Except for data
on price and weight in market transactions, the measurement scales used are almost always nominal.

The most notable example of the tabulation approach
is Sol Tax's *Penny Capitalism* (1953). In this work he
collected vast amounts of economic data, expressed quantitatively. The procedures for collecting it are unusu-
ally well described, although the sampling procedures
are not always so clear. The quantitative data are used
to build hypotheses and support arguments, not merely
presented as facts. For example, Indian peasants are
judged "good" if not perfect bookkeepers (1953:31), and
the Panajachel Indians are considered "capitalists." On
the other hand, he makes assertions that only can be supported by quantitative data which he did not present.
For instance, Tax claims the price of onions depends to

a degree on the size of the local crop, and that supply
and demand affect the price. Yet he does not support
this statement in any way with quantitative data (1953:
112). This is not a trivial point, for the nature of
peasant marketing systems is at issue. This question
is particularly significant, because we have a wealth
of contradictory hypotheses but very little information
on how peasant markets really function.

Kelly and Palerm (1952) present enormous amounts of
quantitative materials on the Tajin Totonac, derived
from relatively large samples. While I feel that the
data are accurate, both the sampling and presentation
create problems. It is clear that the universe they
studied is stratified, at least by wealth, yet the sample is not.

Kelly and Palerm present rich data on many kinds of
variables. They had an excellent opportunity to study
the relationship between variables, but they did not do
so. And it is impossible for us to do it, since, as in
many of the older monographs, the data are not arranged
by household. Thus one cannot, using the household as
the unit, learn whether land holding varies with other
material possessions, language, etc. The same is true
of Drucker's study (1963). A reanalysis of the Chan Kom
materials (Goldkind 1965, 1966) has been possible primarily because one is able to associate traits with particular households. I have pleaded elsewhere (Hunt 1968:
1010), as has Leach (1961), that authors should provide
detailed tables of data so that other students can do
further analyses. If census material is gathered on
many households, covering several variables, it is a
loss to the profession if this information is not shared.
Properly published, such data can be manipulated statistically by other scholars for different scientific purposes.

Associations by inspection. In the 1960's both the number and sophistication of quantitative studies increased
rapidly. Techniques changed, and the kinds of problems
attacked became broader and more complex. By the 1960's,
in addition to economic anthropology, we find studies of
social stratification, differences between Indians and
mestizos, information capacity of naming systems, and
many others. Similarly, the large-sample comparative
literature has developed.

A dominant concern of anthropologists and other social scientists is the establishment of functional relationships between institutions. Quantitative data are
used in the anthropology of Latin America to learn if
two or more variables are associated. Among the more
prominent studies of communities which assess association
by inspection rather than by statistics are Nash (1961)
and Cook (1970). Each study is concerned with correlating variation in sales of locally produced handicrafts
(pottery and stoneware) with the yearly cycle in its agricultural, seasonal, and religious ritual aspects.

M. Nash asserts that there is a negative relationship
between pottery output and land holdings for households
(1961; see also J. Nash 1969, 1970). He finds that peak
production is associated with domestic demand for cash
(in rhythm with the ritual cycle), rather than with high
prices in the market. Nash derives his data partially
from potters' reports, not from first-hand observation.
His sample was extremely small, consisting of the activities of a single potter over a one-year period and two
additional ones for a period of three months. Nash be-
lieves his universe is stratified in terms of low and
high producers. But we do not know how his sample of
three reflects this. His major informant was also a
large producer. There are no data presented on land

holdings per potter. He does attempt to interpret
his quantitative data, however, for he is interested
in the relationship between peasant craft output and
the operation of the money market. He concludes that
output is geared to fluctuating demand for cash on the
part of the household, and not to fluctuating demand in
the market. It cannot be said that this work is based
on sound quantitative research. The sample is too small
to permit confident generalization, the reliability of
the reports on production cannot be determined by the
reader, and the number of observations is very small.
While his conclusions make structural sense and are interesting, strictly speaking they are not conclusions
at all, but hypotheses which remain to be tested. Nash
also claims that the market price of pottery is determined by supply and demand. Although this could be sub-
stantiated with quantitative data, he presents none
(Nash 1961:187).

A second study on the same topic is one by Cook (1970)
on producers of grinding stones (*metates*) in the Oaxaca
valley. His article is an improvement on Nash's. For
twenty-three months he recorded all market transactions
in a single market for all people from one community.
During this period there were variations in sales and
price. Upon inspecting a graph of the sales figures,
he claims that variations in sales must be explained
by using both economic and anthropological variables (supply and demand factors, plus seasonal, ecological, and
cultural factors). His discussion on these points is
convincing.[5]

Again we see a study claiming that supply and demand
determine price. But the generalization is not backed
by evidence. Evaluation of sampling is not much of a
problem in his article, for Cook took all persons selling
in the Oaxaca market. Unfortunately, he does not state

the size of his sample.

We can see in these two studies a significant improvement in method over previous works. Even if his data do
not conclusively support his position, Nash's study es-
tablishes a problem as well as a method for studying it.
Cook, a decade later, improves data-gathering by both
increasing the size of his sample (we assume), and by
increasing the time run of his observations to almost
two years. The next time this is tried, I hope the study
will be designed for the employment of statistical techniques, so we can have a more accurate picture of the
relationships among price and volume of sales, market
forces, and internal community factors.

Other features of social organization have received
some quantitative treatment in the last decade. Drucker
(1963) gathered quantitative data on a large number of
persons in a lowland Mixtec town. She compared *revesti-
dos* (redressed or acculturated Indians) with Indians and
mestizos, making significant suggestions about associations by inspection (cf. Hunt 1968). However, she did
not mathematically analyze associations between variables, and unfortunately she did not present the data
in such a way that secondary analyses could be performed.
Another sophisticated example of association by inspection dealing with the developmental cycle of residence
is Hammel (1961), who compared a slum and a rural village in Peru (see below).

Marvin Harris has investigated ambiguity in the ways
Brazilian subjects assign terms connoting racial types
to standardized pictures of racial phenotypes. A sample
of 100 was chosen and broken down by sex, region, and
socioeconomic status. Each subject was given 72 cards
containing pictures of a face and shoulders. Each por-
trait varied systematically along five dimensions (skin
tone, hair form, lip form, nose form, sex; 3 x 3 x 2 x

2 x 2 = 72). Respondents provided a total of 492 different categorizations (1970:2). Harris's problem was
to analyze this material in such a way as to elicit order while preserving the ambiguity which, he suggests,
is a highly important characteristic of the Brazilian
cognitive system.

To accomplish these aims he studied the association
of the twelve most frequent terms (each having been assigned at least 100 times with the cards). By comparing
pairs of terms, patterns were found, but with larger
groups of terms, little order was discernible (Harris
1970:10-12). Harris concludes that the cognitive system is ambiguous; moreover, the data provide interesting
insights into the functions of ambiguity in a racial
code adopted by a multi-racial, multi-class society.
Harris is admirably explicit about his sampling procedure and its weakness. He quite properly refuses to
generalize (in a technical sense) from his data base.
Unfortunately, he does not attempt to utilize his data
on identified variations among respondents (social class,
rural vs. urban) to see if some of the variation could
be accounted for in this way. Further, it is uncertain
whether socioeconomic statuses are present in the stim-
uli in any way. If they are, they should be eliminated
as sources of order, especially because it is apparently
true that class and phenotype are associated in Brazil
(Harris 1970:1).

Associations measured statistically. The 1960's also
produced studies which used statistical measures of association systematically. Hickman (1962) employed factor analysis and Guttman scaling to analyze relative
degrees of assimilation among all household heads in a
Peruvian village. Hammel presented three papers based
on census materials that he and others gathered for a

valley system in Peru (1961, 1964a, 1964b). In the
first he compares developmental cycles of the residence
profile of domestic groups for the slum of a small city,
and for a nearby rural village. Quantitative data form
the core of his paper. He finds great variation within
and between samples, but also patterns within both samples. He wisely rejects statistical tests of significance, for the samples are too small for some categories, and he wants better and deeper qualitative data
first (1961).

In a second article Hammel compares several characteristics of domestic groups (fertility, age distribution, sex distribution, conjugal unions, occupations,
house structure, and family composition) for whole cities, a rural slum, and several rural villages (1964a:
347-348). He uses chi-square (X^2) "where both sets of
values were nominal and Kolmogorov-Smirnov where at
least one of them was at least ordinal" (Hammel 1964a:
347, n.2). Quantitative data in this paper are extensive, and his statistical measures seem careful and appropriate. He found significant differences between
whole cities, slums, and villages on some variables
(e.g., fertility between urban and rural groups) which
challenge previously accepted generalizations.

In the third article Hammel was interested in establishing the territorial nature of marriage choices in
the same valley system in Peru. Originally, his samples
were not comparable, so he used control procedures which
reduced his sample sizes for the statistical tests. He
does not indicate which statistic was used, although
they were run on an IBM 101, and he cautions that his
small subsample sizes and their nonprobability nature
affect the tests of significance. Data are presented
in terms of cumulative frequencies. He found a territorial unit (which he calls the section) that is statis-

tically endogamous, in the sense that the section-level
endogamy is high while in larger units or across sections
the frequency of endogamous marriages is much lower.
These articles are significant because the uses of the
quantitative data are built into the analysis, and because the author deals with the data elegantly and appropriately.

In 1968 Buchler and Selby demonstrated how, for a
sample of eighty-four households in a town in Oaxaca,
Mexico, decisions about residence for newlyweds are accounted for by a jural rule of virilocality. They also
showed that exceptions to it are explained by differences in wealth. In order for a man to live with his
wife's family, her family must be considerably wealthier
than his own. Again, chi-square (X^2) was the statistic
used (1968:51-52).

A work which seriously emphasizes quantitative methodology is Cancian's work on the Zinacantán officership
system (1965). As part of his research design, Cancian
deliberately took large samples of individual behavior,
matching them not only with each other but also with
normative rules. His quantitative data and analysis aid
him in generalizing about social structure (1965:2). The
book contains many numerical statements of association
(X^2), complete with levels of significance. His numerical data proceed from a tabulation of such individual
activities as participation in the civil-religious hierarchy, farming, and kinship involvement. His measurement scale, derived from enumeration, is ordinal. In
some cases measurement is clear-cut--for instance, where
the cost of an officership is at issue. Other ordinal
measures concern the prestige of a cargo, the number of
a man's brothers and other close male kin, and age. For
purposes of testing associations among these variables,
Cancian dichotomizes all of them, perhaps in some cases

losing the ability to discriminate.

Cancian also solved sampling problems in a satisfactory way. Since population of the municipio is over 7,000, establishing necessary rapport and creating a master list for the population were too difficult, given the resources available. For many of his measures, therefore, he took the entire relevant population from each of three of fifteen hamlets in the entire municipio (Cancian 1965:201-4; Vogt 1969:148). Cancian wonders if this procedure introduced a systematic bias, and he states that it should be empirically tested. His sample sizes are quite large for anthropology, ranging from from 38 to 252 individuals. The samples are specified and drawn adequately; his measures are reasonable, given the nature of the social units; and the statistical procedures he employs are relevant and meaningful. He has also presented a convincing argument for the validity of his conclusions.

Several other researchers have investigated differences between roles in terms of behavioral variables. In these cases, hypotheses are generated partly from participant observation data and partly from expectations based on the ethnographic and theoretical literature on Middle America. O'Nell and Selby hypothesize differences between men and women in two Zapotec towns concerning frequency of *susto* experiences (1968). Hunt, Hunt, and Weitlaner (1968) hypothesize a relationship between frequency of different naming systems and regional geographical location. Hunt and Hunt (1969) hypothesize that Indians and mestizos would use the national court system differently for seven distinct types of cases. In all cases the hypotheses are supported with mathematical studies of quantitative data (x^2 in the first two, Kendall's Tau and Kolmogorov-Smirnov in the third). However, none of the studies can claim to

have conclusively demonstrated its hypothesis, due to
deficiencies in the sampling. Only one study (O'Nell
and Selby) selected one of its two samples randomly.
In none of the cases was the population adequately defined.

Some Middle American studies published in the last
few years exhibit considerable methodological clever-
ness and sophistication. For example, Fábrega (1971)
wanted to know whether a particular kind of medical
practitioner in Zinacantán had more specialized medical
knowledge than laymen. His sample was all thirty-three
practitioners in several hamlets, and thirty-six in a
control group "obtained using a similar procedure"
(1971:28), whatever that means. Each subject was asked
ten questions about each of seventy-six illness terms,
and a matrix was constructed. Using the mode and H, a
non-metric measure of dispersion, his conclusions are startling. The practitioners and the laymen are the same on
the mode and on the dispersion (Fábrega 1971:30-31).
The variability within groups was patterned differently.
The specialists had lower variability in terms of the
kinds of personnel needed for treatment and the existence of remedies, but higher variability on questions
of cause and the need to visit a mountain in treatment.

Fábrega's paper is interesting and productive, but
it must be read with care. First, the sample is not
sufficiently specified. Second, the correlation coefficient is not specified. Finally, special caution must
be used in generalizing from studies of this sort. Good
studies define variables operationally, but they often
assign broad and ambiguous labels to the variables.
Technically, this is the problem of validity. When interpreting the results, the reader must constantly remember the operational meaning of the variable, and not
the label for it. In this case, the label is medical

knowledge, but the operational definition of the variable is found in the responses to ten questions on seventy-six illness terms in an unspecified environment.
The folk and scientific meaning of medical knowledge,
for me, includes diagnostic and clinical skills as well
as verbal response, among other things; these are not
included in Fábrega's operational definition. I am not
arguing that these factors should have been treated in
his study, but merely that the reader should beware of
ambiguous labels when confronted with quantitative studies.

A different kind of quantitative analysis appears in
a study by Collier and Bricker (1970). They investigate
the association between nicknames, ordinary patronyms,
and genealogical membership, using a nonparametric measure of association (Goodman-and-Kruskal's Gamma), as
well as an information theory measure of information.
Rather than draw a sample, they define their universe
as all the married males of a hamlet of Zinacantán. The
paper is interesting primarily because it involves an
application of information theory to the cognitive domains of a culture.

Thompson (1970) has attempted to apply mathematical
principles to quantitative data in a study of changes
in social rank in a Yucatecan city. He took a random
sample of males in the town and had members of the town
judge their social rank according to a six-point scale.
This judging was done also for their fathers, to produce
data on inter- as well as intra-generational mobility.
Thompson uses a product-moment correlation (r) as his
statistic to check the correlation between the status
of father and son, and he tries regression analysis as
well. He did not identify his r, but it apparently is
Pearson's r, the best-known parametric correlation statistic. Finally, he generated a stochastic model in an

attempt to predict future development of the ranking
system (in terms of frequencies for the six categories).
There are many weaknesses in this paper, but I will mention only one here. Thompson attempts to predict the
future with a stochastic model. This prediction appears
futile, for it necessitates correct assumptions about
the relative future importance of the various sources
of variance, and he gives no evidence to justify his
assumptions.

In the last fifteen years two research teams have
worked in the area of Ciudad Sahagún, a new industrial
town recently located in the midst of a rural pulque-
producing area of Mexico. The early study was conducted
by two rural sociologists (F. and R. Young 1966). The
area was restudied by a team of anthropologists headed
by Frank Miller and Pertti Pelto.

One seriously quantitative publication from the second study has appeared so far, that by Poggie and Miller
(1969). Ciudad Sahagún was established in the early
1950's in a valley system which contains twenty-four
other communities. The article is concerned with changes in institutional complexity among the other twenty-
four communities as responses to the presence of the
industrial center. Poggie and Miller took as their universe the industrial center and the twenty-two surrounding villages "that form a geographic and sociometric
network" (Poggie and Miller 1969:190). They utilized
two variables: institutional complexity, which was
measured by means of the Guttman-scale technique with
fourteen scale items, and contact with the center, which
was also measured by a Guttman scale consisting of eight
scale items. Both of these scales had been used by the
Youngs for the 1950-58 period. The Poggie and Miller
effort therefore represents one of the rarest phenomena
in social anthropology, a restudy in which comparable

data are gathered for two points in time. Most restudies have either been contentious (Lewis 1951), or they
have focused on different topics (Redfield 1950; Foster
1967; Leslie 1960).

It is extremely difficult to convince social anthropologists that a time dimension in any study generates
serious implications for the research design. If the
design implies that comparable observations will be necessary at two different points in time, the probability
that the social anthropologist will either not recognize
the problem or ignore it is distressingly high. All
studies of change imply observations at at least two
different points in time. Solutions to this methodological problem vary, of course, from the use of the contemporary ancestor (Graves *et al.* 1969; Hunt 1971) to
genuine restudies (Poggie and Miller). The Poggie and
Miller data were gathered in the same frame as the Young
and Young study, with the same variables, and from the
same sampling units.

The purpose of the Poggie and Miller study was to
"measure growth in complexity by means of the Guttman-
scale technique" (p. 190). Their conclusions are:
among the less complex communities in the sample, rank
change in complexity in the last eight-year period can
be predicted by the degree of contact with the new industrial center; and trends of change are not uniform
or continuous, for the process of growth may suddenly
stop, and it is not always related to contact (p. 190).
It cannot be doubted that their results are significant,
given their problem. What I wish to comment on here,
however, is the nature of the problem they have set for
themselves. The most salient characteristic of this
article is the definition of the problem. They propose
to estimate the variance in community complexity accounted for by an index of contact with the industrial cen-

ter. This is not the same thing as trying to discover
what accounts for variance in institutional complexity.
The purpose of this article is not to explore the structure of institutional differentiation. I suspect most
anthropologists would respond to this research situation
by attempting to understand how and why these communities are changing in complexity. If this were done,
other factors would have been examined. The most obvious is the dynamics of the relationships between *haciendas* and *hacendados*, on one hand, and between *campesi-
nos* and *ejidatarios* on the other, which frequently are
expressed territorially (see Gibson 1964 for the colonial period; see Redfield and Villa 1934 and Friedrich
1970 for twentieth-century cases in Yucatán and Michoa-
cán, respectively).

There is a serious dilemma here. The anthropologist
is encouraged by training and tradition to analyze an
empirical problem in a way that accounts for as much of
the variance as possible. As a consequence, such research tends to be localized and particularistic. The
possibilities of contributing to general theory, therefore, would seem to be reduced. The other strategy involves arbitrarily setting up polar opposites, selecting a variable of universal interest (in this case, contact with a modern center) and estimating the shape and
function of that variable in a particular research environment. This strategy assures universal relevance,
but one misses the conviction that the variable makes
sense in terms of the local situation.

Neither the Young nor Poggie-Miller studies include
any long-term intensive qualitative work which estab-
lishes the variables that make most sense in the local
situation. For example, it may be that the index of
contact used by the Youngs (and by Poggie and Miller)
is not the best one for this particular area. I hold

no brief for some other index; I am merely and hypo-
thetically changing some variables in the design, in an
attempt to imagine other solutions.

If an index generates a distortion, the results are
of unknown value as a contribution to the general theory
of modernization. However, intensive qualitative work
in this case might have led the investigators away from
contact as a prominent variable. As a result, no contribution would have been made to our understanding of
contact as a phenomenon. (This is part of a more general issue concerning research strategies mentioned above
and in the concluding section.) The dilemma is not easily solved.

Modern psychological anthropology lends itself to numerical reporting, particularly for researchers who include interview schedules, systematic observation of
subjects, and projective tests among their techniques.
There have been a few quantitative studies in psychological anthropology. Billig, Gillin, and Davidson (1947-
1948) present results of Rorschach protocols for 25 Indians and 25 *ladinos* from San Luis Jilotepeque; Abel and
Calabresi present similar materials from 106 Tepoztecans
(in Lewis 1951:306-18).

One of the most sophisticated and well-designed cross-
cultural studies is that by the Whitings *et al.*, on socialization in six cultures (B. Whiting 1963). The research design was carefully prepared for cross-cultural
comparisons, statistical manipulation, and hypothesis-
testing. The questions were worked out in advance,
as were the guidelines for collecting and analyzing the
data (J. Whiting, *et al.*, 1966). One field site
was in Oaxaca, Mexico, and a short descriptive monograph
on it has appeared (Romney and Romney 1963). Using factor analysis as the major statistical tool, psychologists
Minturn and Lambert (1964) analyzed the responses to in-

terviews with a sample of mothers in each of the six
cultures. The report contains a chapter on the Mexican
sample, as well as systematic comparisons between the
Mexican and the other five culture samples. One of the
most interesting findings so far is that, in all the
cultures studied, the socialization techniques used by
mothers have more to do with demands of the culture on
the mother's schedule and energy than with either a
conscious plan or blueprint for raising children properly, or unconscious parental motives and anxieties. Further quantitative analyses of anthropological significance should emerge from this project in the future.

In 1970 Fromm and Maccoby published a book on peasant
character and life in the Mexican state of Morelos. The
work is part of a long-term project in which anthropologists participated as field workers. They developed an
extensive questionnaire for analyzing the character
structure of individuals, and they administered the instrument to all adults in a community (N=417) and half
the children (N=187) (1970:41). After the data were
analyzed by frequency in categories, a factor analysis
yielded three major character types. Using the product-
moment correlation, these character types were correlated with other variables such as education, social rank,
and willingness to innovate. Strictly speaking, the
product-moment correlation requires interval data, and
it is hard to conceive of tabulated frequencies on questionnaire responses as interval data. But apparently
psychologists commonly do this, and I am not prepared to
explore this issue here.

My major objection to this work is that, in spite of
the fact that they hired anthropological field workers,
the book shows extreme naïveté about rural Mexican cul-
ture--for instance, the authors do not understand beliefs about the nature of souls and witches, and they

appear to know even less about the institutional context
of the particular village they studied (cf. LeVine 1971).
Yet, if one knows enough about rural Mexico from other
more anthropological works, there is much to be learned
from this book. Its value lies in the workers' having
canvassed the entire population on many socioeconomic
and character traits.

Large-sample comparative studies. Let us now turn from
field studies of single villages to library-based, systematic comparisons of community studies. In anthropology there is an ancient and honorable (if tangled) tradition of investigating the relationship between traits
by the cross-cultural comparative method. This is an
unfortunate term, for comparison is a major premise of
anthropology, and systematic large-sample arrays of
traits constitute only one method, and not the major or
dominant one. But this method has been the primary lo-
cus of quantitative research in anthropology since Tylor
first suggested its use (Tylor 1888).

Many large-sample studies include information from
tribal or peasant groups in Latin America. Because they
cover much more than Latin America and have been recently reviewed in the literature (Naroll 1970), I shall not
discuss them here. Of more direct interest are the
large-sample works which are concerned exclusively with
Latin America. A number of such studies order a set of
communities in an array which supposedly represents a
developmental ranking from least to most "folk" (traditional, undifferentiated, etc.). Redfield's *Folk Culture of Yucatan* (1941) is the classic study, but neither
his nor Mosk's (1954) is quantitative.[6]

In the last ten years, four studies of village modernization have appeared which have amassed frequencies
(Kunkel 1961; Whitten 1965; Young and Fujimoto 1965;

Graves *et al.* 1969). Kunkel, considering economic change
as the independent variable and sociocultural change as
the dependent one, took a sample of fifteen Mexican community studies and found there was a correlation. The
association was derived by inspection of a table. Kunkel
constructed an index of national cultural elements and
formed a scale for his five-part independent variable.
He found a high degree of association between rank ordering on the dependent variable and placement on the
economic scale.

Whitten, on the other hand, took rational power structure as his independent variable. His dependent variable
was composed of ten sociocultural traits, defined as
presence and absence of national elements. After dichot-
omizing each trait in his tabular presentation, Whitten
found a strong relationship between the two variables,
again by inspection. His sample consisted of seventeen
community studies (Chan Kom and Tepoztlán included twice
at different points in time) from eight countries of
Latin America.

Young and Fujimoto chose a sample of fifty-four community studies, all of which had sufficient information
on the socioeconomic traits they were interested in.
They covered twelve countries, but 58 percent of the
works were about Mexico and Guatemala. Arranging the
communities on a Guttman scale of social differentiation, they came up with a scale which has a .82 coefficient of scalability. They found agreement between their
findings and those of Kunkel, but they tested for the independence of Kunkel's variables and found that their own
scale did not permit them to subsume Kunkel's two variables under a single variable of social differentiation.

Graves, Graves, and Kobrin (1969) critically point
out that this use of the Guttman scale was an attempt to
derive historical inferences from arrays obtained from

synchronic data. Besides questioning this position on
theoretical grounds, they visited forty Mexican communities, including those in the Kunkel (1961) and Young
and Fujimoto (1965) samples. They recorded both the
presence and absence of twenty-four variables, plus the
alleged date of adoption of the traits. The developmental scale was correlated with the historical sequences,
which accounted for less than 50 percent of the variance.
Even this level of correlation was accounted for more
completely by using population size as an independent
variable (their correlation was .83 between population
size and scale position [Graves *et al*. 1969:327]). The
authors thus question the internal linear unity of such
scales, and the validity of inferring historical sequences from them. They suggest that the actual processes
of evolution may resemble a multilinear rather than a
unilinear mode of development.

Analysis and Final Reflections

The sampling problem. Of all the issues in quantitative
anthropological research, sampling stands out as one of
the most important and most neglected--the one most need-
ing careful thought and design.[7] Many instances of quantified data in the literature surveyed here fail to mention, much less specify, the universe being sampled.
Many works do not indicate the way in which the sample
was chosen. (Studies by Cancian and other Zinacantán
workers are exceptions.)

Sampling is also critical from a pragmatic point of
view. The anthropologist has operated within an essentially tribal tradition, and this choice has had far-
reaching consequences. Since it has been assumed that
tribes are relatively small and homogeneous, it has been
assumed that they are constructed in terms of mechanical,
rather than organic, integration. It follows that any

small unit of a tribe will yield the same kind of information as any other small unit, and therefore the
choice of the small unit can be made solely on practical grounds, such as ease of access.[8]

When the discipline turned to peasant populations,
the situation changed radically. The tribal assumption
no longer held. By definition, peasants are parts of
states and strongly linked to cities; any peasant community is highly differentiated and organically inte-
grated into a larger society. Furthermore, the territory of a state is subdivided into several layers of
political units (federation, states, counties, town-
ships; or, in much of Latin America, provinces, departments, and counties) which are differentiated by function as well as territorial and population size. In
these systems communities have political-legal statuses
in the territorial organization and, therefore, are differentiated by the same criteria. It follows that no
given community is necessarily the same as any other in
terms of size or political function and structure. Consequently, no single community is necessarily an adequate
sample of all communities within a state or region.

The same argument holds for economic and religious
structures and functions. Territories also are internally differentiated in terms of resources, products,
and access to markets. Their relationships to religious
institutions and personnel also vary systematically. In
sum, states are highly differentiated and organically in-
tegrated systems. The peasant community chosen for analysis must be placed within the proper structural context.

A further consequence of this state of affairs has
not been given sufficient attention. As David Kaplan
has suggested to me, the studies of peasant communities
in Middle America which are noted for their fullness of

data (and their use of quantitative materials) have been
based on the work of many investigators, either simultaneously by teams or serially over long periods (Foster
1948; Lewis 1951; Belshaw 1967; the Zinacantán studies,
such as Cancian 1965; Vogt 1966, 1969). Three reasons
for this situation should be obvious. First, studies
of peasants treat much larger populations than the typical tribal settlement. Second, the communities are internally differentiated, in terms of both social rank
and occupational specialization. Third, many of the decisions which are made in such a community are made with
reference to several outside systems, including the legal system, government agencies, political parties,
church bureaucracies, markets, corporations, other towns,
groups of patrons, clients, and friends and associates
who live elsewhere--to mention just a few.

The combination of size and complexity means that a
single investigator, with the standard field-work time
of one to one and a half years, is simply incapable of
collecting sufficient information on many different subjects over the whole community. Again the classical
tribalist field-worker assumption does not hold. The
consequences of these facts are plain: since whole populations cannot be investigated, one must resort to sampling. Therefore, what is to be sampled, and how, must
be carefully considered.

As one possible solution, the lone investigator might
confine himself to a single cultural subsystem, a single
stratum of the society, or a single, small, and well-
defined problem. But the dilemma this strategy raises
is clear: how is such an investigator to master the
rest of the social and cultural structure enough to
specify context to his own and other anthropologists'
satisfaction? Another procedure is clear, although rarely feasible because of funding problems. Team efforts

greatly reduce sampling problems, as shown in the Vicos project in Peru. Still another strategy is to work in the same community for a long period, as Foster has done in Tzintzuntzán. Possibly the best procedure is to combine the two strategies, as Vogt and his students have done in Zinacantán, where large numbers of researchers have worked in the municipio over a long period. This permits focusing on clearly defined and ethnographically relevant problems and hypotheses in sequential fashion. The results have been productive.[9]

Costs and benefits of quantitative research. There are clearly major benefits from good quantitative research. These include a significant reduction of ambiguity, and efficient descriptions of large amounts of data. In other words, with quantitative techniques anthropologists can unambiguously state the range of the data, the analytic procedures, and the conclusions, provided the readers know as much as the author does about quantitative techniques. Qualitative reporting appears much more ambiguous, although not less "scientific." The efficiency in describing and presenting data quantitatively is impressive to the layman and relatively unambiguous to the professional. Thus the benefits are substantial and are relatively well understood.

The costs are far less understood in social anthropology; for that reason they will receive more attention here. Major costs involve time needed for design and analysis, data-gathering difficulties, loss of serendipity, and spurious generality.

Proper use of quantitative techniques in testing hypotheses means the design must be completed before the data are gathered. The hypotheses must be formulated, the data-gathering techniques highly specified, the sample defined, and the statistical techniques selected,

all before one datum is collected. It is difficult to
do this in the first anthropological field experience;
the really good quantitative designs are typically done
either on second or later field trips, or (for a society
which is already well known) from the literature. Zinacantán is illustrative.

The actual gathering of the data is an extremely ex-
pensive process in social anthropology. Most anthropological field work is organized so that large amounts of
information are collected by a single researcher from
small samples of individuals, at least for the first
field experience. Quantitative research typically demands small amounts of data from larger samples. The
cost in investigator-hours is very high. Many social
anthropologists do not have the resources to hire or
direct large numbers of effective research personnel,
even if they take their own students to the field.

Concerning the restriction on serendipity, I adopt the
viewpoint of the conceptualist, rather than the large-
sample comparativist. If good quantitative research is
the goal, serendipity must be relegated to a secondary
role. Gathering and analyzing materials can be repetitive
and tedious. If there is a research design to execute, it
must be carried out completely. Therefore, one cannot follow hunches in other directions, no matter how tempting,
if they distract from the task at hand.

Perhaps the most important cost involves distortion
embedded in the operational definitions which most people generate for quantitative work in social anthropology. In order to get comparable bits of information
from many instances, quantifiers must define their information units carefully enough to be sure they are observing the same thing each time. Consequently, in almost all quantitative studies the scientist ends up with
very narrowly defined concepts. In fact, in most cases

he resorts to using indices. One result is spurious
generality from giving a variable with a general meaning
a narrow operational definition (see the above discussion
of the Fábrega study on Zinacantán illness terms).

In sociocultural anthropology one often hears impreca-
tions against mere head-counting--in fact, against all
quantitative work. This criticism is not altogether unjustified, given the triviality of some quantitative
work. But there seems to be another source of resistance
to quantitative analysis. There are two distinct traditions in modern sociocultural anthropology, each of which
has a distinct goal. One is focused primarily on expanding the lexicon and refining the conceptual tools with
which we try to understand human behavior (e.g., defining
the concept of witchcraft or marriage), usually in the
context of reporting on a single society. The other is
directed primarily to generalizing about human behavior,
usually involving empirical comparisons of two or more
societies. Between these two traditions there is only
limited common ground, although a few anthropologists
move freely between them (e.g., Claude Levi-Strauss).

If one attempts to generalize about all human behavior, the field must have concepts which are applicable
to the entire universe of societies. These should be
univocal, clearly defined, and analytic or scientific
rather than folk in origin. But some conceptualists
argue that this is not possible, since every society is
unique (Evans-Pritchard 1963; Leach in Naroll 1964;
Goodenough 1970).

The comparativists tolerate lack of fit between univocal concepts and multivocal ethnographic symbols in
order to get on with their job of generalizing. On the
other hand, the conceptualists often are not willing to
accept any lack of fit between a concept and their particularistic ethnographic reality; witness the discus-

sions of caste, or of non-African unilineal systems.
Both approaches are productive and necessary. We need
better general conceptual tools, but we also need concepts which do not force ethnography into procrustean
beds. Especially needed is more work which attempts to
bridge the two traditions, such as Goodenough's.

The field worker's dilemma is acute. There are benefits in having a large sample and quantified material
which can be manipulated statistically, but the price
in loss of time, in serendipity, and especially in distortion is one which a conceptualist frequently finds
extravagantly high. One partial solution is to work on
identified, well-designed problems in which the ethnographic context is sufficiently clear. The work on Zinacantán shows that this is a viable strategy. Rather than
investigating new groups, researchers could productively
revisit many communities and regions, and large projects,
however desirable, will not be absolutely necessary.

In sum, I argue not that good quantitative research
is impossible in social anthropology, but simply that it
is hard to do. The difficulties presented here can be
found in almost all studies surveyed. That they can be
solved satisfactorily, at least for research on peasants
and city-dwellers, is shown by the successful efforts of
Hammel and Cancian. Their studies illustrate that the
basic problems are methodological, rather than technical
or practical.

Conclusions. Techniques and strategies for numerical
analysis exist in abundance, and many can easily be
transferred to the kinds of problems that interest social anthropologists. However, quantitative techniques
have not been popular tools in the anthropology of Latin
America. Using them effectively means having adequate
theoretical and practical training, which is the respon-

sibility of graduate schools. Many social anthropologists obtain their doctorates having no more than an elementary course in statistics. Usually they learn a little about probability theory in reference to poker games,
but seldom do they discover why any of the formulas presented to their innocent eyes have any relevance to their
profession. Obviously, more adequate statistical training is required.

Two changes in graduate training are needed. First,
graduate students must be made aware of the need for
and possibilities of such work. This means that those
who teach them must have a clearer idea of what is relevant and possible. Second, the methods and opportunities
for doing such work should be taught more effectively.
It is useless to teach quantitative methods and techniques without at the same time showing when, where, and
why they should be used.

We may not be able to mount long-term team projects
as a standard form of research for many years, given increasing restrictions on funding and the demands for
salvage ethnography. But two other strategies are clear.
We should bury forever the notion that an anthropologist
"owns" the town or area he works in, and encourage others
to work there so that cumulative knowledge results. We
can also turn our attention to critical problems that
will respond to quantitative field research before a
total ethnography is generated.

Effective numerical analysis is difficult. Research
design, sample design, data gathering, and data analysis
are all exacting and time-consuming tasks, particularly
when combined with other stresses of field work. Therefore, the results of such work should be worth the effort. This in turn requires a careful definition of
problems that deserve treatment by these techniques. It
is easy to be trivial, for the availability of techniques

leads to their indiscriminate use. On the other hand, effectively used quantitative techniques can be productive indeed, considerably advancing our understanding of societies and cultures. They may also serve to clarify the premises of our discipline and to question, upon occasion, our professional goals.

NOTES

[1] Part of the work on which this paper is based has been supported by grants from NIMH, entitled Modernization in Rural Mexico (MH 16166-61, and MH 17-722-01), which I gratefully acknowledge. I especially want to thank my colleague (and wife) Eva Hunt for editing this paper with painstaking care. She performed an invaluable service by encouraging me to challenge my own assumptions.

[2] Phillips (1966) points out that the numerical properties of phenomena are not inherent in the phenomena themselves. Instead, they are the results of human inventions, which are particular observational techniques. No anthropologist can reasonably conclude that the variables of interest to him are nonquantifiable in nature. Although a good means for quantifying them may be currently unavailable, this does not preclude the invention of such a technique.

[3] For much of the material below I am indebted to several chapters in Bernard Phillips's text, *Social Research, Strategy and Tactics* (1966). Phillips's discussion is remarkably sophisticated in terms of the ability to separate the culture of the observer from the things to be observed (which Cicourel [1964], for example, seems not to understand). Phillips offers a clear presentation of number theory and the premises of measurement scales. Siegel also has a lucid discussion (1956:21-30).

[4] I have been able to review only those materials published no later than the summer of 1971.

[5] However, Cook's quantitative data are perhaps underused. His materials could be reworked, if sample size and other conditions were met, and an analysis of variance performed, since he indicates that different variables account for differential amounts of scale variation.

[6] They are both important for the ideational framework they propose for the study of community evolution; since they are the parents of later works, they should not be ignored.

[7] The reader should not conclude, however, that sampling is rel-

evant only where quantitative research is involved. Sampling is involved in any kind of empirical research, and the strictures which follow apply to qualitative research as well.

[8]This assumption is similar to the one made in linguistics, that any native speaker of normal intelligence is an adequate source for structure in the language. This may be valid, but it is subject to empirical scrutiny, and I know of no example of such a study.

[9]This strategy raises other problems for individual workers, because the career model for social and cultural anthropologists has long been based on a pseudo-monopoly of information from a particular settlement or ethnic group (for a particular time span). As a profession we have little experience in solving problems of rights of access to data which may arise in joint projects.

REFERENCES

Adams, Richard N.
1970   *Crucifixion by power*. Austin, Tex.

Arensberg, Conrad
1961   The community as object and as sample. *American Anthropologist* 63:241-64.

Attolini, José
1949   *Economía de la cuenca del Papaloapán: agricultura*. Instituto de Investigaciones Económicas. México.
1950   *Economía de la cuenca del Papaloapán: bosques, fauna, pesca ganadería e industria*. Investigaciones Económicas. México.

Belshaw, Michael
1967   *A village economy: land and people of Huecorio*. New York.

Billig, O.; Gillin, J.; and Davidson, W.
1947-48 Aspects of personality and culture in a Guatemalan community. *Journal of Personality* 16:153-78; 238-68.

Buchler, Ira, and Selby, Henry
1968   *Kinship and social organization*. New York.

Cancian, Frank
1965   *Economics and prestige in a Maya community*. Stanford, Calif.

Cicourel, Aaron V.
1964   *Method and measurement in sociology*. New York.

Colby, B. N., and van den Berghe, P.
1969   *Ixil country: A plural society in highland Guatemala*. Berkeley, Calif.

Collier, George A., and Bricker, Victoria R.
1970   Nicknames and social structure in Zinacantán. *American Anthropologist* 72:289-302.

Cook, Scott
1970   Price-output variability in a peasant-artisan stoneworking industry in Oaxaca, Mexico: An analytical essay in economic anthropology. *American Anthropologist* 72:776-801.

Drucker, Susana
1963   *Cambio de indumentaria*. Col. de antropología social. Instituto Nacional Indigenista. México.

Evans-Pritchard, E. E.
  1963   *The comparative method in social anthropology.* Hobhouse
         Memorial Lecture. London.

Fábrega, Horacio
  1970   On the specificity of folk illnesses. *Southwestern Jour-
         nal of Anthropology* 26:305-14.
  1971   Some features of Zinacantán medical knowledge. *Ethnology*
         10:25-43.

Foster, George
  1967   *Tzintzuntzán.* Boston.

_____, with Ospina, Gabriel
  1948   *Empire's children: the people of Tzintzuntzán.* Smith-
         sonian Institution, Institute of Social Anthropology,
         Publication No. 6. Washington, D.C.

Friedrich, Paul
  1970   *Agrarian revolt in a Mexican village.* Englewood Cliffs,
         N.J.

Fromm, Erich, and Maccoby, Michael
  1970   *Social character in a Mexican village.* Englewood Cliffs,
         N.J.

Gibson, Charles
  1964   *The Aztecs under Spanish rule.* Stanford, Calif.

Goldkind, Victor
  1965   Social stratification in the peasant community: Red-
         field's Chan Kom reinterpreted. *American Anthropologist*
         67:863-84.
  1966   Class conflict and cacique in Chan Kom. *Southwestern
         Journal of Anthropology* 22:325-45.

Goodenough, Ward H.
  1970   *Description and comparison in cultural anthropology.*
         Chicago.

Graves, T.; Graves, N.; and Kobrin, M.
  1969   Historical inferences from Guttman scales: the return
         of age-area magic? *Current Anthropology* 10:317-38.

Hammel, E. A.
  1961   The family cycle in a coastal Peruvian slum and village.
         American Anthropologist 63:989-1005.
  1964a Some characteristics of rural village and urban slum
         populations on the coast of Peru. *Southwestern Journal
         of Anthropology* 20:346-58.
  1964b Territorial patterning of marriage relationships in a
         coastal Peruvian village. *American Anthropologist* 66:
         67-74.

Harris, Marvin
    1970   Referential ambiguity in the calculus of Brazilian racial
            identity. *Southwestern Journal of Anthropology* 26:1-14.

Helm, June (ed.)
    1967   Essays on the problem of tribe. *Proceedings* of the an-
            nual meeting of the American Ethnological Society, Se-
            attle.

Hickman, John
    1962   Dimensions of a complex concept: a method exemplified.
            Human Organization 21:214-18.

Hunt, Eva, and Hunt, Robert
    1969   The role of courts in rural Mexico. In *Peasants in the
            modern world,* Philip K. Bock (ed.), pp. 109-39. Albu-
            querque, N.M.

Hunt, Robert
    1968   Review of Drucker, Cambio de Indumentaria. *American
            Anthropologist* 70:1009-10.
    1969   Centers and hinterlands in Mexico: toward a model for
            regional analysis. Paper presented at the annual meet-
            ing of the American Anthropological Association. New
            Orleans.
    1971   Premises concerning time in large-sample studies of com-
            munity modernization in Latin America. Paper presented
            at the annual meeting of the American Anthropological
            Association. New York.

_____; Hunt, Eva; and Weitlaner, Roberto
    1968   From parallel-nominal to patri-nominal: changing Cuicatec
            personal names. Instituto Nacional de Antropología e
            Historia. *Anales* 19:191-223. México.

Kaplan, David
    1971   Personal communication.

Kelly, Isabel, and Palerm, Angel
    1952   *The Tajín Totonac.* Part I. History, Subsistence, Shel-
            ter and Technology. Smithsonian Institution, Institute
            of Social Anthropology, Publication No. 13. Washington,
            D.C.

Kunkel, John
    1961   Economic autonomy and social change in Mexican villages.
            Economic Development and Cultural Change 10:51-63.

Leach, Edmund
    1961   *Pul Eliya.* Cambridge, England.

Leslie, Charles
    1960   *Now we are civilized.* Detroit.

Lewis, Oscar
    1951   *Life in a Mexican village: Tepoztlán restudied.* Urbana,
            Ill.

LeVine, Robert
    1971   Review of Fromm and Maccoby, Social character in a Mexi-
            can village. *Science* 171:271-72 (3968).

Minturn, Leigh, and Lambert, William
    1964   *Mothers of six cultures: antecedents of child rearing.*
            New York.

Mosk, Sanford
    1954   Indigenous economy in Latin America. *Inter-American
            Economic Affairs* 8:3-25.

Naroll, Raoul
    1956   A preliminary index of social development. *American An-
            thropologist* 58:687ff.
    1964   On ethnic unit classification. *Current Anthropology* 5:
            283-312.
    1970   What have we learned from cross-cultural surveys? *Amer-
            ican Anthropologist* 72:1227-88.

Nash, June
    1969   *Social relations in Amatenango del Valle.* CIDOC Cuaderno
            No. 43. Cuernavaca, México.
    1970   *In the eyes of the ancestors: belief and behavior in a
            Maya community.* New Haven, Conn.

Nash, Manning
    1961   The social context of economic choice in a small society.
            Man 61:186-91 (219).

O'Nell, Carl W., and Selby, Henry
    1968   Sex differences in the incidence of susto in two Zápotec
            pueblos. *Ethnology* 7:95-105.

Phillips, Bernard S.
    1966   *Social research: strategy and tactics.* New York.

Pi Sunyer, Oriol
    1967   Zamora: a regional enclave economy in Mexico. Middle
            American Research Institute. *Publication* 29:95-180.

Poggie, J. J., and Miller, F.
    1969   Contact, change and industrialization in a network of
            Mexican villages. *Human Organization* 28:190-98.

Redfield, Robert
    1941   *The folk culture of Yucatan.* Chicago.
    1950   *A village that chose progress.* Chicago.

Redfield, Robert, with Villa Rojas, A.
  1934   *Chan Kom*. Chicago.

Romney, Kimball, and Romney, Romaine
  1963   *The Mixtecans of Juxtlahuaca, Mexico*. New York.

Siegel, Sidney
  1956   *Non-parametric statistics for the behavioral sciences*.
          New York.

Tax, Sol
  1953   *Penny capitalism, a Guatemalan Indian economy*. Smith-
          sonian Institution, Institute of Social Anthropology,
          Publication No. 16. Washington, D.C.

Thompson, Richard A.
  1970   Stochastics and structure: cultural change and social
          mobility in a Yucatec town. *Southwestern Journal of
          Anthropology* 26:354-74.

Tylor, E. B.
  1888   On a method of investigating the development of institu-
          tions: applied to laws of marriage and descent. *Journal
          of the Royal Anthropological Institute* 18:245-72.

Vogt, Evon (ed.)
  1966   *Los Zinacantecos*. México.
  1969   *Zinacantán, a Maya community in the highlands of Chiapas*.
          Cambridge, Mass.

Whiting, B. (ed.)
  1963   *Six cultures*. New York.

Whiting, John, *et al.*
  1966   *Field guide for a study of socialization in six cultures*.
          New York.

Whitten, Norman
  1965   Power structure and socio-cultural change in Latin Amer-
          ican communities. *Social Forces* 43:320-29.

Young, Frank, and Fujimoto, Isao
  1965   Social differentiation in Latin American communities.
          Economic Development and Cultural Change 13:344-52.

Young, Frank, and Young, Ruth
  1966   Individual commitment to industrialization in rural
          Mexico. *American Journal of Sociology* 31:373-83.

ARCHAEOLOGY

George L. Cowgill

Many contemporary archaeologists working in Latin America, including myself, view themselves as social scientists with humanistic interests. They want to chronicle the past in detail, discerning ancient events and dating them as accurately as possible. Beyond that, they try to reconstruct histories of ancient peoples, putting events in their social and cultural contexts. They do not merely attempt to discover *what* happened *when*; they also try to understand *how* and *why* it happened. This leads one to generalize about human behavior (for individuals, groups, or systems). Archaeologists are thus involved with social science theory--either as consumers (interpreting their data), or preferably as producers (generating and testing theory). In terms of objectives, much archaeology is palaeoanthropology, or even palaeosociology, palaeoeconomics, palaeohuman geography (see Binford and Binford 1968).

Archaeology nonetheless has a number of problems more or less peculiar to itself. Such problems include organizing and summarizing data describing material forms (ranging from single objects to whole settlements); and determining chronological sequences and spatial distributions (Taylor 1948). All these tasks absorb a great deal of time, energy, and thought. Without adequate con-

trol of this basic framework, however, it is almost futile to move on to other areas.

Much of what we want to deal with includes things
other scholars, equipped with a time machine, would like
to tackle. I have in mind historians, social anthropologists, geographers, economists, political scientists,
even psychologists. And when I say that it may be futile
to tackle these problems without adequate control of the
historiographic framework, I do not mean that we must
wait until "all the facts are in" before we can theorize.
Almost from the outset of research in a given region, data
are adequate for some kinds of gross social scientific
theory testing and theory generation. However, archaeological data probably will never be totally adequate, or
at least very good, for testing or developing some topics
in modern social science.

An obvious question arises: why bother to collect
archaeological data to test social science theory if the
testing can be done more easily and effectively by studying living people? Obviously, one should not bother, unless there are advantages to using archaeological data
which offset the difficulties.

In fact, there often are advantages. First, scholars
may have a direct interest in past societies and cultures
on their own terms. This interest is particularly per-
tinent in Latin America, where until recently the past
of the indigenous population was either scorned and neglected or distorted by romanticization. For this essentially historical interest, archaeological data are invaluable.

Second, there are important types of societies or cultures, and major kinds of human events, which cannot be
observed adequately (if at all) among contemporary peoples. For example, we need to know more about hunting
and gathering as a way of life, in the days before food-

producing peoples took over large portions of the best
hunting territory and began to influence surviving hunters. We also need to explore the apparently long and
complex series of events which led to food production
as a major means of subsistence (Byers 1967; Flannery
1968; MacNeish 1971). Similarly, it is important to
know more about the events involved in the rise and functioning of so-called pristine civilizations--those which
developed more or less independently and spontaneously
(Adams 1966). For all these problems, archaeological
data are indispensable.

Finally, to the extent that theory deals with long-
term processes that span more than the period of adequately documented history, there is again no recourse but to
archaeological data. Moreover, knowledge of what has or
has not been done by previous occupants of a region, and
of what has and has not worked before, ought to be available and taken into account when predicting or planning
future developments. In some instances modern technology,
transportation, or politics may differ so much from the
past that what happened before is really without relevance. Yet the general relevance of the past hardly needs
to be stressed for Latin America, where adequate documentation from nonarchaeological sources never goes back
more than a few centuries.

As one example, in the study of contemporary regionalization (see companion papers by Gauthier and Hunt),
it is important to know the time depth of regions. To
what extent are modern regions similar to or different
from those of colonial or pre-Conquest times? Even the
elementary matter of pre-Conquest population densities
remains open to radically different estimates in many
regions and cannot be resolved without archaeological
data. To what extent are similarities between ancient
and modern regions due to ethnic and cultural continui-

ties or to environmental and geographic features (or
other factors) which may persistently override ethnic
or technological shifts? To what extent are differences due to new peoples, new production or transportation
technologies, differing levels of political and economic
integration, different power centers, varying policies
or concepts of regional use, or other factors? Over the
past few millennia of pre-Conquest times, how stable or
well defined have regions been? What processes of regional development or change can we discern in the past,
and how do they compare with contemporary processes?
Some important examples of regionally oriented archaeological studies include those of the Teotihuacán Valley
(Gamio *et al.* 1922; Sanders 1965; Lorenzo 1968; Sanders
et al. 1970; Millon 1970), the Tehuacán Valley (Byers
1967; MacNeish *et al.* 1967, 1970), the Basin of Mexico
(Parsons 1968), western Morelos (Litvak 1970), the
Nochixtlán Valley (Spores 1969), the Valley of Oaxaca
(Flannery *et al.* 1967), and the Virú Valley of Peru
(Willey 1953). All of these studies include important
information about contemporary regional patterns. Almost all recent archaeological studies have been regional, in the sense that they involve either a survey of
sites within a region or a consideration of the environmental setting and the uses of resources at a single
site. The works cited are outstanding examples of studies paying explicit attention to environment and relations between settlements within a more or less well-
defined region.

We cannot assume that the past is bound to repeat itself, but surely a clearer understanding of pre-Conquest
events and the complexities of past relationships will
be of great value for contemporary planners and social
scientists. For example, some prehistorians hold dia-
metrically opposed views regarding the Amazon Basin.

Only through a clear archaeological understanding can
we hope to discern whether the Basin was an important
source and center of cultural innovation, or an irre-
deemable cultural sink in which relatively elaborate
cultures from the Andean highlands occasionally left a
few noteworthy relics before devolving to much simpler
levels (Lathrap 1970; Silva and Meggers 1963).

Here I wish to survey the formal or mathematical
methods which go beyond the simple tabulations, percentages, or occasional chi-square that have been applied to analyses of Latin American archaeological data.
I include published reports of computer projects and an
overview of the scope, problems, and methods of noncom-
puter work. I omit formal stylistic studies, linguistic studies, and work on deciphering hieroglyphic texts,
since these seem less relevant for social scientists in
other disciplines. My aims are threefold: to review
all the work on this topic in Latin America (through
early 1971), to provide guidance for archaeologists
planning such work, and to emphasize data, problems,
techniques, and findings of interest to other social
scientists. Although I refer mainly to Latin American
data, the methods and problems discussed include examples of most of the major formal and mathematical methods that have been applied to archaeological data anywhere in the world. A good deal of the most innovative
work in quantitative archaeology uses Latin American
data. From the viewpoint of methods and problems, then,
the scope of the paper is more nearly worldwide than
hemispheric.

There is an important distinction between problems
and methods which involve managing and arranging archaeological data, and those involving manipulation of the
data for historical and theoretical purposes. In the

former case the data are organized, managed, stored, retrieved, summarized, and analyzed essentially in their own terms. If tests or measures of association are used, they are mainly for description. In this category we include problems of chronological ordering and much (though not all) classification of ceramics, artifacts, or assemblages. To be sure, some notions about human behavior may be invoked to suggest that one way of dealing with the data might be more useful than another, but generally these notions are broad and simple. For instance, if object A looks something like B and something like C, while B and C resemble each other less than either resembles A, and all three are from the same locality, then object A was presumably made at a time between the construction of B and C. On the other hand, if archaeological data are used in connection with social science generalizations, it is rarely, if ever, possible to deal with them directly. The data are taken as indicators of human behavior or some underlying variables--the real focus of interest. While this dichotomy is not without intermediate cases, I think a fairly clear distinction can be drawn.

In general, there are two ways in which the sophistication of archaeological work can vary. One concerns the adequacy or relevance of the models or assumptions about human behavior which are tested or used for interpreting data. In essence, how good are our questions? The other concerns the manner in which one connects archaeological observations with behavioral models, the ingenuity with which this is done, and the quality of judgments concerning what constitutes an adequate demonstration that the inferences regarding the behavioral model are really validated by the observations. That is, how good are our answers?

Quantification in Latin American Archaeology

For most "housekeeping" work (including typologizing, arranging things in the most plausible sequence, data storage, and data retrieval), one is concerned with associations of features on objects or among sets of objects (usually assemblages from single site components). Regarding the latter, one often need only demand that trends in the proportions of different kinds of objects accurately reflect trends (not necessarily actual proportions) in their use by the human groups which the various assemblages can be thought to represent. However, if quantities of archaeological objects are intended to reflect differing values of a set of underlying variables which represent the central concern, the matter becomes more complicated. I will return to this point later.

In view of the need for careful, reliable, and comparable methods of data collection as a precondition for worthwhile quantitative analysis, it is curious that (as far as I know) only three papers dealing with Latin American data explicitly consider this topic (Vescelius 1960; Cowgill 1964; Litvak 1969). Nonetheless, a number of worthwhile studies exist. For example, in cases where the data units were grave lots, ordinary competent field methods serve to recover all imperishable materials. In other cases either reasonably reliable and consistent methods of data collection seem to have been used, or the problems and methods were relatively insensitive to sizeable deviations from optimal procedures. Nevertheless, more thought and sophistication about sampling designs and techniques is desirable. Ragir (1967) provides a useful review of this topic.

One important technical problem that archaeologists face is the chronological ordering of materials in cases where methods like stratigraphic superposition or radio-

carbon dating are inapplicable or insufficient. Often
the units are grave lots or assemblages associated with
briefly occupied sites. Here an important strategy is
to seriate the units (i.e., arrange them in a sequence
whereby the most similar are closest together). The
logic of this procedure is that arrangement by similarity constitutes a relatively accurate estimate of the
true chronological sequence. Of course, one can try to
do this intuitively, but to do so for large numbers of
units is both difficult and time-consuming.

It is of historical interest that the first formal
and quantitative procedure for this purpose was developed
in connection with problems encountered in the chronological ordering of Mayan ceramics in northern Yucatán
(Brainerd 1951; Robinson 1951). Each unit was characterized by the percentage frequency of each type of object
found. Definitions of types in this and in most subsequent seriation efforts involved subjective judgments.
By summing the absolute values of the percentage differences for each type, and subtracting the total from 200
(which is the maximum possible sum of percentage differences for two units with no types in common), any two
units can be compared using Robinson's coefficient of
agreement. With coefficients for all possible pairs of
units arrayed in a square symmetric matrix, the seriation problem is reduced to a strictly formal one. The
task is to find the sequence of units which best approaches the ideal that, as one moves in any direction
away from the principal diagonal of the matrix, the coefficients are equal to or smaller than those closer to
the principal diagonal. But formalization of the problem did not make the work much easier until the advent
of computers, when a number of programs were developed
for Brainerd-Robinson seriation (see Hole and Shaw 1967,
and Cowgill 1968a for reviews). Yet difficulties per-

sist. For example, the seriation of a sizeable number
of units can overwhelm even a computer. Moreover, using
this approach, one is limited inherently to one-dimensional sequential representations of the resemblances
between units.

Work on alternative approaches to seriation continues.
One important illustration can be found in the work of
Victoria von Hagen Bordaz and Jacques Bordaz (1970),
using data from Nayarit, Mexico. They apply a clustering program to ninety excavation units characterized by
the presence or absence of sixty-nine attribute combinations. The clustering program seeks optimally compact
clusters (as defined by the Tanimoto distance function)
and finds a most typical unit for each cluster. These
typical units are then used to build a skeleton matrix
by hand, basing judgments about the sequence of clusters
on the patterns of second-best clusters for units which
fit into more than one cluster. Remaining units are
brought into the sequence according to their membership
in the clusters. Precise sequential locations within
each cluster group can then be determined by inspection,
according to the criterion that as few new characteristics as possible be introduced at any one time. Intuitive judgment is used to locate the few units which the
program did not assign to any cluster, and in a few cases
to reassign units to clusters that were second choices in
terms of the clustering program criteria. Since there
was a good deal of stratigraphic evidence which was not
used in the seriation study, it was possible to evaluate
the seriation sequence in terms of the stratigraphic
data. The agreement proved excellent. The advantage of
this technique is that up to 500 units can be handled at
once. Its main difficulty seems to be that a substantial
part of the work must still be done by hand.

Another alternative to the Brainerd-Robinson approach

is the multidimensional scaling technique of Shepard (1962) and Kruskal (1964a, 1964b). This technique involves more efficient computer algorithms and permits solutions in more than one dimension. However, contemporary programs are limited to fifty or sixty units, or perhaps a hundred in some circumstances. Since there often are many fewer important types than there are units, it would be more economical if it were possible to derive seriations from matrices of associations between types, rather than similarities between units. I have recently developed such a technique and applied it to approximately 550 grave lots from a collection of over 1,000 from northwest Argentina; Alberto Rex González kindly made the data available to me (Cowgill 1972). The essence of the technique lies in treating the points of the multidimensional configuration (if the configuration in two dimensions is sufficiently linear to suggest a one-dimensional ordering) as estimated midpoints of the time spans of the corresponding types. The probability of occurrence for each type in a unit is treated as a simple function of the unit's distance from the estimated midpoint. Each unit is placed at the point in the sequence which maximizes the product of the probabilities of occurrence for all types observed in the unit. The program has worked well in recovering the original sequences for invented test data sets, and it has provided a seriation of the Argentinian data which looks very good, at least from a formal point of view.

True and Matson (1970) provide an instance in which it would make little sense to seriate a set of units in a one-dimensional sequence. They studied material from twenty pre-ceramic sites in the province of Tarapacá, Chile, and multidimensional scaling yielded four important dimensions of variation. One was interpreted as a shift in subsistence orientation over time, another seemed to reflect different cultural traditions, a third separated sites on the basis of emphasis on core tools, and the last was interpreted as reflecting the amount of data available on the sites. True and Matson arranged these sites in a dendrogram based on the average-linkage cluster analysis method of numerical taxonomy which Sokal and Sneath (1963) describe. Both cluster analysis and multidimensional scaling yielded results which are in agreement with conventional intuitive evaluations.

A basic reason for turning to formal and computer methods is the sheer size of archaeologists' data files. In a single season a project will yield hundreds of thousands of objects and observations. These include mostly sherds of broken pottery, but also artifacts of stone, flint, obsidian, bone, and other materials; structures of varying size and elaboration; architectural features such as tombs and storage pits; and observations on the character of the depositional layers or constructional stages in which the objects occur. It is axiomatic that modern archaeologists should keep close track of the precise location where each object was discovered in a site, and of structural features and other objects it was associated with, as well as quantities of objects. The sheer volume and intricacy of such data suggests that computer files can be of considerable value in storage, retrieval, and summarization of such information. By 1962 personnel of the New World Archaeological Foundation were already tabulating sherd frequencies by computer (Anderson 1963; Matheny 1963; Green and Lowe 1967).

To my knowledge, only two projects in Latin America have attempted to put a major part of their field data onto punch cards (and subsequently onto tape or disk). One of these is the Teotihuacán Mapping Project (directed by René Millon), with which I have been associated since 1964 (Millon 1964, 1967, 1970; Cowgill 1967,

1968b). The other is the Kaminaljuyú project of William
Sanders and Joseph Michels (Sanders and Michels 1969;
Michels 1969). The Teotihuacán project involved detailed
surface reconnaissance, mapping, and collecting from all
tracts bearing any evidence of pre-hispanic occupation or
utilization over the roughly eight square miles covered
by the ancient city. The study was concerned with understanding Teotihuacán as a functioning and changing city.
For the computer file numerous observations were recorded
on vegetation, cultivation, alterations, and other contemporary features of the tracts; visible floors, walls, and
other architectural features in place; various kinds of
building debris; architectural and functional interpretations of the ancient features; counts of some 150 categories of ceramics, stone, and obsidian artifacts; and
data such as area of tract and location (in multiples of
ten meters from the map center). In its present form,
the computer file involves over 4,000 units (mainly apart-
ment compounds or other structural units), information on
over a million objects, and approximately 50,000 punch
cards. Since fill containing debris from earlier periods
frequently was reused for later buildings at Teotihuacán,
our surface collections represent early as well as later
periods. Although material collected may not always reflect the activities carried out in the specific building
where it was found, it often does, and it clearly reflects
activity in the close vicinity of the collection point.

The elementary task of getting the data recorded, coded, punched, and corrected was a tedious job. In order
to produce a clean, worthwhile data file involving 50,000
punch cards, one must spend a great deal of time checking
the accuracy of the work at every stage. Nevertheless,
the work was not disproportionate to the much greater
total effort of the project or the value of the file that
now exists. The greatest complicating factor was that

the original survey record forms were not designed specifically for computer input. This required transcrip-
tion of the original records onto code sheets, demanding
additional labor and creating more possibilities for error. Attempts to fit observations into a formal code
when they had originally been part of a narrative description were particularly time-consuming; the time,
effort, and ambiguities involved in trying to have a
coder (rather than the original observer) do this were
often too great to make it worthwhile. In effect, it
was frequently not feasible to code types of observation
or interpretation that had not consistently received explicit attention from the original field parties. Clearly, there is a dilemma here. It would have been best if
one knew from the beginning all the categories desirable
in the final code, so that the initial code forms could
have been completed in the field. Keypunchers could
then have worked directly from copies of original field
records. But one never knows all the categories that
will ultimately be important until the project is well
along, or even nearly over. This problem should become
less serious with time, however, as later projects benefit from the experience of earlier ones. Meanwhile, it
is always valuable to begin preliminary analyses of the
data in the early stages of a large project, so that
ideas about new categories and observations can be in-
corporated before many of the data are recoded.

One important use of our file is basic inventory and
data tabulation--for example, summary statistics, lists
of locations of rare kinds of observations, and occur-
rences of specific combinations of observations. A further important use of the file is producing distribution
maps, which extensively document differences in the absolute or relative abundances of distinct kinds of ceramics and artifacts in different parts of the city. The

maps can show either absolute quantities or proportions
(e.g., material of one period relative to that of another, or of one ceramic category belonging to a certain
period relative to all ceramics of that period). The
possibilities are almost limitless. For such maps it is
important that the collecting be done uniformly and that
the mapping be based on adequately large samples (or
neighborhood aggregates) so that fluctuations due to random error in small samples or to collector bias will be
small, relative to the differences being mapped. At
first we experimented with maps prepared by the computer,
but now we prefer to have the computer generate the list
of numbers for each structure or small neighborhood, and
then to superpose contours by hand on copies of our archaeological map (see Millon 1970 for this map, interpreting Teotihuacán as we think it looked around A.D.
600). Such contour maps help to identify workshops or
other specialized activity areas; to recognize neighborhoods of varying types and social status; to trace changes in overall intensity of utilization of regions of
the city; and to trace changes in distribution of specific artifact types.

We have not used computer methods much for generating
Teotihuacán's chronology, because of the extensive work
on this topic done by other means. However, I have run
a number of correlation studies designed to test the
ceramic sequence. Generally they provide confirmation
of previous ideas, and they help pin down the time range
of some of the less clearly dated categories. Another
approach has involved testing associations of various
ceramic and other artifact categories with various types
of structures (e.g., those interpreted by us as temples,
residences of the elite or of persons of intermediate or
low status, or structures thought to have had other functions). Many of the categories of objects (such as in-

cense burners, obsidian scrapers, grinding stones, or
cooking utensils) had fairly obvious uses; other categories (such as finely decorated pottery) presumably reflect status or wealth differences. Surprisingly little
was known about the actual relations between various
categories and various kinds of structures when we began our work.

Studies of associations between categories and types
of structures can serve at least three purposes: to
clarify, refine, and correct our functional interpretations of the structures; to help identify contexts and
infer uses for categories; and to help infer the ranges
of activities characteristically carried out in, or adjacent to, various types of structures, or in various
neighborhoods. These questions carry us well into the
area of inferences about "underlying" variables, and
into the problems of passing from sherd counts to measurements of activity intensities.

The underlying assumption of all such "functional interpretations" is that the more intensely a particular
activity was carried out, the more refuse that activity
will have produced. This does not mean that we can use
absolute abundances of material collected to infer activity intensities, since many other things affect size
of collections, including size and surface condition of
the area. Standardizing for number collected per unit
area is helpful, but it may not eliminate these problems
completely. It seems we are on firmer ground if we compare relative abundances or percentages of different
categories collected on and adjacent to different kinds
of structures. But if we compute correlations between
these percentages, a serious problem arises. Since the
percentages necessarily total 100 percent, complex constraints are built into the resulting set of correlation
coefficients (Chayes 1971). At Teotihuacán we have mea-

sured differential tendencies in the relative abundances of various categories collected from different kinds
of structures. It seems that category vs. structure comparisons avoid the difficulties encountered in category
vs. category comparisons. Indeed, preliminary work along
these lines has shown considerable previously unrecog-
nized differences in the relative quantities of objects
found around different types of structures at Teotihuacán.

In the case of category vs. category associations, we
have been provisionally using counts. By partitioning
the total sample in various ways, we can control for the
possibility that the patterns may be artifacts of fortu-
itous associations in a few collections with uncommon
abundances. While the resulting matrices of association
coefficients can be factor analyzed to extract groups of
highly associated categories, there are many cases in
which the linear correlation model implied by factor
analysis may not be particularly appropriate. We have
often had better results from the multidimensional scaling methods of Shepard (1962) and Kruskal (1964a, 1964b).

In the Kaminaljuyú project (Michels 1969) well over
two million objects are reported to be in the computer
file. It includes data from the valley-wide settlement
pattern surveys, but especially from several hundred
test trenches and mound excavations at Kaminaljuyú. The
material from each level of a given excavation unit is
washed, cataloged, and classified into some 160 ceramic,
obsidian, stone, bone, and miscellaneous categories. A
hierarchy of zone (five square kilometers), area (one
square kilometer), sector (fifty square meters), excavation unit, and level provide the necessary provenience
information. The provenience data, bag number, and category counts are transcribed onto code sheets for key-
punching, and they are eventually transferred to magnetic

tape. The file has been used to produce several kinds
of catalogs: lists of all material for each excavation
unit, lists of artifact categories with the catalog numbers numerically ordered, and lists of all catalog en-
tries arranged by catalog number in numerical sequence.
Many kinds of percentages and summary statistics also
have been produced. Plans are underway for the production of distribution maps, on a regional basis as well
as for Kaminaljuyú itself. In addition, the data will
be explored extensively using multivariate statistical
analyses.

Computerized data storage and analysis, along the
general lines of the Teotihuacán and Kaminaljuyú projects, are planned for the project now underway at Tula
under the direction of Richard Diehl of the University
of Missouri. Robert Benfer is providing guidance for
the computer analyses. Another project involving vast
amounts of material is the work on electronic storage
and analysis of archaeological materials at the Museo
Nacional de Antropología in Mexico City. Jaime Litvak
and his assistants have reported on this project (Litvak
1968, 1969; Litvak and García 1969; Castillo and Litvak
1968; Flores 1968, 1969).

Systems theory has found some applicability in Latin
American archaeology, notably in a paper by Flannery
(1968). He uses a cybernetics model to account for the
transition from hunting and gathering to an emphasis on
food production in ancient Mesoamerica. Briefly, he
suggests that food procurement systems of hunters and
gatherers tended to be self-regulating, with a number of
built-in *negative* feedback mechanisms which tended to
maintain system stability. When emphasis on the collection of certain wild plants, especially maize and beans,
led to new selective pressures on the wild varieties
(which apparently developed new strains accidentally),

this process encouraged still more emphasis on them as food sources, leading to a *positive* feedback. This feedback created system instability; increasing use of the resources encouraged even greater change, which in turn encouraged more use. The result was the full domestication of a number of wild species and a transformation of the way of life. Doran has criticized Flannery's application of systems theory on the grounds that systems theoretical ideas play a limited role in the discussion, and he suggests that perhaps in this case systems theory was "simply a neutral vehicle for Flannery's own clear thinking" (Doran 1970:291). Doran points out that the systems network Flannery has in mind is not exhibited very clearly. But the value of the systems approach simply as an aid to clear thinking should not be minimized. At any rate, Flannery's analysis of the situation carries us far beyond the naive view that hunting and gathering people became farmers simply because sooner or later it was bound to occur to them that farming was a better way of life.

By far the most elaborate application of a formal model in Latin American archaeology is in the recent work of Jaime Litvak (1970). He has developed and applied a statistical model for regional archaeology to data from the Valley of Xochicalco in western Morelos, basing his study on decorated ceramic categories from twenty-three sites divided into eight epochs or phases. Litvak defines some 250 categories, each of which includes far less variation than do most archaeological types (they might be called microtypes). Thus, although the region covered is only about eighteen by twenty kilometers, many of his categories or taxonomic units are quite localized in their distribution. He defines several basic quantities for each site and for each phase. These include the *value* of the site, V, which is the

number of different taxonomic units collected at the
site for the given phase. A second basic quantity, T,
represents the number of all other sites with which the
given site shares one or more taxonomic units, divided
by the total number of other sites occupied during that
phase. If we think of all sites which share any taxonomic unit being connected by lines, then T is the number of lines which converge on a site, divided by all the
lines which might have been drawn from other sites to
it in the given phase. A third basic statistic, C, is
the *intensity* of contact, which is defined in the following manner. First, one finds a value V (a number between 0 and 1) for each connecting line, representing
the ratio of all taxonomic units shared by the two sites
connected by the line, relative to the total possible
number they might have shared (namely, the total of all
taxonomic units belonging to that phase). To find the
intensity (C), these *values* are now added for all lines
running into the site, and then divided by the total
number of possible lines that were drawn or might have
been drawn from all other sites occupied in this phase.
C would be zero for a site that shared no taxonomic
units with any other site, and 1 would represent a site
which shared all taxonomic units with all other sites.
A fourth basic statistic is the value for a given taxonomic unit for a given phase, Z, defined as the ratio
of all sites where the taxonomic unit occurs, to all
sites occupied during that phase. If a given taxonomic
unit persists into a second phase, its Z value need not
be the same.

A number of other statistics may be calculated from
these basic statistics. These include F, the *focalization* value of a site, which is defined as C/T. A high
F means a tendency to share relatively many taxonomic
units with relatively few other sites, while a low F

would mean that relatively few taxonomic units are shared per site contact. Mean focalization, $\overline{Fx}$, is defined as $(C + T)/2$. Another statistic is H, which is the proportion of taxonomic units found only in a given site, relative to all taxonomic units in that site for that phase. An H value of zero would indicate a site which had no unique taxonomic units, while an H of 1 would indicate a site which shared no taxonomic units with any of the others within the model. Illustrative contrasts include sites with many and strong contacts, many but weak contacts, few but strong contacts, or few and weak contacts.

These data can be analyzed in numerous ways for each period. Computing means and standard deviations or medians and quartile ranges enables us to classify the sites in terms of the degree and type of their participation in the regional network. Perhaps the most striking results are figures which can be superposed on the map of the region, with a circle for each site whose diameter reflects the value of V (number of taxonomic units collected there), while lines depict the connections between different sites.

Each two-dimensional figure can be seen as one layer in a three-dimensional eight-layer sandwich, with time as the third dimension. Litvak notes that each one-phase diagram has the static quality of a snapshot, and he suggests that a more dynamic aspect could be obtained by figures showing the changes between one phase and the next. He also points out that a more complex analysis might consider connectedness in time as well as in space.

Although this pioneering study has used only a limited amount of data, Litvak has extracted a remarkably large amount of important information which would never have been discovered by more conventional methods. Obviously, many other kinds of archaeologically available

data would complement and supplement the information--
including data on contacts involving nonceramic materials; qualitative considerations about the nature of contacts involving trade, taxation and tribute, spoils of
war, changes in residence of individuals or groups, and
specialized centers of manufacture or consumption; and,
perhaps, quantities of shared material in place of presence or absence of shared taxonomic units. Such information would offer further refinements of a project which
Litvak explicitly regards as only initiating a line of
research.

Another group of ingenious and imaginative interpretations of quantitative archaeological data are those of
William Rathje (1970), who calls attention to contrasts
between Early and Late Classic lowland Maya burials in
housemounds at the site of Barton Ramie and in the cer-
emonial center structures at Uaxactún, about seventy-five
kilometers away. At Barton Ramie the Early Classic burials contain a disproportionate number of young adults,
and the average amount of grave goods accompanying young
adults is markedly higher than the average amount in the
graves of mature adults. In Late Classic times there is
a higher proportion of adult burials, and they tend to
include more grave goods than those of young adults. At
Uaxactún an Early Classic temple contained six interments,
four of which were very rich burials of adult males. In
Late Classic times this temple became a palace in which
thirty-eight burials were found, including fourteen male
and fourteen female adults, spanning a range from poor
to very rich in terms of grave goods. Rathje argues that
these data are consistent with the hypothesis that in
Early Classic times social mobility in Maya society was
relatively high, and important offices were achieved
through the accumulation of wealth. Consequently, the
relatively rich burials of young adults in housemounds

are those of young men who died before having accumula-
ted enough wealth to achieve high office, while the relatively few and poor burials of mature adults represent
those men who failed to advance in the system. The more
successful adult males were those found in the rich temple burials at major centers. Rathje suggests that in
Late Classic times population growth led to intensified
competition for roughly the same number of offices, so
men of established families residing in or near the pal-
aces were the only ones with any real chance of achieving high office. People of smaller settlements like
Barton Ramie were effectively blocked from advancement.
This would account for the presence in the graves at
Barton Ramie of more older people with greater wealth
than the younger people there but generally with less
wealth than in contemporary burials at Uaxactún. Although the data used in this preliminary study are far
from ideal, Rathje's inferences about the nature of
Early and Late Classic Maya society seem plausible and
consistent with other knowledge about the Maya. More
recently, Rathje has keypunched data on 1,009 Classic
Maya burials, and he is attempting fuller tests of these
and other hypotheses about ancient Maya society.

A final group of studies involves material obtained
in the past fifteen years from the University of Pennsylvania's project at Tikal, Guatemala. While most data
from this project have not been handled by computer or
mathematical means, several quantitative studies have
been carried out at the University of Arizona (T. P.
Culbert, personal communication; in all cases the pro-
grammer was David P. Adam). Lischka and Culbert have
used factor analysis to investigate nontemporal variation
in Late Classic ceramic distribution, obtaining as the
first factor an axis which shows excellent separation of
archaeological contexts on the basis of status. In a

second study based on Early Classic vessel shapes, Culbert found that factor analysis resulted in a single clear temporal factor and one social factor. Better results were obtained from discriminant analysis and canonical variables, which gave good discrimination for both temporal and social factors. Different variables were identified as primary sources for the two kinds of variation. Rathje attempted an analysis of Early Classic vessel shapes by cluster analysis but obtained poor results, probably because too many rarely occurring variables were included. Finally, Fry has used cluster analysis to investigate regional variation in distribution of Late Classic vessel shapes in survey strips running twelve kilometers away from the center of Tikal, obtaining clear distinctions between samples at varying distances.

Conclusion

The serious application of formal and mathematical methods in Latin American archaeology is a very recent phenomenon--as it is, indeed, for archaeology in general. Except for a few papers on sampling and seriation, none of the work described above was begun before the early 1960's; in fact, most of it is a product of the last few years. It is certain that formal and mathematical methods will continue to develop in archaeology; some methods will be borrowed from other disciplines.

Two broad observations may be made regarding the work surveyed here. On the one hand, it reflects a diffusion of computer and mathematical skills throughout the scholarly world. In archaeology, as in any other field, there are people with this expertise looking for ways to apply their skills. Sometimes this situation has led to work whose aim or rationale was either unclear or reasonably clear but unexciting. On the other hand, much of the work illustrates new and vital uses of archaeological data for historical and social scientific purposes.

REFERENCES

Adams, Robert McC.
1966   *The evolution of urban society: early Mesopotamia and pre-Hispanic Mexico*. Chicago.

Anderson, Lawrence O.
1963   A pilot study in the application of electronic computers in the analysis of ceramics, part I: classification code and mechanics. Paper read at the annual meeting of the Society for American Archaeology. Boulder, Colo.

Antropología Matemática
1968   No. 4. *Nomencladores: Preclásico; Tlatilco; Figurillas*. Instituto Nacional de Antropología e Historia. México.
1968   No. 5. *Correlaciones: Preclásico; Tlatilco; Figurillas*. Instituto Nacional de Antropología e Historia. México.

Binford, Sally R., and Binford, Lewis R. (eds.)
1968   *New perspectives in archeology*. Chicago.

Bordaz, Victoria von Hagen, and Bordaz, Jacques
1970   *A computer-assisted pattern recognition method of classification and seriation applied to archaeological materials*. Archéologie et Calculateurs. Centre National de la Récherche Scientifique. Paris.

Brainerd, George W.
1951   The place of chronological ordering in archaeological analysis. *American Antiquity* 16:301-13.

Byers, Douglas S. (ed.)
1967   *The prehistory of the Tehuacán Valley*. Vol. 1: *Environment and subsistence*. Austin, Tex.

Castillo Tejero, Noemi, and Litvak King, Jaime
1968   Un sistema de estudio para formas de vasijas. *Tecnología 2*. Instituto Nacional de Antropología e Historia. México.

Chayes, Felix
1971   *Ratio correlation: a manual for students of petrology and geochemistry*. Chicago.

Cowgill, George L.
1964   The selection of samples from large sherd collections. *American Antiquity* 29 (No. 4):467-73.
1967   *Evaluación preliminar de la aplicación de métodos de máquinas computadoras a los datos del mapa de Teotihuacán*. Teotihuacán, Onceava Mesa Redonda, México, 1966. Sociedad Mexicana de Antropología. México.
1968a Review of Hole and Shaw, Computer analysis of chronological seriation. *American Antiquity* 33 (No. 4):517-19.

1968b   Computer analysis of archeological data from Teotihuacán,
        Mexico. In *New perspectives in archeology*, S. R. and
        L. R. Binford, eds. Chicago.
1972   Models, methods, and techniques for seriation. In *Models
        in archaeology*, pp. 381-424. David Clarke, ed. London.

Doran, James
1970   Systems theory, computer simulations and archaeology.
        World Archaeology 1 (No. 3):289-98.

Flannery, Kent V.
1968   Archeological systems theory and early Mesoamerica. In
        Anthropological archaeology in the Americas. The Anthro-
        pological Society of Washington, Washington, D.C.

_____; Kirkby, A.; Kirkby, M.; and Williams, A.
1967   Farming systems and political growth in ancient Oaxaca.
        Science 158 (No. 3800):445-54.

Flores García, Lorenza
1968   Diagramas: Preclásico; Tlatilco; Figurillas. *Antropolo-
        gía matemática* (No. 6). Instituto Nacional de Antropolo-
        gía e Historia. México.
1969   Tarjetas con perforación interior. *Antropología matemá-
        tica* (No. 11). Instituto Nacional de Antropología e
        Historia. México.

Gamio, Manuel, *et al.*
1922   *La población del valle de Teotihuacán.* Secretaría de
        Agricultura y Fomento. México.

Green, Dee F., and Lowe, Gareth W.
1967   *Altamira and Padre Piedra, early preclassic sites in
        Chiapas, Mexico.* Papers of the New World Archaeological
        Foundation (No. 20). Provo, Utah.

Hole, Frank, and Shaw, Mary
1967   Computer analysis of chronological seriation. *Rice Uni-
        versity Studies* 53 (No. 3). Houston, Tex.

Kruskal, J. B.
1964a   Multidimensional scaling by optimizing goodness of fit
        to a nonmetric hypothesis. *Psychometrika* 29 (No. 1):
        1-27.
1964b   Nonmetric multidimensional scaling: a numerical method.
        Psychometrika 29 (No. 2):115-29.

Lathrap, Donald W.
1970   *The upper Amazon.* New York.

Litvak King, Jaime
1968   Tarjetas perforadas en las márgenes. *Antropología mate-*

mática (No. 3). Instituto Nacional de Antropología e Historia, México.

1969   Algunas observaciones sobre el muestreo en arqueología. *Anales de antropología* 6:169-81. México.

1970   *El valle de Xochicalco.* Formación y análisis de un modelo estadístico para la arqueología regional. Universidad Nacional Autónoma de México. México.

_____, and Moll, Roberto García
1969   Aplicación de la teoría de conjuntos a la formación de modelos para el desarrollo cultural. *Antropología matemática* (No. 9). Instituto Nacional de Antropología e Historia, México.

Lorenzo, José L. (ed.)
1968   *Materiales para la arqueología de Teotihuacán.* Instituto Nacional de Antropología e Historia, Serie investigaciones (No. 17). México.

MacNeish, Richard S.
1971   Speculations about how and why food production and village life developed in the Tehuacan Valley, Mexico. *Archaeology* 24 (No. 4):307-15.

_____; Nelken-Terner, A.; and Johnson, I.
1967   *The prehistory of the Tehuacán Valley.* Vol. 2: *Nonceramic artifacts.* Austin, Tex.

MacNeish, R. S.; Peterson, F.; and Flannery, K.
1970   *The prehistory of the Tehuacán Valley.* Vol. 3: *Ceramics.* Austin, Tex.

Matheny, Ray T.
1963   A pilot study in the application of electronic computers in the analysis of ceramics, part II: results. Paper read at the annual meeting of the Society for American Archaeology. Boulder, Colo.

Michels, Joseph W.
1969   Application of computer technology to data processing and analysis at Kaminaljuyú. Paper presented at the Annual Meeting of the American Anthropological Association. New Orleans.

Millon, René
1964   The Teotihuacán mapping project. *American Antiquity* 29 (No. 3):345-52.
1967   Teotihuacán. *Scientific American* 216 (No. 6):38-48.
1970   Teotihuacán: completion of map of giant ancient city in the Valley of Mexico. *Science* 170 (No. 3962):1077-82.

Parsons, Jeffrey R.
    1968   Teotihuacan, Mexico, and its impact on regional demog-
            raphy. *Science* 162 (No. 3856):872-77.

Ragir, Sonia
    1967   A review of techniques for archaeological sampling. In
            A guide to field methods in archaeology, R. F. Heizer
            and J. A. Graham, eds. Palo Alto, Calif.

Rathje, William L.
    1970   Socio-political implications of lowland Maya burials:
            methodology and tentative hypotheses. *World Archaeology*
            1 (No. 3):359-74.

Robinson, W. S.
    1951   A method for chronologically ordering archaeological de-
            posits. *American Antiquity* 16:293-301.

Sanders, William T.
    1965   The cultural ecology of the Teotihuacán Valley. Depart-
            ment of Sociology and Anthropology, Pennsylvania State
            University. University Park, Pa.

_____; Kovar, A.; Charlton, T.; and Diehl, R.
    1970   The Teotihuacán Valley project. Final report--Volume 1.
            The natural environment, contemporary occupation and
            16th century population of the Valley. *Occasional Papers
            in Anthropology* (No. 3), Department of Anthropology,
            Pennsylvania State University. University Park, Pa.

Sanders, William T., and Michels, Joseph W.
    1969   The Pennsylvania State University Kaminaljuyú project--
            1968 season. Part I--The excavations. *Occasional Papers
            in Anthropology* (No. 2), Department of Anthropology,
            Pennsylvania State University. University Park, Pa.

Shepard, Roger N.
    1962   The analysis of proximities: multidimensional scaling
            with an unknown distance function. *Psychometrika* 27
            (No. 2):125-40, and 27 (No. 3):219-46.

Silva, Fernando A., and Meggers, B. J.
    1963   Cultural development in Brazil. In *Aboriginal cultural
            development in Latin America: an interpretative review*.
            Washington, D.C.

Sokal, Robert R., and Sneath, Peter H. A.
    1963   *Principles of numerical taxonomy*. San Francisco.

Spores, Ronald
    1969   Settlement, farming technology, and environment in the

Nochixtlán valley. *Science* 166 (No. 3905):557-59.

Taylor, Walter W.
    1948   *A study of archeology*. American Anthropological Associa-
            tion, Memoir No. 69. Menasha, Wis.

True, D. L., and Matson, R. G.
    1970   Cluster analysis and multidimensional scaling of archeo-
            logical sites in northern Chile. *Science* 169 (No. 3951):
            1201-3.

Vescelius, Gary S.
    1960   Archaeological sampling: a problem of statistical in-
            ference. In *Essays in the science of culture in honor
            of Leslie A. White*. G. Dole and R. Carneiro, eds. New
            York.

Watson, P. J.; LeBlanc, S.; and Redman, C.
    1971   *Explanation in archeology*. New York.

Willey, Gordon R.
    1953   *Prehistoric settlement patterns in the Virú Valley, Peru*.
            Washington, D.C.

GEOGRAPHY

Howard L. Gauthier

Nine years ago, in his review of the contribution of
geography to Latin American Studies, James Parsons (1964)
noted the lack of studies using quantitative techniques.
He attributed this to the absence of reliable statistical data, which restricted research possibilities,
and the low level of development of the field in which
quantitative procedures have been employed most frequently, namely, economic geography. Admittedly, these are
serious constraints on the use of quantitative methodology in research on Latin America as a region. Yet they
alone do not explain why the introduction and development of mathematical models and methods in the regional
geography of Latin America have not kept pace with such
developments in other regions, notably Africa.

Parsons's comments on the prospects for future quantitative research are revealing. He observes: "The
vogue for statistical correlations is most evident among
those with the least field exposure. . . . Among its
practitioners there are confidence and high hopes for
mechanistic approaches to the understanding of reality.
Planning and development agencies, seduced by the easy
confidence of figures and formulas, provide increasingly
ready markets for their wares" (1964:37). Parsons's
skeptical, if not cynical, view of quantitative methods

132

in regional geography is probably shared by most of
those involved in geographic research on Latin America.
The major obstacle to quantitative analysis is neither
data scarcity nor the underdeveloped state of economic
geography. Rather, it is one of attitude. Those interested in model formulation are too frequently portrayed
as academic charlatans who have been so mesmerized by
the flashing lights of a computer console that they are
only capable of generating sterile mathematical abstrac-
tions.

Granted, a critical view of quantitative methodology
is appropriate. Quantification has sometimes been over-
sold as a panacea for the methodological problems facing
geography. There have been too many abuses arising from
the misuse and misapplication of mathematical methods.
Yet little is accomplished by a persistently negative attitude toward the use of all quantitative methodology
in regional research. After all, the main issue is not
quantitative versus nonquantitative geography, but the
importance of the research questions under investigation
and their solutions.

Much geographic research on Latin America focuses on
historical and cultural themes. Perhaps it is true
that, once a geographer gains an intimate feeling for
the culture of a country and develops an adequate com-
mand of the language, he will tend to devote much of his
research energies to cultural and historical themes. It
is equally true that the strong current of anti-quantita-
tive feeling has contributed to a weak interest in contemporary economic and social problems. This is remarkable in view of the increasing concern for such issues
in behavioral geography. It is regrettable that many
problems facing Latin America in the twentieth century
have scarcely been treated by geographers. The neglect
of urbanization processes is a striking example. In ad-

dition, little is known about the spatial impacts of industrial location decisions, and the impact of infrastructural investments on the organization of the space economy is dimly perceived. Problems associated with population dynamics and regional economic development have usually been left to economists, engineers, and politicians.

There are some weak indications that geographers may eventually address themselves to these neglected issues. A few American geographers, trained in quantitative methods and concerned with problems of regional development in transitional economics, are turning their attention to Latin America, especially to Brazil. The preference for Brazil is partly explained by the new research orientation of several Brazilian geographers affiliated with the Instituto Brasileiro de Geografia (IBG). Unlike most geographical institutes in Latin America, which are little more than mapping and surveying organizations, the IBG has assumed greater responsibility in governmental planning processes in recent years.

It is unlikely, however, that the change taking place in Brazilian geography will occur elsewhere in Latin America soon. The number of Latin American geographers presently involved in studying current social and economic issues is negligible. In most countries geographical research consists largely of the production of regional monographs in the tradition of Vidal de la Blanche, and the delimitation of natural regions on the basis of Gallois's concepts. Even when geographers are associated with governmental planning agencies, their role in the decision-making process is marginal at best. As a result, there has been little sponsorship or development of geographical research that either treats contemporary issues or utilizes the analytical models and methods characteristic of geography in the United States.

Given the present state of Latin American-oriented
geography, it is not surprising that the amount of quantitative research is small and that it exhibits a strong
Brazilian focus. In contrast to traditional historical and cultural themes, quantitatively oriented research is concerned with current problems of regional
development and related strategies of planning. The
high priority problem areas include: regionalization,
urban systems and growth poles, regional inequalities,
and transportation. Methodology ranges from conventional statistical models, such as factor analysis, to less
familiar models of graph theory and information statistics.

Regionalization

A review of quantitative research in Latin American
geography during the past several years indicates a
greater emphasis on regionalization than on any other
topic. This is consistent with the discipline's histor-
ic commitment to areal differentiation and spatial organization. It is also a logical consequence of the need
to develop regional frameworks for national planning and
the need to provide sampling frames for census operations.
The interest in identifying homogeneous (formal) regions
arises from a desire to define areas likely to display
common responses to public programs, by virtue of their
common characteristics.

Methodologically, the problem of regionalization is
a fairly simple one involving numerical analysis. Given
a large number of areal units of observation, the objective is to determine different types of spatial variation
present in the data. Do these types of spatial variation,
considered together, create contiguous clusters of relatively homogeneous units (e.g., a formal region)? By
applying a combination of factorial and group clustering

procedures, one can begin to answer the question.

Typical regionalization studies are those on Brazil
by Berry and Pyle (1970) at the national scale, by Faissol and Duarte (1971) at the regional (multistate) scale,
and by Keller (1970) at the state level. Though the
scale of analysis may vary, the methodology is consistent and involves the following steps. *First*, the units
of observation chosen are either *municípios* (counties) or
micro-regions (clusters of *municípios* grouped into a more
manageable set of taxonomic units). For each observational unit, three sets of variables are measured:
reference indicators (population, population density,
and area), productivity indices (the quantity and value
of agricultural output), and proportionality values (the
relative share of the national output attributable to
each product and the percentage of land coverage by each
crop within an observation unit). *Second*, the data matrices are factor analyzed. This involves a) the examination of descriptive statistics for the distributions
of each variable to determine what normalizing transformation may be needed; b) the preparation of a correlation matrix for each variable with every other variable,
and a principal axis factor analysis of the matrix with
communality estimates of unity, to determine the number
and composition of the factors or common patterns of
variation of the variables; and c) the derivation of
factor scores for each observational unit with respect
to each factor, together with the preparation and interpretation of factor score maps. *Third*, several analyses
are generally performed on a given data set, generating
a large number of factor solutions. To obtain economy
in expression, a factor-matching procedure is used. The
correlations between the factor vectors are computed,
and a linkage analysis is prepared connecting all factors with correlations exceeding some threshold value.

Finally, a minimum variance clustering analysis is performed on the factor scores to identify regional grouping of observational units which are statistically homogeneous. These groupings are interpreted as basic
planning regions.

The use of factor analysis in regionalization studies
is not limited to the identification of planning regions.
In a recent study Sheck, Brown, and Horton (1973) have
investigated aggregate changes in regional employment
structures in Central American Common Market (CACM) countries. They compare employment structures in eight sectors of the economies of the five CACM countries for 1950
and 1963. After factor analyzing the data, the authors
present a taxonomy of political subdivisions that is useful in examining spatial changes in employment within the
region. The writers' objectives are to provide both a
policy-oriented schema for classifying areas and a means
of identifying the spatial characteristics of employment
shifts resulting from a regional integration process such
as CACM.

To obtain spatial homogeneity Sheck *et al.* group departments so that each category is uniform with respect
to development characteristics of geographically contiguous departments. They achieve this homogeneity by using
a classification algorithm developed by Veldman (1967).
The algorithm operates on the component scores of the
factor analysis to generate groupings that minimize variance within groups while maximizing variance between
groups.

Applying this procedure to CACM, Sheck *et al.* place
departments in one of five categories: agricultural-
forestry activities, infrastructural related activities,
secondary-tertiary activities, mixed primary, secondary,
and tertiary activities, and mining activities. Using
this classification as a basis for comparing changes in

the spatial pattern of employment for 1950 and 1963,
the authors' conclusion suggests some probable types of
impact of integration on the spatial structure of the
regional economy. They put particular emphasis on the
relationships of infrastructural investments to the development of economic complementarity and resulting
shifts in employment patterns.

Urban Systems and Growth Poles

Urban centers play a key role in most strategies of
national or regional development. They are the major
recipients of investment in directly productive activities and social overhead capital. Urban centers provide
a variety of generalized and specialized services to
surrounding areas and serve as foci for the diffusion
of innovations within and between regions. Yet surprisingly little is known about the spatial structure of
Latin American cities or the role they actually play in
the modernization process. We need answers to basic
questions: What is the structure of the urban hierarchy
in Latin America? What is the spatial dimension of urban growth processes?

To answer these questions for Brazil, Faissol (1971)
has investigated the spatial organization and pattern
of the hierarchy of urban centers with more than 40,000
inhabitants. Using approximately thirty direct and surrogate measures of demographic, economic, and social
profiles, he seeks to identify common dimensions of an
urban typology by using a principal axis factor analysis.
Faissol extracts five factors that explain 80 percent of
the original variance in the data: functional size, socioeconomic status, industrial and commercial structure,
social infrastructure, and specialization in textiles
and foodstuffs. These items provide criteria for iden-

tifying and classifying centers within a hierarchical
structure.

Faissol's objective is not merely to provide a typology; rather, his main goal is to identify the spatial
pattern of the urban hierarchy. Using a group clustering technique, he forces a contiguity restraint on the
distribution of factor scores and interprets the resulting spatial pattern in terms of the center-periphery
model suggested by Friedmann (1966). He identifies two
urban nuclei and two related peripheries: a *central
nucleus* consisting of São Paulo and Rio de Janeiro, and
a subcenter in Pôrto Alegre, with the spatial sphere of
influence of São Paulo as the most extensive; an immediate periphery consisting of intermediate-sized urban
centers, sharing the common impact of economic and social transformations originating in the central nucleus;
a *secondary nucleus* along the coastal region of the
northeast, focusing on Recife and Salvador; and a periphery to this secondary nucleus, consisting of relatively small urban centers which are not affected by the
structural transformations taking place in the metropolitan centers of the secondary nucleus.

Studies by Geiger (1971) support Faissol's conceptu-
alization of core-periphery spatial organization. He
attributes the presence of a secondary nucleus in the
northeast, which has little if any impact on the surrounding periphery, to the policies of SUDENE, the Northeast Development Agency. To develop an industrial base in
the northeast, SUDENE has depended on the federal fiscal
mechanism to transfer capital from the south to the northeast. The most successful transfer mechanism has been a law
which allows corporate entities to cut their tax liability
in half by investing tax savings in projects approved by
SUDENE. As Geiger observes, most of these projects have
been located in the metropolitan centers of Recife and Salvador.

No significant investments have taken place in smaller
urban centers or in agriculture. The result, according
to Geiger, has been the polarization of growth in the
northeast. Recife and Salvador act as Perrouxian growth
poles; their economic linkages are with the central nucleus in the south, rather than with the surrounding urban periphery in the northeast.

In a recent study on Chile, Brian Berry (1969) considers possible relationships between factorial dimensions of urban systems and stages of economic development. Berry observes that urban ecologists in the United States differentiate towns and cities according to
such dimensions as economic power, socioeconomic status
of urban residents, and stages in the life cycle of the
family. Whenever a rigid stratification of society
exists along cultural, regional, class, or caste lines,
these strata will not produce urban dimensions similar
to those of the American experience. Rather, he writes,
"The factor structures will isolate particular status
levels and regional or cultural groups and combine sta-
tus-, age-, and family-patterns" (285). On this basis
Berry contends that it should be possible to array urban
systems of countries on a scale from unidimensional traditional societies, through transitional stages, to modern systems. The characteristics of modern systems include a minimal association of ethnic or cultural variables with economic ones, and a separation of status and
life-cycle variations.

Berry's analysis of Chile focuses on the transitional
type of variation in urban dimensions. He undertakes
several factorial analyses of Chile's urban areas to
clarify different facets of their dimensions, and he observes their stability from 1952 to 1960. Berry interprets the components of these analyses as the principal
dimensions of variation in the Chilean urban system.

The identified dimensions are: 1) the functional size
of centers in the urban hierarchy; 2) the agriculture-
based traditionalism in central Chile; 3) the mineral-
exploiting towns, especially the copper mining communities in the North; 4) the manufacturing centers; and 5)
the rapidly growing towns of the resource frontiers,
which are radical in social and political behavior. Unlike the American experience, socioeconomic status and
population composition in Chile do not appear as separate dimensions of urban variability. Unlike India,
where individual regional cultures might create multiple
factors of differentiation, Chile has a relative homogeneous culture that permits the portrayal of traditional urban patterns of the central valley along a single
dimension drawn from educational and demographic correlates.

Berry shows that the ability to analytically establish clear dimensions of urban variability over time
could be useful for evaluating the Chilean program of
promoting regional growth through a strategy of deliberate urbanization. An indication of the success of these
programs should be revealed in the replacement of traditional urban dimensions by those based on socioeconomic
status and stages in family life-cycles.

Berry's concern with regional economic development
raises the question of polarized space in regional planning. Although many critical questions have been raised
about the theoretical contribution of the notion of
growth poles to developmental planning, the concept continues to exert a strong intuitive appeal. This is particularly true in transitional economies, where the concept's social and political appeal encourages planners
to view the growth pole strategy as essential for promoting regional growth, which, however, is not always
the case.

Although growth pole concepts may be challenged on theoretical grounds, the notion of polarized space poses relevant research issues for Latin American geography. First, there is the analytical problem of understanding the causal mechanism involved and the processes whereby growth impulses are transmitted between poles of varying magnitude, and between poles and their surrounding hinterlands. Second, there is the taxonomic problem of identifying growth poles and the spatial extent of their influence.

The taxonomic theme forms the basis of a study by Semple, Gauthier, and Youngmann (1972) on growth poles in geographic space. To identify growth poles, they employ a type of trend surface analysis which first identifies points in geographic space that may be regarded as growth centers, and then measures regional growth trends associated with the centers. The operational procedure involves the identification of a single point whereby the distances from it to the locations of all urban centers maximally correlate with the growth rates of each center. One achieves this by superimposing a fine grid system over the geographic area to obtain a large set of evenly spaced reference points. For each of these points one calculates a correlation coefficient between the distance from each point to the location of the urban centers, and the growth rates associated with each town. The largest correlation coefficient identifies the point accounting for the largest part of the regional growth trend.

Urban growth rates trends are calculated by subtracting the residuals from the original growth values, such that $T_{ij} = S_{ij} - E_{ij}$, where S_{ij}, T_{ij}, and E_{ij} refer respectively to the original growth values, the growth trend values, and the residuals, with coordinate locations i and j. The residuals form the terms of a second

spatial series associated with urban growth values.
Again one superimposes a grid over the geographical
area and repeats the analytical procedure to identify
a second growth point in the geographic space. The
process is interactive and may be repeated until no
statistically significant trends in regional growth remain.

Semple *et al.* provide an empirical example for the
State of São Paulo. To identify growth centers and
their associated regional trends, a sample of ninety
urban centers of over 10,000 is selected. Nine variables relating to rates of growth in population, manufacturing, and retail services are calculated for the
urban centers. Since many of the variables are highly
correlated, the authors perform a factor analysis to
combine them into fewer composite measures. The factor
scores associated with the first factor component explain much of the variance in the original variables
and are used, therefore, as a measure of urban growth.
The trend surface analysis covers two periods, 1940-50
and 1950-60. In each period three growth poles and
their areas of influence emerge. The three poles relate directly to the urban growth strategies initiated
by the federal and state governments. Two basic types
of poles are evident: natural poles resulting from the
federal program of rapid postwar industrialization, and
planned poles resulting from the state governments' efforts to spatially induce economic growth.

The problem of the transmission of growth impulses
between a growth center and its rural hinterland has
been explored by Brown and Lentnek (1972), who studied
the diffusion of commercial dairying practices in the
state of Aguascalientes, Mexico, during the period 1958
to 1968. They postulated a polyphasic diffusion process
based on the following assumptions: there is a single

market center where purchasers have a monopsony; innovation occurs in the production process, the output of
which is delivered to and sold in the market center; and
many potential adopters of the new process are located
in the rural hinterland of the market center. The response of potential adopters to the new production process is conditioned by several factors: market price,
awareness of the new process from either interpersonal
or impersonal sources, production costs, transport costs,
and opportunity costs of the new process relative to alternative production possibilities.

The diffusion process proceeds in stages. For a giv-
en level of demand and a related market price, a supply
area exists in which some farmers alter their production
to include the new process while others do not. If demand is not satisfied, the monopsonist may increase market prices, causing an expansion in the geographical extent of the supply area. A shift in price may be accom-
panied by an increase in adopters within the original
supply area, as well as within the newly expanded supply
area. Alternatively, the monopsonist may opt for one of
two strategies. He can extend his collection routes to
include previously untapped areas, or he can launch an
informational program to pursuade some nonadopters within the original supply area to accept the new production
process. The choice of strategy involves a comparison
between the marginal effects of price increases, increases in transport costs resulting from servicing the
expanded supply area, and the costs of an informational
program to pursuade nonadopters.

Brown and Lentnek use data drawn from a stratified
0.5 percent sample of the rural households of Aguascalientes state, and a systematic sample of one-third
of the suppliers of raw milk to the Nestlé Corporation.
The data consist of twenty variables measuring socio-

economic characteristics of the respondents, economic indices of the farmsteads, contacts with U.S. agriculture, and accessibility to the urban market. The variables are factor analyzed, and the resultant components are used as independent variables in a regression model.

Based on their analysis, the authors drew three conclusions: the supply area expands in a sequential fashion in which accessibility to the urban market and information availability act as major determinants for potential adopters; within the supply area, age-related factors are the important determinants of adoption; to meet demand, the monopsonist both extends transport routes to include new supply sources and attempts to pursuade nonadopters within the original supply area, giving more attention to the former strategy.

Regional Inequalities in Growth

Any consideration of governmental programs to spatially induce economic growth raises the broader issue of the impact of development planning on regional growth inequalities. Whether governmental programs increase or reduce spatial inequities in growth is a theme of utmost importance in Latin American geography. In Brazil, for example, it has been argued that the postwar policies of the federal government have had a negative impact. At worst, they have aggravated regional disparities in rates of growth; at best, they have eliminated any beneficial effects resulting from governmental efforts to achieve a more equitable redistribution of wealth.[1]

In a recent paper Gauthier and Semple (1971) investigate regional inequalities in growth. More specifically, they consider whether, during the postwar period, the growth strategy of the government has resulted in an increase in per capita income inequalities between the major economic regions of Brazil, and, at the same time, whether the selective geographical character of regional development has increased per capita income inequalities within the major economic regions.

To measure trends in regional inequalities in per capita income, the authors use information statistics. To introduce a spatial dimension into the analysis, the basic measure of inequality is expanded to measure inequalities both between and within regions. Subregional groupings are also considered by proportioning the measure of inequality within regions into two component parts: a measure of inequality between subregions, and a measure of inequality within subregions.

In the Brazilian example, the authors aggregate the twenty-one states into two major regions, creating a north-south dichotomy. In turn, they subdivide these two major regions into six subregions according to major census divisions.[2] Inequality of per capita income is calculated both between and within the major regions and their subdivisions for the period 1947 to 1966.[3]

The results of the analysis do not support the contention that there has been a continual increase in income inequalities between the north and south of Brazil (Table 1). Although increases in regional disparities in per capita income do occur during the early phase of the twenty-year period, this is consistent with expectations, given the prevalent government strategy of industrialization by import substitution, a policy that ignores the spatial allocation of growth. Until the middle 1950's, the pattern of regional growth was principally affected by the industrial sectors selected for development. Much of this growth was concentrated in the industrial triangle of São Paulo, Belo Horizonte, and Rio de Janeiro.

For the past decade the trend has been one of diminishing inequalities in per capita income between the

Table 1. Inequality Measures, 1947-66

Time interval	Total inequality	Inequality between regions	Inequality within regions	Inequality between subregions	Inequality within subregions
1947-48	.3289	.1653	.1636	.0272	.1364
1948-49	.3388	.1717	.1671	.0242	.1429
1949-50	.3553	.1960	.1593	.0194	.1399
1950-51	.3629	.2074	.1555	.0152	.1403
1951-52	.3461	.1980	.1480	.0242	.1239
1952-53	.3651	.1977	.1674	.0240	.1434
1953-54	.3666	.2023	.1643	.0406	.1237
1954-55	.3761	.1905	.1856	.0437	.1419
1955-56	.3702	.2058	.1644	.0402	.1242
1956-57	.3405	.1719	.1686	.0416	.1270
1957-58	.3287	.1675	.1612	.0489	.1123
1958-59	.3461	.1657	.1804	.0559	.1245
1959-60	.2856	.1552	.1304	.0289	.1015
1960-61	.2679	.1374	.1305	.0329	.0976
1961-62	.2666	.1140	.1526	.0313	.1213
1962-63	.2195	.0988	.1207	.0205	.1002
1963-64	.2676	.1309	.1367	.0177	.1190
1964-65	.2348	.1130	.1218	.0186	.1032
1965-66	.2169	.1033	.1136	.0170	.0966

Source: Gauthier and Semple (1971:11).

major regions. In large measure this is attributable
to the impact of income transfer programs which the two
regional planning agencies, SUDENE and SUDAM (Amazon
Valley), administer. While these programs have contributed to a reduction in regional growth inequalities,
they have probably increased inequalities within regions. As noted in Geiger's study of the northeast, a
trend toward concentration of investment in a limited
number of metropolitan centers is evident, with little
or no economic transformation in the intermediate and
smaller centers of the periphery. This fact contributes
to an increasing divergence of growth rates within the
regions.

Transportation

Perhaps nothing has a greater spatial impact on the
organization of a regional economy than investments in
transportation. Yet to a surprising degree geographers
have ignored the role of transportation in transforming
the spatial economy. This has been a serious oversight.
Transportation investments represent the largest single
item in the budgets of most Latin American nations. In
combination with other types of infrastructure expenditures, they receive a greater share of public resources
than do social welfare programs. Furthermore, much of
this investment has been made without the benefit of any
pre-construction analysis as to its probable impact on
the space economy.

In Brazil highway construction programs receive more
public funds than any other transportation expenditure.
To consider the spatial impacts of these programs, Gauthier (1968) investigated the relationship between changing accessibility to highway networks and the growth of
urban centers in the region of São Paulo for the 1940-
60 period. Central to the analysis is the notion that

there is a high degree of interdependence between the development of a transportation system and the geographic pattern of urban growth. Capital investments in transportation networks are "shocks" felt throughout the entire system. These shocks are alterations in the spatial structure of the network that affect the regional accessibility of urban centers. Changes in accessibility, in turn, disrupt existing patterns of spatial competition and have an impact on relative rates of urban growth.

To consider the impact of highway transportation improvements on the structural properties of the network, the highway system is abstracted as a graph and analyzed by graph-theoretic models. To reduce the loss of empirical information that is inevitable in the abstraction process, the network is treated as a valued graph; i.e., the linkages of the highway network are weighted according to transportation costs. The purpose is to differentiate node-linkage associations according to the distance between the nodes, the type of linkage, and changes in line-haul costs resulting from modal improvements.

The accessibility surfaces of the network obtained by a power expansion of the valued graphs yield values that reflect the number of path sequences of circuitry, and the constructional quality of direct and attenuated node-linkage associations (Table 2). To gain insight into the structural pattern of the network, the accessibility surfaces are subjected to a principal components analysis, combined with a varimax rotation to simple structure. The five factors extracted result from the collapse of highly intercorrelated connections between distinctive clusters of nodes which display similar patterns of connectivity.[4]

The results of the analysis of network structure form the basis for answering such questions as the extent to

Table 2. Accessibility Surface of Subgraph of Highway Network, 1960

Center	1	2	3	4	5	Acces- 6
1. São Paulo	x	480.4	363.2	753.9	486.9	473.3
2. Mogi das Cruzes		x	135.9	266.4	173.6	158.9
3. São José dos Campos			x	203.2	132.8	121.1
4. Atibaia				x	282.7	273.9
5. Piracaia					x	182.2
6. Bragança Paulista						x
7. Franco da Rocha						
8. Jundiaí						
9. Campinas						
10. Jaguariúna						
11. Americana						
12. Piracicaba						
13. Limeira						
14. Araras						
15. Rio Claro						

Source: Gauthier (1968:87).

sibility values

7	8	9	10	11	12	13	14	15
572.3	934.9	697.6	314.5	256.4	312.0	188.5	97.3	133.5
203.4	415.7	220.9	96.8	72.1	80.9	47.1	22.5	31.0
155.2	314.7	166.1	72.9	53.9	60.1	35.2	16.9	23.1
328.6	690.9	409.0	183.5	149.1	185.1	119.2	64.2	85.0
209.1	440.6	242.8	117.1	85.9	97.5	63.9	34.8	43.0
195.9	442.2	244.2	139.9	100.4	112.4	87.1	55.6	59.4
x	530.4	320.8	137.7	120.8	154.9	96.8	50.4	70.9
	x	762.6	366.1	350.2	457.3	309.7	175.6	238.9
		x	264.6	337.3	510.2	369.2	223.8	311.4
			x	180.4	247.6	215.9	151.8	175.6
				x	438.3	368.6	248.1	333.8
					x	586.7	394.2	538.2
						x	377.9	482.1
							x	341.7
								x

which changes in network accessibility are related to
the economic growth of the urban center. Operationally,
the structural dimensions of accessibility surfaces provide measures of network accessibility at a subregional
scale. Measures of urban growth are provided by the sur-
rogates of urban population, manufacturing, and retail
trade activity. By using canonical correlation, the relationships between the two sets of measures can be determined.

The time frame of the analysis permits us to ask
whether the relationships between network accessibility
have been balanced or unbalanced. The three surrogate
measures of urban growth constitute a first set of variates, $X^{(1)}$, and the five structural measures of accessibility constitute a second set, $X^{(2)}$. Four possible
time combinations emerge (Table 3): increases in both
sets of variates for 1940 to 1950; increases in both
sets of variates for 1950 to 1960; increases in set $X^{(1)}$
for 1940 to 1950 and increases in set $X^{(2)}$ for 1950 to
1960; and increases in set $X^{(2)}$ for 1940 to 1950 and increases in set $X^{(1)}$ for 1950 to 1960.

The results of the canonical analysis suggest that
some basic objectives of the governmental policy involving highway construction and improvement are being real-
ized. There is a general tendency for highway development to lead economic growth in an unbalanced relation-
ship--in which changes in network accessibility affect
the geographic pattern of regional growth in manufacturing and population. It may be noted also that the unbalanced strategy of growth is consistent with the theoretical arguments of Hirschman (1958).

Data Sources

At best, research applying quantitative methods to
Latin American geography is only beginning. Many deserv-

Table 3. Canonical Analysis of Temporal Relationships between Nodal Accessibility and Urban Growth

Combination of sets of variates	Root	$X^{(1)}$			$X^{(2)}$					$\sqrt{\lambda}$	χ^2	D.F.
		X_1	X_2	X_3	X_4	X_5	X_6	X_7	X_8			
1	1	4.48	-2.09	0.43	2.18	-1.33	0.27	0.24	0.13	.34	24.4	15
	2	-1.08	4.11	-1.32	-0.51	0.73	0.45	0.82	-0.62	.23	9.4	8
	3	0.32	0.37	0.98	-0.19	-0.85	0.08	1.12	-0.18	.09	1.5	3
2	1	3.22	1.03	-0.29	1.83	-1.48	0.16	0.05	-0.72	.28	15.3	15
	2	-1.78	2.15	-0.51	1.08	-1.44	-0.71	0.30	0.46	.18	5.4	8
	3	0.82	0.53	-0.86	1.07	0.30	-0.34	0.97	-0.08	.08	1.3	3
3	1	3.19	-1.12	0.45	2.47	1.60	-0.92	0.85	0.31	.37	29.2	15
	2	-2.30	1.97	0.16	1.31	-1.14	0.47	0.77	-0.13	.26	10.9	8
	3	0.98	-0.58	0.15	-0.11	-1.73	0.40	-0.40	-0.21	.09	1.5	3
4	1	7.13	3.08	1.97	9.61	4.94	-1.42	1.02	0.98	.65	90.8***	15
	2	3.68	6.94	-1.12	1.31	-1.14	3.67	0.77	-0.34	.33	18.2*	8
	3	1.24	-0.59	0.44	-0.25	-0.64	0.11	0.33	0.11	.16	4.0	3

*Significant at .95 confidence level.
**Significant at .99 confidence level.

Source: Gauthier (1968:93).

ing areas of inquiry have been ignored, and the range of
models employed has been limited. Whether there is a
trend toward greater use of quantitative methodology is
not yet clear. Obstacles arising from attitudes about,
and training in, regional geography are still formidable.
However, there is some evidence of a decrease in the sev-
erity of the restrictions posed by low levels of quantity,
quality, and accessibility of data.

In the past decade several data banks have been created to meet social scientists' needs for greater access
to data on Latin America. Their development is largely
a response to an increased interest in theoretical and
empirical research on current issues, and is also a product of the retrieval capabilities of computers. Of these,
the most complete is the Latin American Data Bank (LADB),
created at the University of Florida in 1966 (see description in Appendix). As Antonini (1971) has observed, the
acquisitions of LADB add a new dimension to social science research capabilities.

In developing its data resources, the technicians at
LADB have worked closely with the Getúlio Vargas Foundation in Brazil and the Instituto Torcuato di Tella in
Argentina. As a result, the Instituto Brasileiro de
Geografia e Economia (IBGE), the agency with overall responsibility for data collection and preparation in Brazil, has established an Institute of Informatics. This
institute will provide a data bank for all agencies of
the federal government. For the first time there will
be an agency with clear responsibility for coordinating
official data-collecting activities.

The systematization of collection procedures should
improve the quality of the data and provide a high degree of data comparability. This dimension has been
lacking in the past. Moreover, the coordination of data
storage and retrieval will increase the accessibility of

information for research purposes. All data stored in
the bank will be available either on magnetic tapes or
in card format for authorized research. One feature of
this improved accessibility will be a reduction in the
time required for obtaining the release of official statistics. Such an improvement will be welcomed by those
who have endured the inconvenience and frustration of a
two- to ten-year lag in the release of information.

The improvements taking place in data collection,
storage, and retrieval should facilitate geographic research in at least four major fields. *First*, in urban
geography, new data sources should make it possible to
critically examine the spatial structure and organization
of Latin American cities. Data on urban centers (especially by enumeration zones within the centers) have been
limited or nonexistent, except for the unique case of
Rio de Janeiro. This is an intolerable situation for
Brazil, one of the most rapidly urbanizing nations in
the world. The new data banks should also improve as
their files expand to include information on functional
size, economic structure, socioeconomic status, social
infrastructure, and demographics of urban areas. With
such data it will be possible to carry out comparative
analyses of the social ecology of metropolitan areas
both within and between nations. In addition to providing theoretical insights into urbanization processes in
Latin America, such studies should be useful in the planning of future urban growth.

Second, in location theory, expanding data sources enhance the likelihood that serious research can be done
on the spatial impact of the import-substitution strategy
of industrialization. For example, in Brazil a 60 percent sample of industrial establishments has been completed for nine major metropolitan areas. Specific information is available on type of establishment (four-

digit classification); source and amount of capital investment; number, educational levels, and wages of em-
ployees; source, amount, and cost of energy consumed in
the production process; amount, type, value, and cost of
production; quantity, origin, cost, and mode of transfer
of finished goods; previous locations of the firms; and
number and location of branch or affiliated companies.
In addition, information on economic linkages between
firms will be provided by a special input-output questionnaire in the 1970 manufacturing census.

Third, in population geography, research on migration
patterns has been handicapped by inadequate data. Although some information is available on the socioeconomic
characteristics of migrants, little is known about the
spatial dimensions of the migration process. For instance, what is the role of the village and small town
in rural-urban migration?

Answers to such questions are urgently needed. Data
on migration and the characteristics of migrants have
been gathered by the Oficina de Planificación Nacional
(ODEPLAN) in Chile. Data files on internal migration
at the urban level are being developed by the Oficina
Central de Coordinación y Planificación (CORDIPLAN) in
Venezuela. Recently Brazil's IBGE has completed a series
of questionnaires on migration from the northeast of Brazil.
From a 25 percent sample of migrants, information was obtained on social and educational background, employment
history, economic status, place of birth, previous residences, year of migration to current residence, change
of residence between *bairros*, number of family members
who have emigrated, and their present residences. These
data will be supplemented by the 1970 population census,
which required respondents to furnish information on
place of birth, previous residence, whether it was rural
or urban, length of time in the state of present resi-

dence, and length of time in *município* of present residence.

Fourth, in transportation geography, the state of research on transport systems in Latin America promises to
improve vastly. Data on the origins and destinations of
passengers and cargo, fixed and line-haul costs, and types
and quantity of goods by modal type and modal competition have been based on limited samples and estimates.
As a result, identifying and understanding patterns of
spatial interaction and competition have been elusive
objectives. Fortunately, this situation may soon end,
as various agencies expand their data collections to include infrastructural investments. For example, the inventory on transportation prepared by the IBGE will provide important data on companies engaged in the interur-
ban transportation of passengers and cargo. The inventory will provide specific information on type of owner-
ship; amount and source of capital investment; personnel
employed by type of job; number, description, and capacity of vehicles by date of purchase; operating costs by
category of expenditure; itinerary of cargo movements,
including type of commodity, tonnage, and average price
per ton/kilometer; detailed passenger itineraries, including number of passengers and average price per pas-
senger/kilometer; and plans to expand company operations
for the next five years.

The preceeding discussion represents only a limited
portion of the data now available, or which will be available in the near future. Admittedly, research based on
these data will only be cross-sectional. Time series
analysis will be limited by the incompatibility of these
data with earlier enumerations compiled by a variety of
agencies using different collection procedures for areal-
ly inconsistent observational units. However, it is possible that this constraint will be of relatively short

duration. Current plans for the data banks call for a
continuous program of data updating, with time intervals
ranging from one to five years, depending on the demand
for specific types of information. In addition, the utility of these data sources should improve if the Consejo
Latinoamericano de Ciencias Sociales (CLACSO) is successful in its efforts to create, develop, and modernize social science data archives in Latin America.[5]

Conclusion

Several of the promises and problems of quantitative
research in Latin American geography have been reviewed
here. To be sure, this type of research has only recently been applied in regional geography, and the number of
studies is small. But a new orientation in regional geography is emerging. Quantitative studies are more prob-
lem-oriented and more theoretical than most traditional
geographical studies on Latin America. There is less
concern with traditional historical and cultural themes
and more involvement with current social and economic issues. Problems arising from urban growth, the existence
of growth inequalities, the diffusion of innovations, and
the planning of regional development are subjects of the
new line of inquiry.

Whether there will be an overall increase in quantitatively oriented research in Latin American geography is
still uncertain. Ironically, this uncertainty exists at
a time when definite improvements are occurring in the
quantity, quality, and accessibility of information as a
result of the creation of data banks in the United States
and Latin America. There are indications that geographers
in a few Latin American nations are employing the theoretical models and quantitative methodology developed in
North American geography during the past two decades.
However, it is doubtful that there will be any substan-

tial increase in the number of American geographers who are involved in quantitative research on current Latin American problems. A major obstacle appears to be the generally negative attitude in regional geography toward theory and model development, the two hallmarks of social science research.

NOTES

[1]Werner Baer (1964) presents a good review of this argument.

[2]The divisions are: *north* (subregion 1--Amazonas, Pará; subregion 2--Maranhão, Piauí, Ceará; subregion 3--Pernambuco, Alagoas, Sergipe, Bahia, Rio Grande do Norte, Paraíba; subregion 4--Mato Grosso, Goiás), and *south* (subregion 5--Minas Gerais, Espírito Santo, Rio de Janeiro, Guanabara; subregion 6--São Paulo, Paraná, Santa Catarina, Rio Grande do Sul).

[3]Data were supplied by the Fundação Getúlio Vargas.

[4]When spatially grouped, the five factors are: Greater São Paulo region, Riberão Preto region, Pioneer region, Sul de Minas region, and southern region.

[5]The objectives of CLACSO are discussed by Gustavo Antonini (1971). [Ed. Note: CLACSO abandoned its attempt to organize data archives in 1972.]

REFERENCES

Antonini, Gustavo
    1971   Data banks: a new research tool for Latin Americanists.
            Paper presented at the annual meeting, American Associa-
            tion of Geographers, 1971.

Baer, Werner
    1964   Regional inequality and economic growth in Brazil.   In
            Economic Development and Cultural Change 12:368-85.

Berry, Brian
    1968   Relationships between regional economic development and
            the urban system. *Tydschrift voor Economische en Sociale
            Geografie* 60:283-307.

_____, and Pyle, G.
    1970   Major regions and types of agriculture in Brazil. *Revista
            Brasileira de Geografia* 33:1-22.

Brown, L., and Lentnek, B.
    1973   Innovation diffusion in a developing economy: a meso-
            scale view. *Economic Development and Cultural Change*
            21:274-92.

Faissol, Speridião
    1971   Typology of cities and regionalization of economic devel-
            opment. Paper presented at meetings of International
            Geographic Union, Commission on Quantitative Methods.

_____, and Duarte, A.
    1971   Tipologia e regionalização: uma análise quantitativa
            usando análise fatorial. Paper presented at meetings of
            International Geographic Union, Commission on Quantita-
            tive Methods.

Friedmann, John
    1966   *Regional development policy: a case study of Venezuela.*
            Cambridge, Mass.

Gauthier, Howard
    1968   Transportation and the growth of the São Paulo economy.
            Journal of Regional Science 8:74-94.

_____, and Semple, K.
    1971   Uma análise das desigualdades de crescimento da renda no
            Brasil, segundo os conceitos da teoria de informação.
            Revista Brasileira de Geografia 33:109-117.

Geiger, Pedro
    1971   As cidades do Nordeste: uma análise fatorial aplicada.
            Paper presented at meetings of International Geographic
            Union, Commission on Regional Development.

Hirschman, Albert O.
1958   *The strategy of economic development.* New Haven, Conn.

Keller, Elza
1971   Types of agriculture in Paraná: a factor analysis. Paper for the Fundação IBGE, Ministério de Planejamento.

Morris, F., and Pyle, G.
1971   The social environment of Rio de Janeiro in 1960. *Economic Geography* 47:286-99.

Parsons, James
1964   The contribution of geography to Latin American studies. In *Social Science Research on Latin America,* Charles Wagley, ed. New York.

Semple, K.; Gauthier, H.; and Youngmann, C.
1972   Growth poles in São Paulo, Brazil. *Annals of the American Association of Geographers* 62:591-98.

Sheck, Ronald; Brown, Larry; and Horton, Frank
1973   Employment structure as an indicator of shifts in the space economy. *Revista Geográfica* 73:104-17.

Theil, Henri
1967   *Economics and information theory.* Chicago.

Veldman, D. J.
1967   *FORTRAN programming for the behavioral sciences.* New York.

POLITICAL SCIENCE

Clifford Kaufman

This paper focuses on the potentialities, options, and limitations of the comparative method and statistical analysis for Latin American political research.[1] It concerns basic problems of verification for propositions about political structures, characteristics, events, and behavior. Furthermore, it considers basic problems in using quantified data for political analysis at the national and intranational levels in Latin America.[2]

The first section reviews basic steps in political proposition-building. The second and third sections discuss basic explanation strategies regarding Latin American political phenomena, specifying forms of propositions for which scholars have sought verification through quantitative analysis, and defining the comparative method in relation to forms of attempted verification for such propositions. The fourth and fifth sections explore problems and sources of potential error in research designed for explanation of political phenomena. Specifically, the fourth section defines and evaluates major topical diversity in quantitative political inquiry in Latin America, partly in relation to general problems associated with units and levels of political analysis. The fifth section discusses sources of error in quantitative (mainly regression-based) polit-

ical analysis. Here I focus on problems of statistical
analysis, inference, and interpretation. Furthermore,
I consider briefly procedures for developing complex,
comparative measurement relevant to quantifying political and other phenomena observed in different national
and intranational contexts.

The final section treats three general problems in
Latin American quantitative political inquiry: deter-
minancy and uncertainty in explaining and anticipating
political phenomena, the question of topical priorities
and the normative dimension in Latin American political
inquiry, and the role of Latin American area studies in
relation to political theory-building in general.

Although the discussion draws upon Latin American examples exclusively, this paper is of general use for social scientific inquiry in the developing nations, and
perhaps in advanced ones as well. A major concern is
the evaluation and development of theoretically and
quantitatively based research sensitive to options with-
in--and possible discovery through--the comparative
method and statistical analysis.

Basic Steps in Political Proposition-Building

Through scientifically based inquiry a researcher
seeks to develop theory, namely, a set of systematically
related statements which is empirically testable and
which can potentially include lawlike generalizations
(Rudner 1966). Procedures for the potential generation
of theory include conceptual and operational definition
of the dependent variable and the complex of predictors,
the empirical interrelationship of predictors and the
dependent variable, and the series of replicated attempts
to verify, modify, or falsify this relationship.

One must take certain steps in the construction of
theory, in order to verify empirical generalizations

among phenomena which have nonrandom, persistent relationships. One seeks causal statements of the form "If
X, then Y." These can be described as stochastic or invariant relationships.

In establishing empirical generalizations, the first
step is the specification of concepts or variables to
be interrelated through propositions. I will here consider exclusively empirical concepts, no matter how abstract.

The Latin American literature refers to either vector
or relational concepts. Vector concepts refer mainly to
psychological orientations, or forms of political action
or behavior, as properties of a unit of analysis. As
such, vector concepts have magnitude and direction in
relation to an object of reference toward which there is
an orientation, action, or behavior. Examples include
such orientations as political alienation and efficacy,
and such actions as voting and violence. Typically,
these are considered properties of individuals. Relational concepts refer to the form of relationship between
units of analysis. Examples include political integration, authority, and power. These are considered properties of collectivities.

A second step is the selection of appropriate means
of measurement. For each concept type there is the
question of an appropriate unit and form of measurement--
in other words, the problem of units and levels of analysis. Measurement of vector concepts at the individual
level may be in the form of nonaggregated indicators or
of correlates among individual-level attributes. Further, individual attributes may be aggregated to describe
their degree of presence at the collective level, either
as measurement for vector or relational concepts. However, relational concepts can be measured appropriately
only through transaction/exchange indicators. An example

is the concept of power, which is relational and requires transaction measures (see Walton 1971).

A third step involves establishing two necessary forms of verification for propositions--specifically, we attempt to evaluate the extent to which X-Y relationships are invariant, despite the domain in which they are observed or the form of measurement used for their observation. Indeed, the scope of verification is related to the degree of invariant (positive) relationship between X and Y across a domain of data measured at an equivalent level of analysis. The greater the domain in which we observe such relationships, the greater the scope. (For similar statements, see Campbell and Stanley 1963; Galtung 1970). Further, the generality of verification is related to the degree of invariant relationship between X and Y across diverse levels of analysis. It follows that the greater the scope and generality of verification, the more a proposition assumes a law-like status.

Observing X-Y relationships in differing contexts is a fourth step. Latin American research commonly uses what is termed an endogenous strategy of explanation. This is the attempt to evaluate X-Y relationships for specified units of analysis within the limits of an analytically defined domain--in other words, a parameter or context. Explanation for Y is sought through a complex of X contained within the domain. Endogenous strategy conforms to the common goal of seeking mechanistic, closed-system explanation in the social sciences, and it is closely allied with techniques of regression and correlation.

The endogenous strategy includes two major assumptions for which there are corresponding weaknesses. First, it assumes that a contained set of predictors can be identified toward discovering recurrent, determinant explanation for dependent variables. Critics of this assump-

tion claim that such explanation is insensitive to social realities. They point to uncertainty and variability of temporally lagged relationships between system
components, partly in view of complex feedback and the
potential emergence of new system properties. Consequently, there is little expectation of finding determinant,
asymmetric X-Y relationships that have necessarily predictive or explanatory value through time. Further, they
point to human capacity for reason, rationality, innovation, and purposive behavior. The analogy of a mechanical system imposed analytically on a living system implies unjustified determinism in explaining purposive behavior (see Berrien 1968).

Second, the endogenous strategy assumes that one can
identify autonomous, clearly defined domains, which are
necessary for evaluating the extent of contained, invariant, and determinant explanation for dependent variables.
Here the extent of contingent explanation is determined
by estimating the effect of parameters on X-Y relationships, analogous to the same technique in econometrics
(Christ 1966). Critics argue that few subsystems have
clear enough boundaries and sufficient autonomy for justified parameter estimation. Moreover, boundaries and
internal properties of a domain can change through time
and preclude simple invariant explanation for dependent
variables.

If a determinant, mechanistic explanation is chosen,
there are three major requirements. First, the values
of X and Y must be determined without the influence of
outside forces. Otherwise, it is not possible to meet
the second requirement, namely nonspurious covariation
between X and Y. If the X-Y relationship is explained
through non-endogenous sources, mechanistic explanation
is precluded. Third, causal inference, based on time-
lagged and asymmetric relationships between X and Y, is

justified exclusively on the basis of endogenous variables. As a rule, we limit ourselves to discussing X-Y
covariation and believe that causal interpretation is simply too bold at this stage of development of the social
sciences.

Forms of Propositions in Quantitative
Political Analysis

There are two cases in which the propositional forms
differ substantially. The first involves variations in
which the independent variables (predictors) are associated with the dependent variable at the same level of
analysis, entailing endogenous explanation. In the second, we explore propositional forms which concern inter-
relationships among levels of analysis, a process entailing complex explanation.

*Case I propositional forms: concomitant association
among attributes of the units of analysis.* This type of
analysis typically includes propositions of the form "The
greater the X, the greater the Y." X may include one or
more variables; consequently, propositions may be stated
in bivariate or multivariate form. The literature on
Latin American politics contains mostly bivariate propositions.

Let us consider some examples. At the *national* level
Needler (1968) examines the relationship between political and economic development; Rabinovitz (1969) observes
relationships between various levels of urban and political development, analyzing rank-order relations between
levels of such variables as urbanization and voter turnout. At the *subnational* level Hofferbert, Cameron, and
Henricks (1970) investigate relationships between state
expenditures in diverse policy-output areas, urbanization, industrialization, and communications in Mexico.

At the *urban* level in Mexico, Alschuler (1967) relates
degrees of social mobility, rates of rural-urban migration, characteristics of the development context, and
political participation. A study by Passos (1968) considers the socioeconomic characteristics of Brazilian
states as measures of social tension with voting for
Goulart as a dependent variable. At the *individual* level Silva Michelena (1971) compares political orientations
among diverse samples in Venezuela with such variables as
aspiration and satisfaction levels. And Inkeles (1969)
analyzes the correlates of modern orientations among workers in Chile and Argentina, while Rogers (1969) seeks the
correlates of modernism among peasants in Colombia. Common to all these studies is an attempt to discover concomitant variation among unit-of-analysis attributes, despite differences in the form of inference derived from
the studies and the form of theory used to justify the
studies.

*Case I propositional forms: change in attribute co-
variation.* Similar to the attempt to find covariation
are tests for relationships among variations in values
of unit attributes for specified time periods. Such
analysis can include simple covariation among unit of
analysis attributes, but the form of the proposition is
not "The greater the X, the greater the Y." It is, rather,
"Within specified time periods, changes in X are associated with changes in Y."

Let us cite some examples of this approach. At the
national level Mora y Arauco (1968) examines relationships between shifts in the degree of political instability (conflict) and changes in degree of economic development and structural tension during the same period.
Dean's analysis (1970) treats the incidence of coups
d'état and economic fluctuations over long periods, and

Banks's study (1970) examines political democracy in
relation to socioeconomic modernization through time.
At the *subnational* level Schmitter (1971) examines Brazilian socioeconomic development characteristics and degrees of membership in associations at the state level
for the census years 1940, 1950, and 1960. Powell (1970)
attempts to relate changes in social characteristics of
Chilean provinces and voting patterns between 1958 and
1964, and Bwy (1968b) attempts to explain forms of political violence and observes several relationships
through time at both the national and subnational levels for Brazil, Cuba, the Dominican Republic, and Panama. At the *individual* level Goldrich (1966) analyzes
the dynamic relationships between politicization, political legitimacy orientations, and other psychological
orientations among Panamanian students in the early
1960's. Despite the enormous differences in substantive
interests among these scholars, they all seek to discover
covariation in levels of change among unit-of-analysis
attributes at the same point in time.

*Case I propositional forms: covariation between a com-
plex of interacting attributes and a dependent variable.*
In most Latin American political studies which use statistical analysis, the linear, additive model of regression prevails. The object is to discover how much variation in the dependent variable any single predictor ex-
plains, and to incorporate independent predictors which
account additively for that variance. In reality, such
predictors are often interacting factors, and the interaction contributes to the explanation of the dependent
variable.

One alternative to linear, additive regression is the
multiplicative regression procedure. This has been used
by Soares and Hamblin (1967), who seek to explain provin-

cial-level voting for Allende in the 1952 presidential
election. Taylor (1970), in a study of irregular government change (including Latin American data), claims
that one can substantially increase the amount of variance explained in the dependent variable by accounting
for the interaction of predictors. Soares-Hamblin and
Taylor share the notion that predictors may not act independently in accounting for variance in the dependent
variable. The interaction among the predictors is crucial, because only a certain level or form of relationship among the predictors can account for differences
in the dependent variable. There may be syndromes of
interacting factors in political systems; furthermore,
linear, additive models of regression have too many restricting properties, including the need for independent
variables, which (as essentially discrete factors) account for explanation of the dependent variable in a
statistical sense. Moreover, the linear property of ap-
proximation of the additive regression model may be too
restricting for such problems as development and modernization. It can be hazarded that the greater the complexity and corresponding interdependencies of system
components in a society or polity, the more likely a
multiplicative solution (in contrast to a linear, additive regression solution) will yield a stronger explanation of the dependent variable.

*Case I propositional forms: covariation of attributes
of units of analysis, but as a complex sequencing of
attributes through time.* A well-known hypothesis is
that attributes emerge, persist, and disappear at differing rates and magnitudes in the development of collectivities.
(General problems and potentialities of this form of
analysis are included in Campbell [1963] and Brunner
[1970].) In this view a complex interaction exists

among the attributes--some attributes do not appear or
emerge until others are present. Introduction of new
attributes can contribute to a new form of systemic relationship among the attributes, as well as to the emergence of further complexity in relationships among changing attributes. This approach is often used to discover
patterns or processes of complex sequencing of attributes.

Though this form of analysis is employed rarely in
quantitative Latin American political analysis, Durston
(1970) and Tullis (1970) have tried to use it. In studies of institutional development (as a form of attribute
development) both authors use Guttman scaling procedures,
and they find unidimensional representations of attribute
development in Guatemalan and Peruvian villages, respectively. (Characteristics and problems of Guttman scaling
are discussed in Ghiselli [1964] and W. Scott [1968].)

*Case I propositional forms: covariation among attributes
of units of analysis within a particular range of observational units.* Relationships may hold for particular
ranges of observational cases and not for others; at
least linear approximations of relationship may only hold
for particular ranges of observation. Covariation among
attributes may be contingent on particular contexts, measured by the range of units observed.

Reworking data in the Soares-Hamblin study mentioned
above, Przeworski and Soares (1971) argue for contextual
prediction. They reanalyzed the 1952 provincial election
data for Chile and removed the deviant cases--in particular, the two mining provinces of Arauco and Atacama.
They are thus able to explain 86 percent of the variance
of leftist voting in the 1952 Chilean election at the
provincial level with a single independent variable--per-
centage of population in mining and industry. The analysis shows that a percentage greater than 36 for any

province makes no appreciable contribution to the degree of voting for Allende. One implication is that covariation among attributes holds within a particular range of values for the predictors. Analogous to the concept of marginal utility in economics, for a set of attributes beyond certain ranges there is marginal payoff in their contribution to explaining variance in the dependent variable.

In a study at the national level Hazlewood and Paranzino (1971) argue that dependent variables such as political violence have different explanations in different regions of the world. As with Przeworski and Soares, Hazlewood and Paranzino suggest that statistical explanation and parameter estimation for the dependent variable differ for particular ranges of observations. Consequently, one must observe relationships in different contexts and be ready to find different forms of explanation for similar phenomena in diverse contexts.

Case II propositional forms: seeking exogenous and endogenous explanation. Clear inference from statistical analysis is possible in case I, since all attributes are measured at the same level and all predictors are related to the dependent variable at that level. In case II cross-level analysis is necessary. Either attributes associated with units of analysis are explained by higher levels of analysis, or the relationship among attributes for a unit of analysis is contingent upon some higher level of analysis.

Unfortunately, regression and a number of common statistical procedures apparently do not permit clear inference when variables are to be measured at more than one level (see Przeworski and Teune [1970]). Studies show, however, that we must often consider more than one level in order to explain variations in a dependent variable

at some particular level. In the nonquantitative literature Leeds (1968; 1969) has presented what I consider
the most explicit and exciting attempt in Latin American
research to deal with explanation at different levels.

Multi-level explanation can be illustrated by the following examples of quantitative research. Stinchcombe
(1968) examines differing orientations among the middle
classes in South America; Walker (1967) looks at democratic orientations among students in Latin America; and Walton (1970a; 1970b) considers community politics and power structures in Mexico and Colombia. Each study shows
that explanation for variations in the orientation or
behavior of observed units (individuals, collectivities)
is contingent not only on the endogenous attributes of
the observed unit, but also on variations in national
context. According to Stinchcombe the degree of democratic orientation among the middle classes varies cross-
nationally and is apparently explained by factors associated with social position and national culture. Walker claims that democratic orientations among students
chiefly vary according to personal characteristics of
the students and national context. Walton argues that
a combination of local and national factors appears to
account for variations in community activity levels and
institutional structure in two Mexican and two Colombian
cities. Further, there is complex national sequencing
of political and economic factors that affects local
political activity and power structures.

Studies of collectivities by R. Scott (1965), Zeitlin
(1967), and Goldrich (1966) demonstrate the need to consider more than a single level of analysis. They also
show that system components may be partly a function of
national political characteristics. We need a methodology that includes more than one level of analysis in
seeking endogenous and exogenous sources of explanation.

At present, we test for relationships among attributes
in varied contexts to assess how invariant a relationship appears to be, and we commonly use partial correlation among attributes measured at the same level. The
technique of partial correlation is often used to indicate a spurious relationship among a set of attributes.
True, we already have extensive techniques for the fal-
sification of propositions, but we lack tools designed
for the potential verification of positive relationships
among variables measured at different levels. (See Valkonen [1969] for a general discussion and Teune and Ostrowski [1970] on the context of comparative political
research for the United States and Poland.)

Comparative Method and Proposition Testing

Briefly stated, the comparative method is that set of
procedures employed for evaluating the level of generality and the scope of a proposition. Its purpose in inquiry is the discovery of stochastic or determinant, perhaps invariant, relationships among X and Y variables.

Przeworski and Teune (1970) and Gillespie (1970) consider the comparative method useful for testing propositions and estimating parameters, though Przeworski and
Teune argue specifically that comparative research includes inquiry which permits observation of relationships at more than one level of analysis. Even if we
treat the comparative method largely in relation to proposition-testing, an alternative purpose should be mentioned. Weil (1971) and others have argued that, by observing diverse cases, one may create analogies from
which specific propositions may be derived and tested in
other cases. One creates propositions or relationships
through induction, a process leading to formalization of
what one observes, and to formal testing in diverse contexts in order to assess the scope and generality of

verification. (Clearly, what Weil suggests is similar
to Hanson's argument [1969] on retroduction.)

Options in comparative method. In practice, most studies attempt to increase the scope of a proposition.
Usually one tests for covariation among attributes or
among changes in attributes at the same level across a
greater domain of data. Propositions frequently tested
are those based on the North American experience. They
deal with such diverse areas as voting behavior, state
politics, and national politics. However, the transfer
of concepts and propositions to Latin America from the
United States has created a number of problems. (See
the important discussion by Parrish [1965], where he
spells out conceptual difficulties in comparative Latin
American research.)

Scope is increased if one can show that relationships
among attributes or changes in attributes are statistically significant for diverse circumstances. An alternative approach is to show how a modified proposition
can hold for many diverse circumstances and can account
simultaneously for what is explained by a set of smaller,
more disjunct propositions.[3] Moreover, one may attempt
to show how a proposition holds under particular conditions, particular ranges of attribute values, and the like.

A research design which increases the scope of a proposition is not necessarily complex. Observational units
should be specified in the proposition. Survey analysis
is most useful for measurement or observation at the individual level; aggregate sources of data, for national
and subnational collectivities. Covariation among attributes can be evaluated with a cross-sectional design.
Yet this design does no more than describe the state or
structure of a set of attributes of observational units.
Covariation among changes in attributes can be evaluated

and statements of process can be verified only with a
longitudinal design, if at all.

Making causal inference from comparative analysis
involves a complex research design. Here one might consider the techniques of quasi-experimental research.
(See Campbell and Stanley [1963]; also see the rare use
of a quasi-experimental design for Latin American political research in Boschi [1970].) One might also want
to consider the effects of exogenous factors, at least
in relation to their potential effect on relationships
among attributes of units. In this respect one can con-
duct research in diverse nations to assess whether relationships among attributes of subnational units of observation are invariant, or if they vary systematically
with national characteristics. Fortunately, Schmitter
(1968, 1969) has collected and factor-analyzed national
aggregate data for Latin America. As a next step, one
might choose to test propositions at the subnational
level. Indeed, Schmitter (1969) suggests the use of
paired comparisons of subnational units in Latin American (or Latin American and other regional) cases in a
case-study approach to parameter estimation. Addition-
ally, Kaztman (1968) has shown some fairly consistent
relationships between the degree of involvement in the
international economy and the internal structure of
Latin American nations. One may look at nations with
varying degrees of international involvement to assess
the extent to which international factors mediate relationships found at the national level in Latin America.
Finally, Alschuler (1967) has classified Mexican cities
on the basis of factor analysis, permitting one to make
informed and deliberate selections of urban research
sites in Mexico.

Despite some efforts to increase the scope of propositions, there are few attempts to increase generality.

Perhaps it is because the scope of the propositions is
so narrow, and confidence in current propositions is
correspondingly low. However, it may be that some of
the propositions only appear to have narrow scope because they have been tested at a level on which the proposition is not likely to be verified. Some propositions
conceivably have broad scope and low generality. Perhaps
this is what some researchers obtain when they derive a
proposition from the literature relevant to the collective level and test the proposition at the individual
level. Kahl (1968), for example, derives a series of
propositions about the modernization of collectivities
and evaluates them at the individual level of analysis.
And in his study of violence Bwy (1968b) deliberately
attempts to test propositions at two levels of analysis,
in differing national contexts, and with longitudinal
data. Data results differ by nation, by levels, and
through time. In brief, my point is analogous to Type I
and Type II errors in probability statistics: a proposition should not necessarily be considered false because
of a few nonverifications; an inappropriate range of data
or level of analysis may have been used. On the other
hand, despite initial successful tests, one should not
claim verification for a proposition too hastily; it may
prove to have narrow scope or low generality after repeated tests. Scope and generality are established only
after extensive comparative research through repeated
tests in diverse circumstances and at various levels.

While the purpose of the comparative method can be
abstractly stated, inference from comparative analysis
is more complex. It cannot be overemphasized that the
importance of research findings is not simply what is
termed statistical significance. Findings of relationships, verified or not, have a direct bearing on theoretical inquiry. Without some notion of theory, or with-

out a grasp of cumulative research, there is little opportunity to evaluate data findings. One example is the
"crucial test," familiar to sociologists, in which one
attempts a deliberate evaluation of several competing
explanations for the same dependent variable to determine which is most effective (see Stinchcombe [1968])
in particular contexts. We should not be misled by such
conveniences as the level of correlation as an exclusive
criterion for distinguishing good propositions from bad
ones. It is a matter of finding correlations consistent
with one's expectations of relationship levels among X
and Y variables. Indeed, low correlations in one context and high ones in another may provide clues as to
how propositions should be modified to increase their
scope and generality. The use of raw correlation figures
can never replace rigorous training in political science
and Latin American culture (see Needler [1970]).

We now need more subnational research in Latin America. In particular, little work has been done at the urban and provincial levels. National politics is supposedly "where the action is" in Latin America, but important decisions about the distribution of socioeconomic
goods are made at the subnational level as well. Besides, cities are growing rapidly and becoming differentiated ecological units in which politics is likely to
develop in a complex fashion. Urban studies provide an
opportunity to confront statements about the complex sequencing of attributes, among other propositional forms,
which may be explored through the comparative method.

Fallacies and Topical Diversity in Quantitative
Analysis of Latin American Politics

I have argued for proposition-building in Latin American political analysis, and I have specified some basic
requirements in establishing X-Y relationships with scope

and generality. Now I shall proceed from necessary components in quantitative political analysis to types of
potential error in establishing such relationships.

Forms of fallacy. One form of fallacy concerns inference from data findings in evaluating the scope and generality of propositions. The most basic requirements in
proposition testing include the specification of analytical units for which we expect X-Y relationships to hold,
valid measurement for both X and Y at the level of the
specified units, and the observation of positive X-Y relationships through repeated tests. Even when these
basic requirements are satisfied, there remains a possibility of error in inferring scope. X-Y relationships
can be spurious if they are dependent on particular contexts or exogenous variables, or if other endogenous
variables which account for variations in predictors
have not been identified. Consequently, contextual fallacy and spuriousness may limit scope. Proposition testing at one level does not imply generality, despite broad
scope at that level. To be sure, we can have a cross-
level fallacy, if inference from our data findings is
made at a level higher or lower than the unit at which
proposition-testing is conducted. Where the unit of
analysis for which we seek inference is higher than the
unit of analysis in which we observe X-Y relationships,
we face the possibility of aggregation fallacy (assuming
the proposition does not have high generality). Where
the unit of inference is lower than the unit of analysis,
we have the possibility of ecological fallacy, again assuming the proposition does not have high generality.
(Description and terms for these forms of fallacy are included in Alker [1969a].)
    Another major type of fallacy concerns the inference
from data findings that include relationships among dif-

ferent concept types. Both vector and relational concepts can be measured with aggregated individual data.
However, in one instance we can measure vector concepts
at the collective level, and in another we can measure
relational concepts with available, though not optimal,
data. In relating measures of the two concepts at the
aggregate-individual level, we can have respectable correlates. Logically, but not necessarily empirically,
vector and relational concepts are difficult to relate
because a complex of the former does not adequately describe the latter. Thus there is a possibility of false
interpretation when using empirical relationships to infer what otherwise is a logically problematic relationship.

Topical diversity. Diversity has been substantial.[4]
Topics include variations in political structures, characteristics, events, and behavior. One finds inquiry
designed for intended inference at several levels of
analysis--individuals, organized subcomponents of national systems (such as urban areas and provinces), and national political systems. Dependent variables include
both vector and relational types, and they vary considerably in complexity and dimensionality. For example,
voting behavior is a fairly simple concept, while policy
outputs and modernization are multidimensional and highly complex concepts. Measurement of highly complex concepts is problematic though necessary. Although simpler
variables (e.g., voting and political violence) may lend
themselves to easier data collection and definition, for
many political systems they are of little interest.

In Table 1 representative cases of topical diversity
are summarized; studies and topics are classified according to units of observation (analysis) and, partly, the
intended levels of inference. Such studies often include

analyses of diverse units of observation, and several
levels of inference are frequently discussed. Studies
are classified according to their overt analytic purpose
(i.e., topical intent) and according to at least one
unit of observation. In some instances I have selected
only a portion of a large study in order to illustrate
examples of various combinations of observational units
and inference levels. Finally, studies are cited only
if they include some form of relational statistics,
though the variables in the study may be measured only
at the nominal level.

Much of the literature is subject to potential contextual fallacy or spuriousness of X-Y relationships.
By and large, there has been little comparative testing
of propositions, either cross-sectionally or longitudin-
ally. In fact, such testing requires large-scale research support for original data collection. Therefore,
we can identify for Latin America only a handful of
cross-national studies (Goldrich [1970], Inkeles [1969],
Kahl [1968], and Miller [1970]) or systematic comparative projects within nations (Bonilla [1970a], Rogers
[1969], Schmitter [1971], and Silva Michelena [1971]).
These researchers have collected some of their data at
the individual level, but their inference is often aimed
at the level of the national political system or its components. There are a few studies with longitudinal designs and multiple observations of X-Y relationship
through time--Ames (1970), Banks (1970), Bwy (1968b),
Mora y Arauco (1968), Powell (1970), and Schmitter (1971).
These studies use aggregate or census data, and all are
subject to potential contextual fallacy. However, in
view of their comparative testing of propositions, they
are among our most reliable assessments of degrees of
X-Y relationship.

Few studies include multivariate data analysis, though

Table 1. Representative Topical Diversity in Latin American Quantitative Political Analysis, Classified According to Units of Observation and Levels of Inference

Unit of observation

Individual

Level of inference

Individual	Organized sub-component of the national system	Characteristics of the national political system
Modern political orientations (Rogers 1969)	Local influence and power structure--composition of local political elites; political mobility and recruitment patterns (Bastos/Walker 1970; D'Antonio *et al.* 1968; D'Antonio/Form 1965; Holden 1967; Miller 1970; Hoskin 1968; Wanderley 1968b) Mass (and elite) support for local political institutions (Behrman 1970; Pratt forthcoming)	Mass political orientations (a) support for national political institutions and/or policy-outputs (Bonilla 1970b; Cintra 1968a, 1969; Glazer 1967; Goldrich 1962, 1966; Jutkowitz 1970; Kaufman 1971; Martins Rodrigues 1970; Nasatir 1968; Reading 1968; R. Scott 1965; Snow 1969; Stinchcombe 1968b; Walker 1967; Zeitlin 1967) (b) Political radicalism (Cornelius 1969; Kahl 1968; Portes 1970a, 1970b; Soares 1965; Wanderley 1968c) (c) Political modernism (Behrman 1971; Smith/Inkeles 1966) Mass political activity in national politics (Flinn/Camacho 1969; Goldrich 1970; Goldrich et al. 1970; Inkeles 1969; Mathiason 1967; Nie et al. 1969b; Roberts 1970) National political elite composition, orientations, and behavior (Bonilla 1970a; Imaz 1964; Payne 1968; Petras 1969; Silva Michelena 1967a; Welch 1971)

Unit of observation

Subnational	Political alienation and radicalism (Petras/Zeitlin 1967; Soares/Hamblin 1967) Community power and complexity (Durston 1970; Kaztman 1967; Lamounier 1968; Tullis 1970; Walton 1970a, 1970b, 1971) State policy outputs (Hofferbert et al. 1970) Electoral behavior (Powell 1969) Urban and state (electoral) political participation (Alschuler 1967; Schmitter 1971)	Political integration and conflict (Cornelius forthcoming) Support for national political institutions and/or policy outputs (Silva Michelena 1965, 1967b, 1971) Electoral behavior (and political radicalism) (Ames 1970; Cintra 1968; Johnson 1967; Martz/Harkins 1970; Passos 1968; Powell 1970) Political violence (Bwy 1968b)
National	Empty cell Urban policy outputs (Rabinovitz 1969)	Political integration and conflict (Kaztman 1968; Mora y Arauco 1968; Wanderley 1968a) National political structure (democracy, authority patterns, constitutional government) (Banks 1970; Fitzgibbon 1967; Fitzgibbon/Johnson 1961; Needler 1968; Snow 1966) National policy outputs (Cutwright 1965; Schmitter 1968) Irregular government change (coups d'état, political instability) (Dean 1970; Duff/McCamant 1968; Putnam 1967; Taylor 1970) Political violence (Bwy 1968a; Ferraz 1968; Hazlewood/Paranzino 1971)

exceptions include Hazlewood/Paranzino (1971), Inkeles (1969), Kahl (1968), Kaufman (1971), Soares/Hamblin (1967), and Portes (1970a). Despite the obvious difficulty in controlling the context in which X-Y relationships are observed (and the ever present possibility of excluding unknown endogenous variables from a given study), such analyses represent attempts at avoiding spurious relationships.

Though topical diversity is substantial, quantification requires available and appropriate data. Consequently, there is often a disparity between the data requirements for appropriate testing of propositions and the actual observational units employed for evaluating X-Y relationships. The lack of appropriate data often forces researchers to follow a less than optimal strategy.

There are also instances of potential aggregation fallacy--for example, studies using individual units of observation to evaluate propositions related to such concepts as political modernism (e.g., Inkeles 1969). Although certain relationships may exist at the individual level for a variable such as political modernism, mass orientations and behavior do not necessarily help to explain degrees of modernization in national politics in any simple aggregative way, even assuming agreement as to the meaning of that concept. There is, unfortunately, no easy way of aggregating data about individuals or components of collectivities which would permit one to make clear inferences for higher levels of analysis. Unless one correlates X and Y measured with aggregated individual data at the national level, a procedure which requires a domain of several nations, inference from individual data to the national level is highly problematic.

Some studies contain a potential for ecological fallacy. Collective-level, aggregated individual data may be readily available, but they do not necessarily permit

inference at the individual level (or at the level of
national political system components). Rabinovitz (1969)
incorrectly uses national data to make inferences at the
urban level, and Petras and Zeitlin (1967) use *município*
data to infer individual political behavior.

The fallacy in interpretation can also be illustrated
in studies on Latin America. Where aggregated individual survey data are used to measure vector concepts such
as political orientations, and inferences are drawn about
complex, relational concepts (e.g., political development), this fallacy may occur. Silva Michelena (1971)
uses aggregated individual survey data for inference at
the collective level on political integration and democracy in Venezuela. Indeed, vector concepts are mainly
studied in the Latin American context through individual
or aggregated individual measurement, either from surveys or census data. Electoral data and survey results
are usually used for political and other orientations.
Though researchers study relational concepts, generally
they lack available transaction/exchange indicators.
There are notable exceptions using economic data, event-
scoring for actions such as violence, and budgetary figures as indicators of public policy output. Cornelius's
study on political integration and conflict (1973) is an
encouraging example.

The literature on social science methodology stresses
the myriad problems in making inferences at a unit of
analysis higher or lower than the unit of observation;
but fortunately, such topics as electoral behavior and
violence in Latin America have been considered in propositional form over diverse units of analysis and across
a wide domain of data. Other topics such as leftist
radicalism, political support, policy outputs, and modernization have also been considered across diverse units
of analysis and observation. The existing literature

therefore should be helpful in assessing the scope and generality of verification of propositions, and useful in modifying them.

Options and Limits of Statistical Analysis

Measurement error of the X and Y variables. A major source of error in statistical analysis in Latin America is found in measurement. (On problems of data collection, see Frey [1970], Patch [1970], and Portes [companion essay].) Let us first consider the problems of obtaining reliable and valid data for interval scale measurement suitable for regression and correlation analysis.

Latin American data reliability is often low. In aggregate data analysis, the estimates for national and subnational attributes reported by national and international agencies are often questionable. Data provided by Latin American governments are frequently collected poorly, based on inadequate sampling frames, and sometimes intentionally biased for favorable international images. Uneven levels of reliability can occur for particular variables or measures within particular nations. Consequently, problems exist even at the simple level of comparing estimates for different attributes for one nation at one time. To complicate matters, data collection procedures vary through time for certain nations, thus creating problems in comparing levels of attributes for particular nations at different times, or changes in attributes for particular nations through time. In addition, if one opts for comparative national or subnational analysis, the problems of securing reliable data for various nations through time on a series of attributes are enormous.

For regression and correlation analysis, nonreliability tends to bias correlation coefficients in the direction of underestimation. Indeed, uneven levels of re-

liability for diverse attributes can produce serious
distortion in value estimates for the predictors and the
dependent variable. The result is problematic interpretation of regression and correlation findings.

Another source of measurement error involves validity.
This problem arises when indicators do not provide appropriate measurement for variables included in regression and correlation analysis. Where direct measurement
is used for such relatively simple concepts as voting,
the problem of validity is often not serious, though data reliability may be problematic. Where measurement is
inferred for such complex concepts as political development or modernization, validity is a major problem.

Furthermore, in measuring complex concepts in varying
national or subnational contexts, the problem of measurement equivalence intrudes.[5] Such a problem arises when
comparative political analysis is conducted in different
contexts, and when multi-indicator inferred measurement
is necessary for valid estimation of levels of particular
attributes for varied levels of analysis. Factor analysis has been useful for obviating the problem, though it
has not been used frequently for the development of complex, comparative measurement in the Latin American literature. One of the few attempts is by Kahl (1968), who
attempts to create scales of degree of modern orientations for Mexicans and Brazilians.

Factor analysis can be used to determine the number
of meaningful dimensions of separate measurement necessary for a complex concept (see Przeworski and Teune
[1970]). This process is facilitated through principal
components analysis, which reveals the structure of indicators and the extent of relationship (through factor
loadings) of particular indicators to the dimensions.
The greater the extent to which face-valid indicators
are related with high factor loadings to only one dimen-

sion (independent of the number of dimensions), the
greater the likelihood that one can infer internal consistency of the indicators and, perhaps, corresponding
construct validity. (On validation in measurement, see
Campbell and Fiske [1959].)

Using factor analysis in comparative analysis of sets
of identical or equivalent indicators for particular
concepts helps establish equivalent measurement. Assuming identical measures related to a particular concept,
one may then wish to determine if, in different contexts,
such measures have a similar or equivalent structure.
Similarity can be assessed on the basis of the number of
dimensions apparently necessary to describe the indicators, and the degree of relationship of each indicator
with separate dimensions. In comparative analysis one
seeks the greatest number of identical indicators for
concepts measured in diverse contexts, though the structure of indicators must be considered in each context.
Equivalence is the similarity of construct validity in
varied contexts in which measurement is conducted.

Accordingly, similarity of structure of identical indicators can be tested in diverse contexts. If there
is equivalence of structure, we can infer comparative
measurement and validity for the indicators in diverse
contexts; we can also assess the extent to which a subset of indicators has construct validity in diverse contexts. If this subset is sufficient for comparative
measurement of a complex concept, it can be used. If
the subset is insufficient, then measurement in each of
the diverse contexts can be supplemented with context-
specific indicators, provided that each relates in an
equivalent way to the structure of the subset of identical indicators measured in each context. This equivalence of context-specific indicators is established
through similarity of factor analysis solutions in each

of the diverse contexts.[6]

Another source of error can be the inclusion of non-interval data where interval data are required.[7] However, nominal and ordinal data often are used for measurement of indicators and can be interpreted as having interval properties. This is a matter of judgment; for example, a number of attributes may be measured originally with nominal, dichotomous data, for which the presence of an attribute is scored 1 and the absence, 0. If such data have direction, they may be considered to have interval properties and be entered into a regression analysis. Correlations among such variables may be produced, though interpretation of correlation coefficients can be problematic. Beyond this, a fine line exists in deciding whether data are of ordinal or interval levels. In questionnaires, a format for closed-end questions is the "disagree strongly" through "agree strongly" procedure, which produces what are normally considered ordinal data. Interval data are created by assuming that the distance between "agree a little" and "agree strongly" is equal to the distance between "agree a little" and "disagree a little."

A series of questions in such a format can be correlated. On the basis of the correlations, the data can be factor-analyzed and respondents can be given factor scores. Such scores are treated as interval data. Some of the relevant procedures are illustrated in studies by Kahl (1968), Kaufman (1971), Pastore (1969), and Rogers (1969).

Multicollinearity. To assess the independent effects of each predictor in explaining the dependent variable, the predictors must be essentially uncorrelated in linear, additive regression. Because predictors are frequently intercorrelated, the problem of multicollinearity arises.

Since predictors can have a high degree of shared variance, the independent contribution of each predictor
cannot be evaluated (Palumbo 1969a; Tufte 1969).

Unfortunately, the problem of multicollinearity is
not considered extensively in Latin American statistical
analysis. Though it is difficult to completely avoid
problems of multicollinearity, there are procedures for
reducing its effect. These procedures are useful for
assessments of independent contributions of predictors.
They are also helpful in using multivariate, linear,
additive regression as a technique in assessing asymmetric relationships which are not subject to spurious correlation and which perhaps yield some causal interpretation.

In assessing whether a subdimension of a complex concept is related to the dependent variable, factor analysis can produce potentially uncorrelated dimensions of
the concept, which can be used in correlation analysis
with the dependent variable. Moreover, given a diverse
data set, factor analysis can produce dimensions, each
of which may be a separate variable measured with multi-
indicators. Each dimension should be essentially distinct and can be correlated with the dependent variable.

Another technique is stepwise regression. This procedure usually calls for an initial identification of
the highest correlation between the predictor and the
dependent variable. Next, partial correlations are produced between each of the remaining predictors and the
dependent variable; the predictor with the highest partial correlation is then selected. New predictors are
entered either until the predictors are exhausted or until an insufficient F-value appears, precluding the inclusion of further predictors. By obtaining a series
of partial correlations for sequencing the entry of
predictors into the regression, the researcher attempts

to avoid multicollinearity and to eliminate the problem
of shared variance as an obstacle to assessing the independent contribution of predictors. While stepwise regression has been used in Latin American research (see
Kaufman [1971] and Rogers [1969]), the technique is still
controversial because it may artificially reduce the degrees of freedom bearing on the partial correlations
used for the entry of predictors, thereby distorting the
level of correlation (Kane [1968]). Second, this technique biases the information about the interrelationship
among the predictors. It may be preferable to use a
form of causal or path analysis to evaluate more complex
patterns of interrelationship among the predictors and
the dependent variable, while guarding against spurious
correlation among variables. (See Alker [1969b], Blalock
[1964, 1968], and Forbes and Tufte [1968] on causal analysis; Duncan [1969] and Land [1969] on path analysis.)
One can also examine high-order partial correlations
among the predictors and the dependent variable, in order
to guard against spurious correlations among X and Y variables. One example for Mexican research is Kaufman
(1971).

*Interaction among the elements in the unit-of-analysis
set (Galton's problem).* Galton's problem is the interaction of exogenous and endogenous variables (Blalock
[1969], Christ [1966], and Cnudde [1970]). It is especially important for anthropologists (Naroll [1968],
Gillespie [1970]), who often seek endogenous sources of
explanation for variations in the structure and functioning of communities--analytically described as self-con-
tained. Because attributes of given communities interact with attributes in other communities, nomothetic or
idiographic correlations may be spurious insofar as they
yield explanations with causal interpretation.

Borrowing structural-functional language and analysis in the study of political development, researchers have perforce adopted certain perspectives on Latin American nations. We tend to treat them as independent units, though we realize fully the interaction of such units with external and internal factors. Diffusion effects can be substantial in Latin America, resulting in Galton's problem.

Galton's problem introduces major difficulties in interpreting cross-national aggregate data for Latin America (see Gillespie 1970). Though high levels of correlation are often found among predictors and dependent variables, the sources of explanation for some correlations may be exogenous; that is, they may be located in the international system or in the interactions among the units of analysis themselves (in this case, the nations). If so, exogenous or interactive factors may systematically mediate and bias correlations found among endogenous attributes of Latin American nations. Kaztman (1968) finds that Latin American nations' involvement in the international economy is related strongly and consistently with several internal structural features, such as rural-urban imbalance. There is strong evidence that endogenous factors may not provide a set of causal factors for explaining many of the national attributes of Latin American nations. On this point, students of linkage politics in Latin America form the vanguard in explaining a number of political variables (see Chalmers [1969], McCoy [1971], and Pratt [1970]).

Because of Galton's problem it is difficult to accurately assess the independent contributions of endogenous attributes to the characteristics of Latin American nations. Unfortunately, Galton's problem has no clear solution.[8]

Conclusion

Finally, let us consider three broad issues in political inquiry. First, to what extent should research be designed exclusively for the discovery of invariant, determinant X-Y relationships? Mechanistic explanation in the social sciences and the use of regression analysis for the evaluation of such relationships are aimed at establishing deterministic solutions for political and other problems. An alternative is to search for probabilistic relationships between X and Y, in the context of an open systems analysis and with the expectation of uncertainty and variability of such relationships through time. But to what extent will criticisms from general systems theory be translated into the study of political development in Latin America? Happily, some first steps have been taken through the study of linkage politics, but this perspective has yet to specify its explanatory concepts and might be considered a part of the general systems approach.

Second, to what extent are we to be explicitly normative in selecting topical priorities for empirical work in Latin America? Our normative concerns have typically been designed to conform to the political and public policy goals of government agencies. To what extent is social science inquiry in Latin America to be intentionally instrumental for public policy design and implementation?

Third, what is the role of Latin American area studies in the development of political and social science? A satisfactory answer requires a specification of what is distinct about the Latin American region in order to attempt to avoid the contextual fallacy. This may require the development of a conceptual and scientific language that permits truly cross-national inquiry beyond Latin America.

NOTES

[1]I am grateful to Robert Backoff, Randal Cruikshanks, Leo Hazle-wood, Jerry Medler, Barry Rundquist, and Steven Sinding for helpful advice and criticism. All errors and omissions are, of course, my responsibility. Though this paper includes a basic discussion of the components of conceptually based and comparative political inquiry, some readers may wish to consult other introductory sources. I recommend: Paige (1964), Holt and Turner (1970), Merritt (1970), Przeworski and Teune (1970), and Blalock (1969).

[2]I share with Portes the argument that the logical and technical components of social scientific inquiry are relevant for diverse domains of data, including Latin America. Consequently, Latin American studies, as a subunit of social scientific inquiry, can benefit from advances in methodology in social science research on any area of the world.

[3]Where new, perhaps more complex propositions are suggested, a modification of the concepts is usually necessary. On the logic and problems of empirical concept formation and levels of appropriate concept abstraction for comparative analysis, see Kalleberg (1966), Sartori (1970), and Naroll (1971).

[4]Diversity in political science research on Latin America is discussed in Ranis (1968), Schmitter (1969), and Martz (1971).

[5]This problem is considered in Przeworski and Teune (1966-67, 1970), Teune (1968), Jacob (1971), Merritt (1970), Naroll (1971), Janda (1971), and Triandis (1971).

[6]Scaling can be constructed through other clustering techniques--see Portes (companion essay). In Latin American research, clustering techniques are used by Welch (1971) for the study of leadership, and by Smith and Inkeles (1966) for the study of attitudes characterized as modern. See also the criticism of the latter study by Behrman (1971).

[7]See Mueller *et al.* (1970) and Palumbo (1969b) for discussions of statistical techniques for handling nominal and ordinal data.

[8]Yet through clustering techniques one could at least seek distinct regions (as domains composed of specified units of analysis) to reduce exogenous and endogenous variable interaction. One might obtain clusters based on transaction/exchange indicators to form such units of analysis. For discussions of clustering techniques, see the essays by Gauthier and Cowgill in this volume.

REFERENCES

Alker, Hayward R., Jr.
  1969a A typology of ecological fallacies. In *Quantitative
         ecological analysis in the social sciences*, Mattei Dogan
         and Stein Rokkan, eds. Cambridge, Mass.
  1969b Statistics and politics: the need for causal data anal-
         ysis. In *Politics and the social sciences*, Seymour Mar-
         tin Lipset, ed. New York.

Alschuler, Larry R.
  1967   Political participation and urbanization in Mexico.
         Ph.D. dissertation, Northwestern University.

Ames, Barry
  1970   Bases of support for Mexico's dominant party. *American
         Political Science Review* 64:153-67.

Banks, Arthur S.
  1970   Modernization and political change: the Latin American
         and Amer-European nations. *Comparative Political Stud-
         ies* 2:405-18.

Bastos, Tocary A., and Walker, Thomas W.
  1970   Political parties and political forces in Minas Gerais,
         Brazil: an empirical approach. MS, Department of Po-
         litical Science, University of New Mexico.

Behrman, Lucy C.
  1970   Political development and secularization in two Chilean
         urban communities. Paper presented at the annual meet-
         ing of the American Political Science Association, Los
         Angeles.
  1971   The convergence of religious and political attitudes and
         activities among workers in Santiago, Chile. Paper pre-
         sented at the annual meeting of the American Political
         Science Association, Chicago.

Berrien, Kenneth
  1968   *General and social systems*. New Brunswick, N.J.

Blalock, Hubert M., Jr.
  1964   *Causal inferences in nonexperimental research*. Chapel
         Hill, N.C.
  1968   Theory-building and causal inferences. In *Methodology
         in social research*, Hubert M. Blalock, Jr., and Ann B.
         Blalock, eds. New York.
  1969   *Theory construction*. Englewood Cliffs, N.J.

Bonilla, Frank
  1970a *The failure of elites*. Cambridge, Mass.

1970b   Rio's favelas: the rural slum within the city.   In
          Peasants in cities: readings in the anthropology of
          urbanization, William Mangin, ed.   Boston.

Boschi, Renato Raul
1970   População favelado no Rio de Janeiro: história de um
          trabalho.   *Dados* 7:179-87.

Brunner, Ronald D.
1970   Data analysis, process analysis, and system change.   Pa-
          per presented at the annual meeting of the American Polit-
          ical Science Association, Los Angeles.

Bwy, D. P.
1968a   Political instability in Latin America: the cross-cul-
          tural test of a causal model.   *Latin American Research*
          Review 3 (No. 2):17-66.
1968b   Correlates of political instability in Latin America:
          over-time comparisons from Brazil, Cuba, the Dominican
          Republic, and Panama.   Paper presented at the annual
          meeting of the American Political Science Association,
          Washington, D.C.

Campbell, Donald T.
1963   From description to experimentation: interpreting trends
          as quasi-experiments.   In *Problems in measuring change,*
          Chester W. Harris, ed.   Madison, Wis.

_____, and Fiske, Donald
1959   Convergent and discriminant validation by the multitrait-
          multimethod matrix.   *Psychological Bulletin* 56:81-105.

Campbell, Donald T., and Stanley, Julian C.
1963   *Experimental and quasi-experimental designs for research.*
          Chicago.

Chalmers, Douglas A.
1969   Developing on the periphery: external factors in Latin
          American politics.   In *Linkage politics,* James N.
          Rosenau, ed.   Glencoe, Ill.

Christ, Carl F.
1966   *Econometric models and methods.*   New York.

Cintra, Antônio Octávio
1968a   Partidos políticos em Belo Horizonte: um estudo do
          eleitorado.   *Dados* 5:82-112.
1968b   Educação e protesto político: estudo preliminar de uma
          hipótese.   *Dados* 4:169-85.
1969   Values, policy-preferences and political participation:
          explorations on modernization and social structure in
          Belo Horizonte, Brazil.   Mimeo MS circulated through

the Survey Research Center, University of California, Berkeley.

Cnudde, Charles F.
1970   Problems in evaluating complex models in cross-national research. Paper presented at the annual meeting of the American Political Science Association, Los Angeles.

Cornelius, Wayne A., Jr.
1969   Urbanization as an agent in Latin American political instability: the case of Mexico. *American Political Science Review* 63:833-57.
1973   Nation-building, participation, and distribution: the politics of social reform under Cárdenas. In *Crisis, choice, and change: historical studies of political development*. Gabriel A. Almond *et al.*, eds. Boston.

Cutright, Phillips
1965   Political structure, economic development, and national social security programs. *American Journal of Sociology* 70:537-48.

D'Antonio, William V., *et al.*
1968   Institutional and occupational representations in eleven community influence systems. In *Community structure and decision-making*, Terry Clark, ed. San Francisco.

D'Antonio, William V., and Form, William H.
1965   *Influentials in two border cities: a study in community decision-making*. Notre Dame, Ind.

Dean, Warren
1970   Latin American golpes and economic fluctuations, 1823-1966. *Social Science Quarterly* 51 (No. 1):70-80.

Draper, N. R., and Smith, H.
1966   *Applied regression analysis*. New York.

Duff, Ernest A., and McCamant, John F.
1968   Measuring social and political requirements for system stability in Latin America. *American Political Science Review* 62:1125-43.

Duncan, Otis Dudley
1969   Contingencies in constructing causal models. In *Sociological methodology 1969*, Edgar F. Borgatta, ed. San Francisco.

Durston, John W.
1970   Institutional differentiation in Guatemalan communities. *Economic Development and Cultural Change* 18:598-616.

Ferraz, Francisco
    1968   Correlates of civil violence in Latin America. Mimeo MS
            circulated through the Survey Research Center, University
            of California, Berkeley.

Fitzgibbon, Russell
    1967   Measuring democratic change in Latin America. *Journal of
            Politics* 29 (February):129-66.

_____, and Johnson, Kenneth F.
    1961   Measurement of Latin American political change. *American
            Political Science Review* 55:515-26.

Flinn, William L., and Camacho, Alvaro
    1969   The correlates of voter participation in shantytown
            barrios in Bogotá, Colombia. *Inter-American Economic
            Affairs* 22 (Spring):47-58.

Forbes, H. D., and Tufte, E. R.
    1968   A note of caution in causal modeling. *American Political
            Science Review* 62:1258-64.

Frey, Frederick W.
    1970   Cross-cultural survey research in political science. In
            The methodology of comparative research, Robert T. Holt
            and John E. Turner, eds. New York.

Galtung, Johan
    1970   *Theory and methods of social research*. London.

Ghiselli, Edwin E.
    1964   *Theory of psychological measurement*. New York.

Gillespie, John V.
    1970   Galton's problem and parameter estimation error in com-
            parative political analysis. Paper presented at the
            annual meeting of the Midwest Political Science Associa-
            tion, Chicago.

Glazer, Myron
    1967   The political attitudes and activities of Chilean univer-
            sity students. Paper presented at the conference on stu-
            dents and politics, sponsored by the Harvard Center for
            International Affairs and the University of Puerto Rico.

Goldrich, Daniel
    1962   *Radical nationalism: the political orientations of Pana-
            manian law students*. Bureau of Social and Political Re-
            search, Michigan State University.
    1966   *Sons of the establishment: elite youth in Panama and
            Costa Rica*. Chicago.

1970   Political organization and the politicization of the
        Poblador. *Comparative Political Studies* 3 (July):176-
        202.

_____; Pratt, Raymond B.; and Schuller, C. R.
1970   The political integration of lower-class urban settle-
        ments in Chile and Peru. In *Masses in Latin America*,
        Irving Louis Horowitz, ed. New York.

Hanson, Norwood Russell
1969   *Patterns of discovery*. New York.

Hazlewood, Leo A., and Paranzino, Dennis
1971   Regions, regionalism, and violence: "groups" of politi-
        cal systems as problems in comparative analysis. Paper
        presented at the annual meeting of the International
        Studies Association, San Juan, Puerto Rico.

Hempel, Carl G.
1966   *Philosophy of natural science*. Englewood Cliffs, N.J.

Hofferbert, Richard I.; Cameron, David R.; and Henricks, J. Stephen
1970   Urbanization, industrialization, and integration in five
        countries: a comparison of subnational units. Paper
        presented at the annual meeting of the American Political
        Science Association, Los Angeles.

Holden, David
1967   The structure of leadership and its characteristics in a
        Costa Rican community. *América Indígena* 27 (No. 1):55-
        68.

Holt, Robert T., and Turner, John E. (eds.)
1970   *The methodology of comparative research*. New York.

Hoskin, Gary
1968   Power structure in a Venezuelan town: the case of San
        Cristóbal. *International Journal of Comparative Sociol-
        ogy* 3-4:188-207.

Imaz, José Luis de
1964   Los que mandan: las fuerzas armadas en Argentina.
        América Latina 7:35-69.

Inkeles, Alex
1969   Participant citizenship in six developing countries.
        American Political Science Review 63:1120-41.

Jacob, Herbert
1971   Problems of scale equivalency in measuring attitudes in
        American subcultures. *Social Science Quarterly* 52 (June):
        61-75.

Janda, Kenneth
    1971   A technique for assessing the conceptual equivalence of
            institutional variables across and within culture areas.
            Paper presented at the annual meeting of the American
            Political Science Association, Chicago.

Janson, Carl-Gunnar
    1969   Some problems of ecological factor analysis. In *Quanti-
            tative ecological analysis in the social sciences*, Mattei
            Dogan and Stein Rokkan, eds. Cambridge, Mass.

Johnson, Kenneth
    1967   *The Guatemalan presidential election of March 6, 1966:
            an analysis*. Washington, D.C.

Jutkowitz, Joel M.
    1970   Political socialization in Venezuela: the relationship
            between education's influence and perspectives on power.
            Paper presented at the annual meeting of the American
            Political Science Association, Los Angeles.

Kahl, Joseph A.
    1968   *The measurement of modernism: a study of values in Bra-
            zil and Mexico*. Austin, Tex.

Kalleberg, Arthur
    1966   The logic of comparison: a methodological note on the
            comparative study of political systems. *World Politics*
            19:69–82.

Kane, Edward J.
    1968   *Economic statistics and econometrics: an introduction
            to quantitative economics*. New York.

Kaufman, Clifford
    1971   Mass support for national political institutions: the
            lower class in Mexico City. Paper presented at the an-
            nual meeting of the American Political Science Associa-
            tion, Chicago.

Kaztman, Ruben
    1967   Educational stratification in Argentine provinces. *Bul-
            letin des Sociolischen Institüt der Universität Zurich*
            (No. 4).
    1968   Dependency and absorption of social tensions in under-
            developed countries. Mimeo MS circulated through the
            Survey Research Center, University of California,
            Berkeley.

Lamounier, Bolívar
    1968   Política local e tensões estruturais no Brasil: teste
            preliminar de uma hipótese. *Dados* 4:186–98.

Land, Kenneth
 1969   Principles of path analysis. In *Sociological methodology 1969*, Edgar F. Borgatta, ed. San Francisco.

Leeds, Anthony
 1968   The anthropology of cities: some methodological issues. In *Urban anthropology*, Elizabeth Eddy, ed. Athens, Ga. (Southern Anthropological Society Proceedings, No. 2.)
 1969   The significant variables determining the character of squatter settlements. *América Latina* 12 (July–September): 44–84.

Lijphart, Arend
 1971   Comparative politics and the comparative method. *American Political Science Review* 65:682–93.

Martins Rodrigues, Leôncio
 1970   Industrialização e atitudes operárias. São Paulo.

Martz, John D.
 1971   Political science and Latin American studies: a discipline in search of a region. *Latin American Research Review* 6 (Spring):73–100.

_____, and Harkins, Peter B.
 1970   Urban electoral behavior in Latin America: the case of metropolitan Caracas, 1958–68. Paper presented at the annual meeting of the American Political Science Association, Los Angeles.

Mathiason, John A.
 1967   The Venezuelan campesino: perspectives on change. In *A strategy for research on social policy*, Frank Bonilla and José A. Silva Michelena, eds. Cambridge, Mass.

McCoy, Terry
 1971   External inputs and population policy in Latin America. Paper presented at the annual meeting of the American Political Science Association, Chicago.

Merritt, Richard L.
 1970   *Systematic approaches to comparative politics.* Chicago.

Miller, Delbert C.
 1970   *International community power structures.* Bloomington, Ind.

Mora y Arauco, Manuel
 1968   Tensión estructural, desarrollo económico y cambios en el nivel de conflictos. Paper presented at the Centro Latinoamericano de Pesquisas em Ciências Sociais, Rio de Janeiro.

Mueller, John H.; Schuessler, Karl F.; and Costner, Herbert L.
    1970   *Statistical reasoning in sociology.* Boston.

Naroll, Raoul
    1968   Some thoughts on comparative method in cultural anthro-
            pology. In *Methodology in social research,* Hubert M.
            Blalock, Jr., and Ann B. Blalock, eds. New York.
    1971   Conceptualizing the problem as seen by an anthropologist.
            Paper presented at the annual meeting of the American
            Political Science Association, Chicago.

Nasatir, David
    1968   Higher education and the perception of power: the case
            of Argentina. *Social Science Quarterly* 49 (No. 2):321-
            30.

Needler, Martin
    1968   Political development and socioeconomic development:
            the case of Latin America. *American Political Science
            Review* 62:889-97.
    1970   The quality of quantities: the use of quantitative
            data in cross-national comparisons. Paper presented at
            the annual meeting of the American Political Science
            Association, Los Angeles.

Nie, Norman; Powell, G. Bingham; and Prewitt, Kenneth
    1969a   Social structure and political participation: develop-
            mental relationships, I. *American Political Science
            Review* 63:361-78.
    1969b   Social structure and political participation: develop-
            mental relationships, II. *American Political Science
            Review* 63:808-32.

Nie, Norman; Bent, Dale; and Hull, C. Hadlai
    1970   *Statistical package for the social sciences.* New York.

Paige, Glenn
    1964   *Proposition-building in the study of comparative admin-
            istration.* Monograph No. 4, Comparative Administration
            Group, American Society for Public Administration.

Palumbo, Dennis J.
    1969a   Causal inference and indeterminacy in political behavior:
            some theoretical and statistical problems. Paper pre-
            sented at the annual meeting of the American Political
            Science Association, New York.
    1969b   *Statistics in political and behavioral science.* New York.

Parrish, Charles
    1965   The relevance of comparative method to the study of Latin
            American politics. MS, Department of Government, Univer-
            sity of Texas at Austin.

Passos, Aloar S.
1968   Transição e tensão nos estados brasileiros. *Dados* 5:57-81.

Pastore, José
1969   *Brasília: a cidade e o homem*. São Paulo.

Patch, Richard W.
1970   The La Paz census of 1970. *American Universities Field Staff: Fieldstaff Reports, West Coast South America Series* 17 (12).

Payne, James L.
1968   *Patterns of conflict in Colombia*. New Haven.

Petras, James
1969   *Politics and social forces in Chilean development*. Berkeley, Calif.

_____, and Zeitlin, Maurice
1967   Miners and agrarian radicalism. *American Sociological Review* 32:578-86.

Portes, Alejandro
1970a   Leftist radicalism in Chile: a test of three hypotheses. *Comparative Politics* 2:251-74.
1970b   On the logic of post-factum explanations: the hypothesis of lower-class frustration as the cause of leftist radicalism. Paper presented at the meeting of the Rural Sociological Society, Washington, D.C.
1971   Society's perception of the sociologist and its impact on cross-national research. Paper presented at the Conference on Methodological Problems in Comparative Sociological Research, Indiana University, Bloomington.

Powell, Sandra
1969   Political participation in the barriadas: a case study. *Comparative Political Studies* 2:195-215.
1970   Political change in the Chilean electorate, 1952-1964. *Western Political Quarterly* 23:364-83.

Pratt, Raymond B.
1970   The underdeveloped political science of development. MS, Department of Political Science, Washington University, St. Louis.
1971   Parties, neighborhood associations, and the politicization of the urban poor in Latin America: an exploratory analysis. *Midwest Journal of Political Science* 15:495-524.

Przeworski, Adam, and Teune, Henry
  1966-67 Equivalence in cross-national research. *Public Opinion Quarterly* 30:551-68.
  1970   *The logic of comparative social inquiry.* New York.

Przeworski, Adam, and Soares, Gláucio A. D.
  1971   Theories in search of a curve: a contextual interpretation of left vote. *American Political Science Review* 65:51-68.

Putnam, Robert
  1967   Toward explaining military intervention in Latin American politics. *World Politics* 20:83-110.

Rabinovitz, Francine F.
  1969   Urban development and political development in Latin America. In *Comparative urban research: the administration and politics of cities,* Robert R. Daland, ed. Beverly Hills, Calif.

Ranis, Peter
  1968   Trends in research on Latin American politics: 1961-1967. *Latin American Research Review* 3 (Summer):71-78.

Reading, Reid
  1968   Political socialization in Colombia and the United States: an exploratory study. *Midwest Journal of Political Science* 12 (No. 3):352-81.

Roberts, Bryan
  1970   Urban poverty and political behavior in Guatemala. *Human Organization* 29 (Spring):20-28.

Rogers, Everett
  1969   *Modernization among peasants: the impact of communication.* New York.

Rudner, Richard
  1966   *Philosophy of social science.* Englewood Cliffs, N.J.

Rummel, R. J.
  1970   *Applied factor analysis.* Evanston, Ill.

Sartori, Giovanni
  1970   Concept misformation in comparative politics. *American Political Science Review* 64:1033-53.

Schmitter, Philippe
  1968   New strategies for the comparative analysis of Latin American politics. Paper presented at the meeting of the Latin American Studies Association, New York.

1969   New strategies for the comparative analysis of Latin
        American politics. *Latin American Research Review* 4
        (Summer):71-78.
1971   *Interest conflict and political change in Brazil.* Stan-
        ford, Calif.

Scott, Robert E.
1965   Mexico: the established revolution. In *Political cul-
        ture and political change,* Lucian Pye and Sidney Verba,
        eds. Princeton, N.J.

Scott, William A.
1968   Attitude measurement. In *The handbook of social psychol-
        ogy,* Gardner Lindzey and Elliot Aronson, eds. Reading,
        Mass.

Silva Michelena, José A.
1965   Estructura Social y el diseño de políticas. *América
        Latina* 8:27-45.
1967a   The Venezuelan bureaucrat. In *A strategy for research
        on social policy,* Frank Bonilla and José A. Silva
        Michelena, eds. Cambridge, Mass.
1967b   Nationalism in Venezuela. *Ibid.*
1971   *The illusion of democracy in dependent nations.* Cam-
        bridge, Mass.

Smith, David Horten, and Inkeles, Alex
1966   The OM scale: a comparative socio-psychological measure
        of individual modernity. *Sociometry* 29:353-377.

Snow, Peter G.
1966   A scalogram analysis of political development. *American
        Behavioral Scientist* 9 (No. 7):33-36.
1969   The class basis of Argentine political parties. *American
        Political Science Review* 63:163-67.

Soares, Gláucio A. R.
1965   Desarrollo económico y radicalismo político. In *La in-
        dustrialización en América Latina,* Joseph A. Kahl, ed.
        Mexico.

_____, and Hamblin, Robert L.
1967   Socioeconomic variables and voting for the radical left:
        Chile, 1952. *American Political Science Review* 61:1053-
        65.

Stinchcombe, Arthur
1968   Political socialization in the South American middle
        class. *Harvard Educational Review* 38 (No. 3):506-27.
1969   *Constructing social theories.* New York.

Taylor, Charles Lewis
    1970   Turmoil, economic development, and organized political
            opposition as predictors of irregular government change.
            Paper presented at the annual meeting of the American
            Political Science Association, Los Angeles.

Teune, Henry
    1968   Measurement in comparative research. *Comparative Polit-
            ical Studies* 1:123-38.

_____, and Ostrowski, Krzysztof
    1970   Explaining within-system differences: political systems
            as residual variables. Paper presented at the annual
            meeting of the American Political Science Association,
            Los Angeles.

Triandis, Harry
    1971   Social psychological perspectives and solutions to the
            problem of conceptual equivalence. Paper presented at
            the annual meeting of the American Political Science
            Association, Chicago.

Tufte, Edward R.
    1969   Improving data analysis in political science. *World
            Politics* 21:641-654.

Tullis, F. LaMond
    1970   *Lord and peasant in Peru: a paradigm of political and
            social change.* Cambridge, Mass.

Valkonen, Tapani
    1969   Individual and structural effects in ecological research.
            In *Quantitative ecological research in the social sci-
            ences,* Mattei Dogan and Stein Rokkan, eds. Cambridge,
            Mass.

Walker, Kenneth
    1967   Political socialization in universities. In *Elites in
            Latin America,* Seymour Martin Lipset and Aldo Solari,
            eds. New York.

Walton, John
    1970a   Development decision-making: a comparative study in
            Latin America. *American Journal of Sociology* 75:828-51.
    1970b   Political development and economic development: a com-
            parative analysis of the concepts and their empirical
            interdependence. Paper presented at the annual meeting
            of the American Political Science Association, Los
            Angeles.
    1971   A methodology for the comparative study of power: some
            conceptual and procedural applications. *Social Science
            Quarterly* 52:39-60.

Wanderley Reis, Fábio
    1968a   Latin America and the United States: preliminary test
            of some hypotheses. Mimeo MS circulated through the
            Survey Research Center, University of California,
            Berkeley.
    1968b   Explorations in opinion leadership in a transitional
            context. Mimeo MS circulated through the Survey Research
            Center, University of California, Berkeley.
    1968c   Status, education, and political radicalism: some survey
            data from Brazil. Mimeo MS circulated through the Survey
            Research Center, University of California, Berkeley.

Weil, Herman
    1971   Comparison and politics: a methodological perspective.
            MS, Department of Political Science, University of New
            Mexico.

Welch, William
    1971   Toward effective typology construction in the study of
            Latin American political leadership. *Comparative Politics* 3:271-80.

Zeitlin, Maurice
    1967   *Revolutionary politics and the Cuban working class.*
            Princeton, N.J.

SOCIOLOGY AND THE USE
OF SECONDARY DATA

Alejandro Portes

Measurement theory in the social sciences is now sufficiently developed to permit specific applications of
its general logic to problems of research in any country, regardless of its specific sociocultural features.
Discussion of problems encountered when using secondary
data from Latin America does not require the introduction of any new concept, since whatever difficulties
exist fall along the same methodological axes defining
research problems in the United States, Western Europe,
or any other area. Cultural relativists' warnings of
the difficulties of attaining cross-national conceptual
equivalence need not deflect us into alternative concep-
tualizations, because the content of their observations
can be summarized as differences along the four main
parameters of research methodology: data availability,
reliability, validity, and representativeness (Strauss
1969).

The discussion that follows does not introduce any
new dimension; nor, for that matter, does it discuss
cross-national research in general terms. Rather, the
purpose is to present and illustrate, for the specific
case of Latin America, methodological issues well established in conventional measurement theory.

Before plunging into the discussion, it is important

to outline the major approaches to measurement of social
phenomena as a way of delineating the specific area to
be examined. Measurement can be classified according to
the form of data collection and the units of analysis.
Data collection, in turn, can be either primary or secondary. Primary data are those collected by the investigator himself for the special purpose of his study.
Secondary data are those gathered by original researchers which are adapted by other researchers to meet their
specific needs. Units of measurement can be either individual or aggregate. Individual data are based on the
characteristics and responses of persons, as is the case
with survey research. Aggregate data are summary measures of characteristics of a social collectivity. The
scope of aggregate data varies from units which are
small primary groups, to associations, urban communities,
regions, nations, and entire continents. The type of
summary measure also varies, but in most cases is an indicator of central tendency (i.e., mean, proportion, or
median).

Figure 1 presents a cross-classification of these two
dimensions, which yields a fourfold typology. The cells
contain examples of actual studies conducted at each
level. Not all measurement types are equally plentiful.
At the aggregate level, secondary data have been employed
far more frequently than primary data. This is an obvious consequence of individual researchers' difficulty and
expense in measuring characteristics of regions or entire
countries. However, secondary aggregate data have not
always been used in raw form, as provided by local reporting media. Frequently they have been submitted to
some sort of manipulation through statistical transformations, weighting schemes, and event scoring (Schmitter
1969).

The vast majority of studies at the individual level

Figure 1. The Measurement of Social Phenomena

Unit of analysis

		Individual	Aggregate
Data collection	Primary	Smith and Inkeles (1966): the measurement of individual modernity on the basis of a six-nation comparative survey by the authors.	McClelland (1967): national differences in achievement motivation based on scoring tales in grade school readers.
	Secondary	Janowitz and Segal (1970): social cleavage and party affiliation in the U.S., Britain, and Germany on the basis of national surveys conducted by research centers in each country.	Cutwright (1963): the measurement of national political development on the basis of weighted event scoring for each nation. Russett (1964): *The World Handbook of Political and Social Indicators*.

have been based on data collected by the researcher himself. While unquestionably useful at the beginning of empirical research, the current utility of primary individual studies (usually surveys) must be weighed against the rising costs in time and money, excessive duplication, and depleting patience among researched populations. In contrast, survey data which have already been collected offer a vast and growing body of underutilized research opportunities. Because of these largely unmined resources, this paper will focus on the possibilities and problems of analyzing secondary data on individuals. Moreover, it may become necessary to make greater use of such data in the future, given the growing financial and political difficulties of conducting primary social research in Latin America.

Data Availability

The study of Latin American populations is an increasingly difficult undertaking. Since attention has
shifted from international to domestic problems, North
American researchers interested in the area are encoun-
tering greater difficulty in securing financial support.
More important, the legitimacy of U.S.-sponsored research in Latin America is being questioned seriously
in many countries. As Whyte (1969:28) bluntly states:
"The situation has reached the point that any Peruvian
professor who collaborates with any U.S. professor and
receives money from the United States, whatever the
source of those funds, is subject to attack as a tool
of Yankee imperialism. . . . Apparently this is not a
problem peculiar to Peru. The trend seems to be in the
same direction in Colombia and Chile and probably other
countries also."

Without entering into an analysis of this situation,
a topic examined in detail elsewhere (Portes 1972a), it
seems clear that a deteriorating image of U.S. social
science in Latin America is due to three main factors:
first, perception of the connection between U.S.-spon-
sored research in Latin America and American political
and economic interests. The implications of such linkages were made painfully clear by the Camelot scandal
(Selser 1966; Horowitz 1967); as a result, social science projects have become vulnerable to accusations of
imperialism. Second, there are high costs to those involved in U.S. research projects. These include loss
of political prestige to local professionals asked to
collaborate with U.S. researchers (Whyte 1969), and
costs in time and effort to researched populations--es-
pecially to routinely over-researched informants in positions deemed strategic (Blair 1969). Third, there is

the absence of reciprocity, whereby the high costs in-
curred in collaborating with U.S. researchers are not
compensated by tangible improvements among researched
populations or by increased expertise and familiarity
with relevant national problems among local scholars
and officials (Graciarena 1965).

A combination of these factors has changed the research climate in many countries. Whereas U.S. scholars
were previously welcomed, the situation has become one
in which increasingly tough bargaining is necessary before a researcher is allowed to carry out his project
(Form 1971; Portes 1972a). Nonetheless, most scholars--
including graduate students--insist on carrying out their
own surveys, often without adequate exploration of alternative sources of data already available in their area
of interest. There seems to be a fetish about "being
there and carrying out one's own field work" before a
study can be considered complete and worthwhile. While
familiarity with the country, issues, and specific population under study helps immensely in evaluating results,
it does not follow that in every case direct acquaintance
must lead to the interview schedule. The general result
of this orientation is one of inefficient allocation of
resources and excessive duplication, coupled with continuous underutilization of available information sources.
The standard cliché on Latin American studies--"Very
little research has been done in this area" (a remark
most likely calculated to give the neophyte quasi-messi-
anic expectations for his planned research role)--has
contributed substantially to this state of affairs.

While sources of secondary data in Latin America certainly are not as abundant as in the United States, they
are far less scarce than one generally assumes. Governmental agencies, universities, and private research centers carry out a considerable number of surveys in many

countries. From these studies only univariate distributions (raw frequencies and percentages) are generally
reported, usually in mimeographed form. Lack of time,
statistical expertise, and access to computers commonly
prevent further analysis of the data; they are then filed
away largely untouched, and forgotten. A Chilean professor, for example, has conducted yearly surveys of political opinions for nearly two decades. The surveys
are based on probability samples of the population of
Santiago. These data, invaluable for the analysis of
longitudinal trends in Chilean politics, are filed on
IBM cards and tapes in his office after he has published
reports of party preferences and a few other variables.
As the researcher frankly admits, he has neither the
time nor the means to carry out further analyses.

Though utilization of data collected by U.S. researchers tends to be more intensive, only a small portion of
the data in most surveys ever gets analyzed, and an even
smaller proportion gets published. The unused data kept
for future analyses (which seldom take place) constitute
--after several decades of empirical research in Latin
America--a vast reservoir of untapped opportunities for
investigation. Yet only a minimal proportion of survey
data collected by North American researchers in Latin
America ever finds its way into data banks, a pattern
which obviously contributes to underutilization of informational resources.

The existence of data sources is not identical with
availability, since researchers and research centers may
refuse access to them. However, this does not seem to
be the dominant pattern. It is my impression that most
scholars are willing to make their data available to
others for further study, after analyses bearing on the
main topic of interest have been conducted and reported.

In short, availability of survey data for Latin Amer-

ica is more extensive than usually assumed. This re-
inforces the conclusions of Schmitter (1969), who finds
a similar situation at the aggregate level. Sources of
secondary survey data are 1) formal data banks in the
United States, the best-known example being the International Data Library and Reference Service of Berkeley,
California; 2) files of individual researchers who have
conducted surveys in the area (mainly scholars from the
United States and Latin America); and 3) universities,
research centers, and governmental agencies in Latin
America. Data on file in Latin American institutions,
especially universities, include not only those collected research by the institution itself, but also those
deposited by individual scholars, national and foreign.[1]
Absence of relevant data now seems a smaller problem
than the absence of communication channels to relay information on who has data on what,[2] and the lack of mo-
tivation among researchers to locate appropriate data
sources. Both problems are surmountable.

It may be argued that even if data availability does
not constitute a major obstacle to secondary analyses,
the quality of most Latin American survey data leaves
much to be desired. This suggests the convenience of
continuing primary data-gathering as a way of insuring
satisfactory or at least known levels of reliability
and validity. The quality of survey data, in Latin
America as elsewhere, varies widely. There is indeed
a good deal of poorly collected data whose analysis
would serve no useful purpose. Two points deserve attention: first, there are means to assess the quality
of secondary data; second, available reports and the
impressions of those familiar with Latin American data
do not seem to indicate that the data are any worse than
comparable material collected in the United States. My
own experience with data from several countries strongly

supports this contention.

The following sections examine these two points in
detail. Empirical examples illustrate techniques for
evaluating the quality of available information and provide evidence that Latin American survey material is not
significantly inferior. Techniques for analyzing the reliability and validity of secondary data are essentially
the same as those employed with primary data. For this
reason, the examples below utilize primary as well as
secondary survey data.

Reliability

Internally, the quality of a data set is a function
of its reliability and validity; externally, it is a
function of its representativeness or generalizability.[3]
Reliability is the consistency of scores over repeated
measurements or, more generally, the absence of measurement error (Selltiz *et al.* 1959; Bohrnstedt 1969). The
reliability of variable X is represented by the correlation of the variable with itself: r_{xx}. Mathematically,
reliability is given by the equations:

$$r_{xx} = 1 - \frac{s_e^2}{s^2} = \frac{s^2 - s_e^2}{s^2} = \frac{s_t^2}{s^2}$$

Where: s_e^2 = error or random variance in variable X

s_t^2 = true or nonerror variance in X

s^2 = total variance in X which equals the sum
of true plus error variance (Cronbach 1960)

The notion of reliability implies that the scores in a
given variable are a function of some consistent under-

lying dimension, rather than a result of mere chance or error.

Reliability is not a sufficient criterion for evaluating the quality of a variable, because the consistent dimension determining respondents' scores may not be the one we want to measure. An American researcher asking Mexican peasants for their opinions about the United States may find attitudes which are consistently favorable, no matter how many times or in how many different ways he formulates the questions. He has a highly reliable variable, but it may be a consequence of his respondents' desire to please him rather than a reflection of their true attitudes toward the United States. In short, a variable may be reliable without being valid.

Nevertheless, reliability is important, since it conditions the possibilities for adequate testing of hypotheses. Hypotheses involve predicted relationships between two or more variables, and relationships are established empirically in survey research by measures of correlation between or among them. The extent to which variable X correlates with other variables is limited by its reliability. In other words, the proportion of variance in X which is due to error (nonreliable) does not correlate even with itself. Therefore it cannot correlate with any other variable. If a variable has low reliability (i.e., high proportion of error variance) it will produce low correlations with other variables automatically. Thus a hypothesis may be rejected, not as a function of the absence of a real relationship between the variables, but as an artifactual consequence of the low reliability with which one or more of the variables were measured. As a general rule, the correlation of variable X with variable Y cannot exceed the square root of X's reliability:

$$r_{xy} \leq \sqrt{r_{xx}}$$

Two types of reliability can be distinguished: stability, defined as the consistency of scores of the same
variable over time, and internal consistency, defined as
the equivalence of scores over several indicators of the
same variable at the same time. As a general rule, both
stability and internal consistency tend to increase with
the number of indicators composing a variable. Hence,
other things being equal, a variable measured by answers
to a single question tends to have lower reliability
than one measured by a combination of responses to a
large number of questions.

Stability. The notion of stability implies permanence
of scores on a variable over time and constitutes the
logically most compelling form of establishing reliability. Stability is measured by test-retest correlation,
which consists of administering the same set of questions
to the same set (or a random subsample) of original respondents at a later point in time. The interval varies
from two weeks to six months. Short periods between
original test and retest maximize the possibility that
memory, not real permanence of the variable, may spur-
iously increase the correlation. On the other hand,
long intervening periods increase the probability that
real changes will occur in the variable, thus artificially decreasing the stability coefficient beyond the point
actually due to measurement error.

Very few studies are available on the stability of
survey data in Latin America. For this reason, secondary or primary data sets which contain some sort of retest information are especially useful and should be
evaluated carefully. Absence of research on response

stability is not limited, however, to studies in Latin
America. Other areas, including Western Europe, exhibit
the same scarcity, and even in the United States stability assessments of survey results have been largely neglected (van Es and Wilkening 1970). Available data from
Latin America suggest two tentative conclusions. First,
as is the case in the United States, the stability of
objective variables (indicators of biological and social-
positional traits which could be easily reported by persons other than the respondent) is significantly higher
than stability of subjective variables (indicators of
attitudes, feelings, aspirations, intellectual capacity,
and other mental traits). Second, the stability of variables in Latin America does not differ significantly
from stability of comparable variables in the United
States.

It is impossible to establish a general criterion for
differentiating stable from unstable variables. The
point at which a variable should be considered unstable
varies with the setting, the purpose and design of the
study, and the nature of the variable. Stability coefficients above .85 are usually considered good, those
between .65 and .85 acceptable, and those between .50
and .65 marginal.

If .75 is accepted as a crude cutting point, we find
that the large majority of objective variables reach
stability coefficients beyond this point in all Latin
American studies for which relevant data are reported.
In contrast, most subjective variables fall well below
this figure.

The first panel of Table 1 presents results from one
study (Haller 1969) of social stratification in a *município* (county) of rural Brazil. Following the above criterion, variables were divided first into "objective" and
"subjective," and then into "changeable" and "relatively

unchangeable," according to the likelihood that they
would change over a short period. Objective variables
defined as changeable were expected to exhibit lower
stability coefficients than objective, unchangeable variables. All subjective traits measured were defined
theoretically as unchangeable, and hence were expected
to yield high stability coefficients. As the results
show, objective and unchangeable variables did have generally higher stability than objective and changeable
indicators. Both types were far more stable than subjective measures, regardless of how unchangeable they
were expected to be in theory.

Identical patterns were found by Portes (1970b) in
lower-class slum settlements of Santiago, Chile, and by
van Es and Wilkening (1970) in a rural county of Brazil.
The second and third panels of Table 1 present these
patterns. The van Es and Wilkening study employed a
fourfold classification of variables. Two categories,
"demographic variables" and "reports of present behavior," are equivalent to variables defined above as objective. The third category, "reports of past behavior,"
may be termed quasi-objective, since present attitudes
may influence recall and reporting of past experiences.
The fourth category of "evaluative variables" is identical to those above termed "subjective." As expected,
stability coefficients decrease from the first two groups
of variables to the third, and then markedly to the
fourth.

Low reliability of attitudinal and personality measures indicates the need for cautious evaluation of the
large proportion of survey research aimed at their measurement. This pattern is not unique to Latin America,
as comparable results from research in the United States
(presented in Table 1 from van Es and Wilkening) clearly
show. In the United States, as in Latin America, objec-

Table 1. Stability Coefficients in Three Latin American Studies

I   (Haller)

Variable type	Variable	r_{xx}
Objective-Unchangeable	Sex	1.00
	Age	1.00
	Socioeconomic status (7-item index)	.96
	Size of family	.96
	Agricultural-nonagricultural occupation	.94
	Education	.93
	Literacy	.91
	Tools owned	.75
Objective-Changeable	Wage rate	.96
	Prestige of main occupation	.80
	Total family income	.79
	Mass media exposure	.72
	Food consumption	.56
Subjective-Unchangeable	Alienation	.51
	Anomie	.50
	Realistic educational aspirations for sons	.50
	Idealistic educational aspirations for sons	.28
	Realistic occupational aspirations for sons	.17
	Idealistic occupational aspirations for sons	-.09

II   (Portes)

Objective	Sex	1.00
	Education	.97
	Age	.96
	Occupational status	.93
	Trade union membership	.66
	Frequency of newspaper reading	.66
Subjective	Frustration with personal situation (5-item index)	.75
	Political party preferences	.61
	Expected earnings in five years	.60
	Political alienation (2-item index)	.50
	Leftist radicalism (7-item index)	.50

Perception of opportunities offered by country	.30
Belief in attainment of future aspirations	-.16

III   (van Es and Wilkening)

Variable type	Median r_{xx}	Comparative figure from U.S. research
Demographic variables (objective)	.84 (16 variables)	.89 (26 variables)
Current behavior variables (objective)	.79 (23 variables)	.88 (56 variables)
Past behavior variables (quasi-objective)	.70 (21 variables)	.76 (64 variables)
Evaluative variables (subjective)	.57 (20 variables)	.65 (33 variables)

I - Haller's study (1969) of rural stratification in the *município* of Acucena, state of Minas Gerais, Brazil, 1967-68. Retest based on a simple random subsample without replacement of 91 original respondents. Time interval between original and retest interviews: 6-8 weeks.

II - Portes's study (1970b) of determinants of political orientations in lower-class slum settlements of Santiago, Chile, 1968-69. Retest based on a simple random subsample without replacement of 30 original respondents. Average time interval between original and retest interviews: 3 months.

III - van Es and Wilkening's study (1970) of rural geographical mobility and adaptation in the *município* of Itumbiara, state of Goias, Brazil, 1966. Retest based on a simple random subsample without replacement of 115 original respondents. Time interval between original and retest interviews: 6 months. The comparable U.S. data are based on 19 studies published in 7 sociology, psychology, and statistics journals.

tive variables tend to display high levels of stability, while subjective measures fall considerably below the norm. Moreover, differences in median stability coefficients for each group of variables between Brazilian and comparable United States data are not high. This situation occurs despite the fact that the former were collected among rural, poorly educated, low-status groups, which generally are assumed to yield lower reliability figures, while the latter were drawn from different samples, including urban and relatively well-educated sectors. As van Es and Wilkening (1970:202) state: "It is clear that response stability obtained from the Brazilian sample is not greatly different from that of studies done in the United States. . . . The data do not provide evidence that respondents with different cultural background, low socioeconomic status, low levels of education, and little contact with the larger society are exceptionally prone to low response stability."

Internal consistency. The notion of internal consistency implies that scores on several indicators of the same variable should produce equivalent classifications or distributions of respondents. While data on response stability seldom are collected either in Latin America or in the United States, most surveys do tend to operationalize variables, at least the most important ones, through a plurality of indicators. Therefore, tests for internal consistency become the most common method of assessing the reliability of variables.

Reliability established by internal consistency does not have the same meaning, however, as reliability assessed by test-retest correlation, and the two are therefore not interchangeable. This is true because what is defined as measurement error changes from variable to variable. Response stability is less important when the

variable is expected to change with relative ease over
time than when it is defined as a permanent dimension.
Consequently, while low stability coefficients in the
case of age, occupation, and education imply serious
measurement error, equally low coefficients among attitudes toward a specific governmental policy or a political candidate are less important, since they may be im-
puted to actual changes of opinion, rather than to error.

Conversely, assessment of internal consistency is
more important in the case of abstract dimensions, whose
measurement by specific indicators is partial and tentative, than for fairly concrete variables, adequately op-
erationalized by a single indicator. For example, while
five different items designed to measure a person's sex
or age are likely to strike us as unnecessary regardless
of how high the correlations between them are, the same
number of questions may prove insufficient in establishing adequate reliability for measures of alienation,
anomie, or mental ability. Internal consistency is the
degree of redundancy which obtains between different indicators of the same dimension at the same time. In the
case of objective and fairly concrete variables, such as
age or years of education, redundancy can be taken for
granted; in the case of more general variables, it must
be established empirically.

The basic form of assessing internal consistency is
to examine the intercorrelations between indicators of
the same variable. If, for example, evaluation of present occupation and assessment of whether initial income
aspirations have been attained are both indicators of
"degree of satisfaction with present situation," then
the correlation between them should be sizeable and in
the predicted direction.

Employing secondary data collected during 1962 by
Hamuy in Santiago, Portes (1970a) attempts to test sev-

eral theories on determinants of leftist political attitudes. The first step is to build an acceptable indicator of the dependent variable, "leftist orientations."
Three questionnaire items appear relevant to that purpose: general political preferences, classified into
leftist (given a score of 3), centrist (scored 2), and
rightist (scored 1); specific party preferences, classified as Communist-Socialist-FRAP (scored 3), Christian
Democratic (scored 2), and Radical-Liberal-Conservative
(scored 1); and attitude toward the Cuban revolution,
classified into good or very good (scored 3), undecided
(scored 2), and bad or very bad (scored 1).

Although *a priori* each item seems an appropriate measure of "leftist orientations," this fact does not by itself justify their combination into a single index. A
simple way of establishing internal consistency in this
instance is to inspect the intercorrelations between
items (see Table 2). All correlations are positive and,
though not high, they all are moderately so and reach
significance at the .001 level. Therefore, one can conclude that the data do justify a combination of the items
into a "leftist orientations" index.

When there are many items tapping the same dimension,
it may be difficult to assess internal consistency by
simple inspection of the correlation matrix; hence, some
summary measure is required. Four techniques are employed most commonly for this purpose. First, average
intercorrelations of each item with all others are computed. Through this procedure items can be ranked according to their degree of association with others, thus
facilitating elimination of items poorly correlated with
the rest (Schnaiberg 1970).

Second, item-to-total correlations may be computed by
adding up the standardized scores of all items into a
general index, which is then correlated with specific

Table 2. Zero-Order Correlations between Indicators of Leftist
          Orientations in Hamuy's 1962 Santiago Survey

Items	-X1- General political preferences	-X2- Specific party preferences	-X3- Attitude toward the Cuban revolution
-X1-	--	.49*	.42*
-X2-		--	.35*
-X3-			--

*p < .001

Source: Portes (1970a)

items. This procedure also allows ranking of items from
the most to the least internally consistent. However,
item-to-total correlations tend to convey an artificially
high impression of internal consistency, for the simple
reason that each such correlation contains the correlation of the item with itself as part of the total index.
Thus, if there are four items, each item shares at least
one-fourth of the variance with the total index and, as
a result, item-to-total correlations cannot go below .50
($r_{it} = \sqrt{1/4} = \sqrt{.25} = .50$). Obviously, the greater the
number of items, the smaller the artificial inflation of
item-to-total coefficients, since self-correlations of
individual items become diluted in the process. Nevertheless, it seems convenient, as shown in the work of
Schnaiberg (1970), to include floor levels of correlation
when reporting item-to-total coefficients as measures of
internal consistency.

A third technique is the procedure Bohrnstedt (1969)

presents, which permits direct computation of item-to-
total correlations, subtracting the effect of self-
correlations. Table 3 illustrates this procedure with
data from Portes's (1970b) study of political orientations among lower-class slum-dwellers in Chile. The
table presents intercorrelations between items selected
as components of the Leftist Radicalism Index (LRI), un-
corrected item-to-total correlations, and corresponding
coefficients corrected for self-correlation. Components
of LRI include: 1) attitude toward a popular revolution
in Chile, ranging from "very good" to "very bad"; 2) attitude toward breaking diplomatic relations with the
United States, dichotomized into "very important that
it be done" versus "should not be done or not very important that it be done"; 3) attitude toward reestablishing
friendly relationships with Cuba, dichotomized in the
same way; 4) attitude toward expropriating the properties
of the rich and putting them under state control, also
dichotomized in the same way; 5) comparison between two
alternatives ("Social change should not be revolutionary.
It is necessary to preserve many things from the past,"
and, "Social change should be revolutionary. It is necessary to sweep away the whole past"), with responses
trichotomized into agrees with the first, agrees with
neither, and agrees with the second; 6) comparison between another set of alternatives ("The best way for a
progressive government to attain power is through democratic elections," and, "The best way for a progressive
government to attain power is through a popular revolution"), with responses trichotomized in the same way;
and 7) comparison between these alternatives ("To achieve
true social change, it is necessary to use force against
the powerful," and, "Force does not lead anywhere. To
achieve true social change, it is necessary to seek the
cooperation of all"), also trichotomized in the same way.

Table 3. Intercorrelations between Indicators of Leftist Radicalism
          and Item-to-Total Correlations in Lower-Class Chilean Sample

Variables	-X1-	-X2-	-X3-	-X4-	-X5-	-X6-	-X7-	LRI (I)	LRI (II)
-X1-	--	.32	.38	.19	.49	.54	.34	.71	.57
-X2-		--	.24	.27	.41	.32	.30	.62	.46
-X3-			--	.31	.28	.32	.20	.59	.42
-X4-				--	.25	.24	.30	.56	.38
-X5-					--	.50	.43	.73	.60
-X6-						--	.51	.74	.62
-X7-							--	.67	.52

-X1- Attitude toward revolution in Chile
-X2- Attitude toward breaking U.S.-Chile relations
-X3- Attitude toward reestablishing Chile-Cuba relations
-X4- Attitude toward expropriation of the rich
-X5- Attitude toward preservation of past institutions
-X6- Attitude toward means for attaining power
-X7- Attitude toward use of force

LRI- Leftist Radicalism Index
      (I) - Item-to-total correlations
      (II)- Item-to-total correlations corrected for self-
            correlations

Source: Portes (1970b)

On all of the above items, leftist radical responses were coded highest. Impressions of very high internal consistency are moderated considerably by subtracting the contribution of self-correlations. Nevertheless, corrected item-to-total correlations range from moderate to sizeable, all significant beyond the .001 level. Results can be interpreted as indicating an acceptable level of internal consistency among these items.

A fourth technique to assess internal consistency is the use of summary measures which indicate the level of internal consistency for the entire set of items, rather than for individual ones. Most frequently employed are the Kuder-Richardson formulas 20 and 21 and Cronbach's Alpha (Cronbach 1960; Bohrnstedt 1969). All are applicable to data for which intercorrelations between indicators of the same variable are available. KR20 is computationally more difficult, but more accurate, than KR21. Alpha seems in general the best coefficient, being an approximate average of all possible intercorrelations between items.

A more refined though more complex technique for evaluating internal consistency is factor analysis. The basic assumption of factor analysis is that correlations between a set of variables are due to their being jointly determined by a smaller set of basic dimensions. Factor analysis is a mathematical procedure designed to extract from a correlation matrix the underlying dimensions accounting for whatever relationships exist between variables. A corollary of the above assumption is that once the basic factors have been extracted, residual correlations between variables will approximate zero.

The logical link between factor analysis and internal consistency can be seen by recalling that the latter is defined as the extent to which a group of items are equivalent or redundant indicators of the same basic di-

mension(s). If they are, intercorrelations between them
will be consistently high, and a factor analysis of the
correlation matrix will yield one or a few factors accounting for practically all common variance in the items.

In most cases the general variable that a series of
items aims at measuring is defined theoretically as unidimensional. That is, items are assumed to correlate to
the extent that they represent a single basic variable.
Among the various methods of factor extraction, the principal axes technique seems best suited to test this assumption, since it is designed to maximize the common
variance extracted by the first factor (Fruchter 1954).
To the extent that unidimensionality exists, loadings
(factor-item correlations) of items on the first factor
will be sizeable and significantly greater than on subsequent factors. By the same token, proportion of common variance explained by the first factor will be significantly greater than that accounted for by secondary
factors. Absence of unidimensionality, on the other
hand, implies that whatever relationships exist between
variables are due to more than one factor or that no
common dimensions underlie the variables (in which case
the matrix will contain a large number of near-zero
coefficients).

Whenever a theoretically important variable has been
measured by a sizeable number of items, and the researcher has the means at hand, it is recommended that he assess internal consistency by factor analysis. This method yields information not conveyed by simpler procedures
about the underlying structure of the variable. My own
familiarity with factor analytic results from several
Latin American surveys indicates that Latin American
data are no less reliable than those from the United
States or other countries (Portes 1970b, 1973). Moreover, results have often yielded meaningful factorial

structures.

One of the above studies (Portes 1973) explores the question of whether the concept of individual modernity can be identified empirically as a cluster of consistent psychosocial variables. For this purpose, data from a sample of lower-class respondents in urban, rural white (*ladino*) and native Indian (Cakchiquel) areas of Guatemala were analyzed. Table 4 presents results of factor analyzing available indicators of individual modernity by the principal components method.[4] Results from this twenty-item set indicate that a unidimensional modernity dimension can be detected empirically, thus supporting the findings of Smith and Inkeles (1966) and Schnaiberg (1970), among others. Loadings on the first (modernity) factor are usually at least moderate (> .30), reaching higher values in many instances. Moreover, all run in expected directions. The first factor, as predicted, accounts for a significant proportion of the common variance (21.8 percent), almost three times the percentage explained by the next most powerful factor. Further exploration of these results yielded a meaningful structure after a varimax factor rotation. These results indicate that while a basic modernity dimension may exist in reality, other more specific but theoretically interpretable dimensions also can be identified empirically.

Additional methods. The above methods of assessing reliability belong to the standard arsenal of empirical researchers. When confronted with a new set of secondary data, however, it is important to look for additional and less conventional ways of evaluating reliability.

The Guatemalan data discussed above offer one such opportunity. This survey, conducted by the Central American Institute of Population (Amaro 1968), concerns the socioeconomic determinants of modernity and fertility.

It is based on simultaneous but separate interviews with husbands and wives in 875 couples. The feature of independent simultaneous interviews permits assessment of a variant of inter-rater reliability by checking the extent to which husband and wife give similar responses to questions which they are expected to answer in the same manner. For example, both husband and wife should give identical answers to the question of whether their marriage is legal or common-law. Absence of agreement (i.e., low husband-wife correlation) would indicate that, for whatever reason, the variable is not being appropriately measured.

Table 5 presents zero-order correlations between husband and wife responses to those items where agreement is expected. As shown in Table 5, the two variables where total agreement should occur--marital status and report of dwelling conditions--do yield high correlations. Religious affiliation is generally expected to be the same for husband and wife, and so are the occupational aspirations they hold for their sons. However, there is greater room for disagreement in both variables, since there can be mixed marriages and parents can have different aspirations. Thus one can anticipate sizeable but somewhat lower correlations. As Table 5 indicates, this is what happens. Knowledge and use of contraceptive methods should also be similar, unless we assume low intramarital communication and much extramarital sexual activity. Hence, the lower husband-wife correlations encountered in these two variables, especially in knowledge of contraceptive methods, sensitizes us to the possibility that a significant amount of response error exists in these variables. Reluctance of respondents to discuss such intimate topics, especially in the case of women, may be advanced as an initial explanation for these results. At any rate, they lead us to conclude

Table 4. Unrotated Factor Loadings for Modernity Indicators in Lower-Class Guatemalan Sample

Variables	I (Modernity)	II	III	Factors IV	V	VI
Knowledge of population increase in Guatemala	.32	-.05	.02	-.06	-.31	.68
Attendance at mass	-.33	.46	.22	-.25	-.54	.01
Frequency of communion	-.53	.46	.10	-.22	-.31	.02
Favorableness to wife's work outside home if she desires	.26	.25	.16	.32	-.19	-.23
Favorableness to wife's autonomy from husband	.40	.43	.20	.19	.06	-.25
Favorableness to children's autonomy from parents	.46	.38	.24	.01	.19	-.14
Definition of family as nuclear rather than extended	.34	-.34	.11	.16	-.27	-.28
Favorableness to urban life	.48	-.25	.08	.22	-.30	-.14
Belief that cities corrupt people	-.25	-.28	-.10	-.12	-.36	-.42
Occupational aspirations for sons	.73	-.03	.15	.05	-.11	.05

Numerical definition of "small" family	.46	-.11	.11	-.61	.06	-.12
Numerical definition of "large" family	.36	-.21	.16	-.64	.15	-.18
Favorableness to letting an interval pass between children	.20	-.15	-.34	-.13	-.35	.02
Knowledge of contraceptive methods	.67	.17	-.14	.04	-.02	.11
Disposition to learn more about contraceptive methods	.29	.08	-.60	-.05	-.08	-.03
Attitude toward use of contraceptive methods by poor families	.52	.02	-.31	.02	.01	.05
Communication with spouse about sexual matters	.24	.41	-.57	-.08	.04	-.21
Use of contraceptive methods	.48	.32	-.06	-.03	-.03	-.04
Years of education	.63	.20	.16	-.15	.07	.17
Years of urban residence	.78	-.23	.17	.11	-.13	.04
Percentage of variance explained	21.8	7.8	6.3	6.0	5.3	5.1

Source: Portes (1973)

Table 5. Husband-Wife Correlations as Reliability Indicators
          in Lower-Class Guatemalan Sample

Variables	r_{hw}
Marital status (legal vs. common law marriage)	.96
Status of dwelling	.90
Religion (Protestant vs. non-Protestant)	.67
Occupational aspirations for sons	.61
Religion (Catholic vs. non-Catholic)	.56
Use of contraceptive methods	.53
Knowledge of birth control methods	.38

Source: Portes (1973)

that though the reliability of these data generally
seems satisfactory, findings based on the latter two
variables should be interpreted with caution.

Validity

   Validity is the degree to which empirical measures
represent a relevant theoretical dimension. While reliability is concerned with the problem of whether some
variable is being measured consistently, validity asks
whether that dimension is in fact the one we wish to
measure (Selltiz *et al.* 1959). Logically, reliability
is a necessary condition for validity; validity in turn
is a sufficient condition for reliability. Theoretically, the question of validity is more important; it is
also the more difficult to evaluate (Nagel 1961). Figure
2 summarizes graphically the role of reliability and validity in measurement.

   The question of validity, which implies a vertical
relationship between the theoretical definition of a

Figure 2. The Role of Reliability and Validity in Measurement

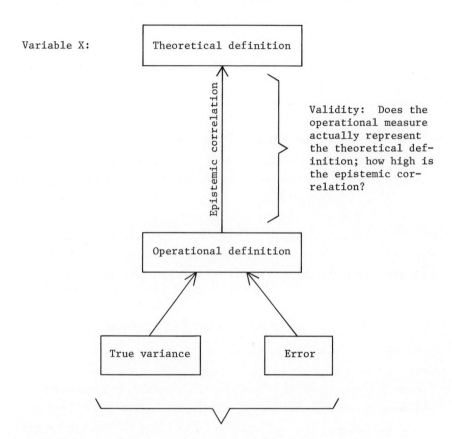

Reliability: Is the proportion of true variance significantly greater than the proportion of error?

variable and its actual empirical measure or operational
definition, can never be conclusively established because
there is no way of directly assessing the theoretical
meaning of the variable. For this reason, techniques
for establishing validity always involve assumptions.
These are examined below.

Assessing validity of measures within a specific data
set is not identical to determining whether a particular
measure is representative of the same theoretical variable across surveys conducted at different points in time
and space. If the researcher desires to describe cross-
national differences in n-achievement, he must demonstrate that his measures are valid not only within a specific national sample but also between a series of such
samples. It becomes necessary to establish the fact that
the same empirical indicator measures the same dimension
in the same manner across countries--to assess the extent to which "phenomenal identity" of a measure also
carries "conceptual equivalence" (Strauss 1969). Alternatively, the researcher must demonstrate the extent to
which the same measure coded in different ways, or different measures, yield conceptual equivalence cross-
nationally.

Fortunately, the serious difficulties involved in this
task are bypassed by using secondary data to test hypothesized relationships within specific populations. In
most cases interest does not center on the description
of the behavior of a single variable across regions or
countries, but rather on the ways two or more variables
are related in particular settings. Obtaining this information requires establishing only the validity of relevant variables for the specific population involved
(Schmitter 1969). Use of secondary data for hypothesis-
testing is methodologically less difficult and scientifically more important. For purposes of theory-building,

it is less important to know absolute scores on variable
X than its causes, consequences, and correlates. Testing hypotheses within specific countries by use of secondary data can form the basis of a more efficient comparative approach, which examines similarities and differences in the ways variables relate in different countries.

Predictive validity. The validity of a measure can be
assessed if different degrees of whatever the variable
represents are likely to lead to different behavioral
outcomes. If so, scores in the measure can be correlated with ensuing behaviors. A high correlation indicates substantial validity, since the former could have
been used to accurately predict the latter (Cronbach
1960). This method of validation rests on the assumption that the behavior that serves as a criterion does
in fact reflect the theoretical meaning of the variable.
For example, if a test of mental ability is validated
against grade point average five years later, it is because we assume that, in the long run, academic grades
do reflect mental ability.

Evaluating the validity of secondary data through
this method is difficult, since variables do not usually
carry a clear prediction of specific patterns of behavior. In cases where they do, information on these behavior patterns seldom exists. However, there are some
instances where predictive validation is possible. For
instance, one can validate data on political attitudes
collected on the basis of probability samples of administrative units (such as municipalities, counties, or
provinces) by correlating results with electoral outcomes in these areas.

A variant of this procedure was employed to validate
the Leftist Radicalism Index (LRI) presented above. The
Chilean municipal elections of 1969 took place at the

time data collection was almost completed. All parties, including the extreme left alliance of communists and socialists, took part in the election. No significant leftist organization, not even the most extreme sectors of this alliance, abstained. Data had been collected on the basis of simple random samples of family heads in four lower-class slum areas of Santiago (one area divided into two sectors). These areas should rank in the same order by using our indicators of leftist extremism (assuming they are accurate) as they would by using more objective measures of support for the extreme left during the pre-election campaign. As in other countries, all parties made intensive use of electoral posters. Posters in public places meant little for our purposes because they could be put up by mobile teams. However, posters affixed to houses could not stay there without the consent of the dwellers. Thus it appeared that counting the number of communist and socialist posters affixed to dwellings would give us a good independent measure of support for the extreme left in different areas. Accordingly, two interviewers were sent to each slum settlement on the same day to count the number of posters. They counted independently and the final score was the average of their counts. This score, in turn, was standardized for all areas by taking the ratio of number of posters to number of dwellings. Once LRI had been developed, it was possible to compare rankings of settlements according to proportions of leftist radicals (LRI) and to ratios of extreme left posters to dwellings. Table 6 presents the results. The rank order is almost identical in both cases. Though this finding could be due to other factors, it provided, together with other evidence, initial support for the validity of the index.

Concurrent validity. A measure can be validated by cor-

Table 6. Extreme Left Posters Displayed in Dwellings and Proportions of Leftist Radicals in Slum Settlements of Santiago (Chile)

Settlement	% Leftist Radicals* (LRI)	Number of extreme left posters	Number of dwellings**	Ratio of posters to dwellings
Lo Valledor Norte	11.3	60	850	.071
Parque Sta. Monica	11.9	69	850	.081
La Faena – 1st Sector	14.4	194	2,000	.097
La Faena – 2nd Sector	29.2	141	500	.282
Herminda de la Victoria	29.2	432	1,200	.360

*Percent Leftist Radicals includes those having scores on or above one standard deviation in the radical direction in the total distribution of the index.

**Figures provided by the Chilean Housing Corporation (CORVI).

Source: Portes (1970b).

relating scores in it with those obtained in a well-established indicator of the same variable. For example, a new test of mental ability can be validated by administering it to a sample of subjects together with the Stanford-Binet scale. A high correlation between the new test and the Stanford-Binet would indicate high concurrent validity (Cronbach 1960). This type of validation obviously depends on the assumption that the criterion (Stanford-Binet) does in fact measure the relevant theoretical variable.

Though useful to psychometricians, concurrent validation is never employed in assessing the quality of secondary survey data. The obvious reason is that if the data contained a valid measure of the variable, there would be no need to validate alternative, imperfect indicators.

A variant of concurrent validity, however, furnishes a useful technique for data evaluation. This consists of correlating two general (usually composite) measures of the same variable. If a survey measures individual modernity by using two different scales (e.g., Smith and Inkeles's and Kahl's), then the correlation between scores in the two scales would provide a measure of convergent validity (Campbell and Fiske 1959). A high correlation would be expected, since both scales are supposed to tap the same dimension. There is no need for assuming that one scale is initially more valid than the other. Hence, it is not the case that the superior measure validates the inferior one, but that each reciprocally validates the other.

There is a close similarity between the logic of convergent validation and that of reliability by internal consistency. In both cases one correlates a plurality of simultaneous indicators of the same variable. The difference is this: while internal consistency involves relationships between isolated and tentative items, convergent validation involves the association between two or more composite, generally well-established measures.

Parallelism between reliability and validity can be extended by noting the correspondence between the two forms of reliability assessment and the two methods of validation already discussed. While both internal consistency and convergent validity are concerned with the degree of redundancy between different indicators of one basic dimension, stability and predictive validity refer to the relationship between a measure and a related outcome in the future. In the case of stability, the outcome is repetition of scores in the same measure; in predictive validity, it is enactment of a theoretically re-

Figure 3. Reliability, Validity, and the Time Dimension

Measures taken at:

	same time	at least two times
Reliability	**Internal consistency:** Redundancy of a plurality of indicators of the same variable	**Stability:** Consistency of scores on one or more variable indicators over time
Validity	**Concurrent (convergent) validation:** Redundancy of two or more general measures of the same variable	**Predictive validation:** Consistency of behaviors with those expected from previous measurement of the variable

lated behavior. Figure 3 summarizes these relationships.

A variant of convergent validation was employed to provide additional evidence for the validity of the Leftist Radicalism Index (LRI) discussed above. The questionnaire contained a series of items asking respondents whether different groups and organizations would promote or hinder social change in Chile. Each group possessed a definite political connotation such that it was possible to predict the direction of the correlation between responses to each item and LRI. For example, those scoring high in the index would be expected to answer that the rich would hinder social change, producing a significant negative correlation between the item and LRI. Conversely, leftist radicals would be expected to endorse the workers and the Communist party as promoters of social change, yielding positive correlations with the index.

Convergent validity is established in this case by

examining whether the general index and the series of group items correlate as they would be expected to do theoretically. If LRI is a valid indicator of leftist extremism, it should yield significant correlations in the predicted directions in all or most cases. As Table 7 demonstrates, all correlations run in the expected directions. Though several coefficients are small, all reach statistical significance at the .01 level or higher. The results can be interpreted as providing additional support for the validity of the index.

Positive results from convergent validation should be interpreted carefully, for the method depends on the assumption that the basic variable which a high correlation between different measures reflects is in fact the relevant one. Although internal consistency is concerned only with whether several indicators measure the same variable, convergent validation asserts that this variable is indeed the one we want to measure. While this may be the case, it need not be so, and the strength of convergent validation is relative to the number and plausibility of alternative hypotheses (i.e., alternative basic variables) accounting for results.

Construct validation. The third and most generally applicable method for evaluating validity consists of correlating not different measures of the same variable, as in concurrent validation; but measures of different variables. Formally, construct validation is identical to hypothesis-testing, except that the content of what is tested and the assumptions are reversed (Cronbach 1960; Schnaiberg 1970). In hypothesis-testing we assume valid measurement of variables in order to examine whether postulated relationships hold. In construct validation we assume that certain relationships do hold, in order to examine whether the measurement of the variables is

Table 7. Zero-Order Correlations between Leftist Radicalism Index
          (LRI) and Attitudes toward Different Groups as Promoters
          of Social Change in Chile

Group	Expected direction of correlation with LRI	Actual correlation
Rich	Negative	−.30*
Catholic Church	Negative	−.19**
Workers	Positive	.26*
Army	Negative	−.19**
Socialist party	Positive	.32*
Peasants	Positive	.22*
U.S. government	Negative	−.42*
Miners	Positive	.25*
National party (rightist)	Negative	−.26*
Landowners	Negative	−.26*
Communist party	Positive	.31*
Christian Democratic party (centrist)	Negative	−.42*
Large industrialists	Negative	−.29*

*p < .001

**p < .01

Source: Portes (1970b).

Figure 4. The Logic of Hypothesis-Testing and Construct Validation

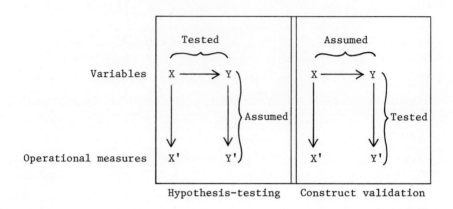

valid. Figure 4 summarizes the two alternative situations.

Although appropriate information for evaluating predictive or convergent validity is rare in secondary data,
almost all surveys contain sufficient information for
some form of construct validation. This process involves
searching for variable relationships which have been well
established by past research. If they do not hold in the
present data set, this fact may indicate invalid measurement.

Measures of individual modernity should correlate positively with socioeconomic status and years of urban living (Lerner 1958, Smith and Inkeles 1966); political
opinions should be significantly associated with objective socioeconomic status and subjective class identification (Portes 1970a); and the latter two variables
should be positively correlated (Centers 1949). Most
surveys contain information on occupational status, income, and education--indicators of socioeconomic position

which have been found to be consistently correlated
across nations. They furnish an excellent point of de-
parture for assessment of the quality of secondary data
since in most cases they should be at least moderately
intercorrelated.

This strategy of construct validation was applied to
Hamuy's 1962 Santiago survey, yielding the coefficients
presented in Table 8 (Portes 1970a). Correlations between education and occupational status and between education and income are only moderate; the correlation between occupational status and income is sizeable. Moreover, all three variables correlate positively with subjective class identification, as expected. Income, in
turn, correlates moderately with perceived adequacy of
income. The last two variables, plus occupational status, correlate significantly and predictably with satisfaction with life situation. Education does not correlate significantly with this last variable; that fact
is not surprising, since educational attainment is a
contingent (not a direct) indicator of present level of
living. Results therefore appear to furnish a fair
amount of initial support for the validity of these data.

It should be emphasized that construct validation depends on the assumption that two or more variables are
in fact empirically related. As a result, the strength
of the method is contingent on the number, quality, and
consistency of previous studies which have examined these
relationships. Moreover, the relationships that are assumed in order to establish construct validity cannot be
part of the set of hypotheses to be tested. This would
load the dice in the researcher's favor, because if the
relationships held, they would both validate the measures and support the hypothesis. If they did not, this
fact could be blamed on faulty measurement. Through
this procedure a hypothesis could never be conclusively

Table 8. Correlations between Variables in All-Santiago (Chile) Sample as Indicators of Construct Validity

Variables	-X1- Education	-X2- Occupational status	-X3- Income	-X4- Class self-identification	-X5- Perceived adequacy of salary	-X6- Satisfaction with present life
-X1-	—	.38*	.36*	.31*	--	.09**
-X2-		--	.65*	.48*	--	.26*
-X3-			--	.48*	.46*	.31*
-X4-				--	--	--
-X5-					--	.33*
-X6-						--

*p < .001

**n.s.

Source: International Data Library and Reference Service, Survey Research Center, University of California (Berkeley), "Stratification and Mobility in Four Latin American Cities--The Santiago Survey," survey conducted by Eduardo Hamuy (University of Chile), 1962.

rejected--a situation which would violate a basic canon
of scientific research.

Convergent and discriminant validity. The logic of convergent and construct validity have been combined elegantly in Campbell and Fiske's (1959) multitrait-multi-
method matrix. The general rationale of the procedure,
rather than the specific technique, is relevant to secondary data analysis. As defined above, convergent validity is the degree to which independent measures of the
same variable correlate. Construct validity, on the
other hand, is the degree to which independent measures
of different but theoretically related variables correlate. A combination of the two procedures yields the
notion of discriminant validity. Briefly stated, a correlation between related but different variables (construct validity) should be high, but not higher than correlation between two measures of the same variable (convergent validity). In other words, knowledge of scores
in one measure of a variable should help predict scores
in another such measure better than those in a theoretically close but different variable. Again, one measure
of a variable should be substitutable for another of the
same variable more perfectly than a measure of a different variable.

While seldom employed in survey analysis, the procedure outlined by Campbell and Fiske constitutes one of
the most logically compelling forms of assessing validity. Confidence can be placed in measures which have
passed this test for a number of reasons. First, the
measures have been required to correlate to the extent
that they tap the same basic variable. Second, they
have been required to correlate to the extent that they
are different but theoretically related. Third, the
measures must meet the final criterion that coefficients

in the first set be higher than those in the second.
Moreover, the procedure is not an unreachable methodological ideal; it can be applied to survey data with relative ease. Indeed, its applicability is far greater than
that of predictive or concurrent validation.

In the absence of available results from Latin America, Table 9 illustrates this method with data on measurement of individual modernity from a Chicago sample (Armer
and Schnaiberg 1971). Several waves of interviewing were
carried out in this study to assess response stability.
Of these, results for the first two have been analyzed.
In each case four measures of modernity were administered:
Smith and Inkeles's (1966), Kahl's (1968), Armer and
Youtz's (1971), and Schnaiberg's (1971). Socioeconomic
status was also measured in both waves. Srole's (1956)
anomie scale was administered in the first wave and Middleton's (1963) alienation scale in the second; both are
designed to measure personality dimensions conceptually
close to modernity.

Convergent validity was measured by average intercorrelations of scores on each modernity scale with the
others. As Table 9 shows, correlations were sizeable in
both waves. Construct validity was assessed by correlations between modernity scales and measures of anomie
and socioeconomic status (first wave) and alienation and
status (second wave). As expected, correlations of modernity scales with socioeconomic status were positive
in all cases, ranging from moderate to high. As expected, correlations of modernity with anomie and alienation
all were negative and sizeable.

Thus the first two validation criteria provide strong
evidence in support of the four modernity scales. But
examination of discriminant validity yields a different
result: convergence coefficients were not significantly
higher than construct ones, and the latter were higher

Table 9. Convergent and Discriminant Validity Coefficients of Modernity Scales in Uptown (Chicago) Sample (Corrected for Attenuation)

Modernity scales	WAVE I (N = 156)			WAVE II (N = 109)		
	Convergence:	Discriminance:		Convergence:	Discriminance:	
	Average r	Anomie	Socio-economic status	Average r	Alienation	Socio-economic status
Smith and Inkeles's	.79	-.67	.81	.78	-.86	.69
Kahl's	.77	-.85	.53	.71	-.90	.46
Schnaiberg's	.63	-.65	.61	.62	-.77	.63
Armer and Yountz's	.87	-.84	.71	.66	-.67	.53

Source: Armer and Schnaiberg (1972).

than the former as often as not. In other words, measures of anomie, alienation, and socioeconomic status sub-
stitute for or predict modernity scores in each of the
scales almost as well as or better than other modernity
scales. The authors conclude that this fact leads to rejection of the notion of modernity, at least as currently
measured, for the unique psychosocial syndrome it is supposed to represent cannot be empirically isolated from
other, conceptually close dimensions. In their words:
"Either 'modernity' does have some independent empirical
reality, and our present measures have not captured this;
or there is no culturally universal concept of 'modernity,' save in the minds of social scientists. Regardless
of which of these positions one takes, the notion that
social science has been able to develop a valid culturally universal measure of modernity appears to be false"
(Armer and Schnaiberg 1972:623).

Generalizability

When application of several of the above methods demonstrates satisfactory levels of reliability and validity, a set of data can be employed for a variety of purposes. The importance of the third parameter of data
evaluation, generalizability, is contingent upon the
uses to which the data are put. Generalizability refers
to the degree to which results are applicable to populations more inclusive than the sample from which data were
collected. In almost all cases, surveys aim at being
representative of a larger population (city or county,
province or region, or entire nations). High generalizability is always preferred. However, the importance of
meeting this goal depends on the function of the survey.
One conducts surveys either to estimate average values
of one or more variables in the larger population (the
descriptive function) or to analyze the extent to which

hypothesized relationships among a series of variables
hold empirically (the theory-building function [Hyman
1967]).

One almost always employs secondary data for the second rather than the first function. Paradoxically, data
representativeness is less important when our purpose is
to analyze relationships than when it is to estimate population parameters. When a survey is representative only
of the sample from which it was collected, its utility
for estimation of population values is nil; yet it may
still be quite useful for examining the strength of postulated relationships. A nonprobability sample of several thousand Lima residents would be practically worth-
less to establish means for years of education, income,
occupational prestige, and age for Lima, but it would be
invaluable to test whether hypotheses which hold in the
United States also hold among Peruvian respondents.
Thus, while generalizability is always desirable and
should be assessed, its relative absence should not deter
us from analysis when the data possess adequate levels of
reliability and validity, and when our purpose is theory-
building rather than description.

Statistical inference of univariate parameters or relationships with a larger population is only justified
when data have been collected from a probability sample--
that is, when each member of the relevant population has
had an equal chance of being selected as a respondent.
This requires the use of an adequate sampling framework
and maintenance of a constant sampling fraction for individuals at the end of the different stages of sampling
(Kish 1967). When evaluating the representativeness of
a sample, it is important to consider not only selection
procedures but also the sampling frameworks on which they
are based. In other words, one must establish clearly
whether the data are representative, and precisely what

they are representative of. For the 1969 study of lower-
class settlements in Santiago (discussed above), 10 percent simple random samples of family heads were drawn
from each area selected. Thus the data were representative of the four specific settlements, not of the entire
urban slum population.

Although the only means of establishing statistical
representativeness is through appropriate sampling procedures, one can employ another technique to establish
the tentative generalizability of results. If results
are available from larger and/or more representative
samples of the same population, these can be compared
with figures from our secondary data set. To the extent that results over a number of variables approximate
each other and follow the same trends, this fact would
provide initial evidence that our data are as generaliz-
able as those with which they are compared. This test
is often applied to probability samples as an independent
check on the representativeness of data.

The rationale of the technique is akin to that of concurrent validation, except that it does not involve mere
duplication, because the nonprobability data set may contain important variables not present in the more representative one. If both data sets contain measures of
exactly the same variables, obviously it would be unnecessary to use the less representative one. When a secondary data set is based on a population coterminous with
one of the administrative units recognized by the census
office, it is possible to employ census figures—presumably based on the entire population of the area—as the
criterion (Amaro 1968).

Table 10 illustrates this method with data from the
1969 Chilean slum settlement survey. Several variables
from this study were measured also in a larger survey by
the Latin American Population Center (CELAP), based on a

two-stage probability sample of the entire peripheral slum population of Santiago. A few other variables correspond to those in a nonprobability census of the entire adult population of a large number of slum settlements in Santiago, a survey conducted by the Chilean Corporation of Housing Services (CORHABIT). More than 70,000 slum settlers were interviewed in this census.

Comparison of figures between a specific data set and the census criterion should be based on two considerations: the closeness of results and the similarity of trends in variables for which several categories are reported. As Table 10 illustrates, results from the 1969 study largely meet these criteria. Parallel figures are fairly close. More important, distributions in such variables as educational attainment and type of occupation follow the same frequency patterns in both sets of results. Consequently, we can be cautiously optimistic that these data are representative, and we can conclude that the findings suggest tentative generalizability of results to the entire Santiago lower-class periphery.

The use of tests of significance to establish whether figures from a specific data set are in fact similar to those from a census criterion study is usually not recommended. Difference of means or difference of proportions tests employed for this purpose are very sensitive to sample size. Large numbers of cases in the data set and especially the census criterion reduce standard errors considerably, yielding statistical significance even if differences are quite small (Blalock 1960). Moreover, many researchers tend to employ the usual .05 or .01 levels of statistical significance for such tests without realizing that in this instance one should strive to minimize the probability of finding no difference when in fact one exists, rather than that of finding differences when in fact none exist. In other words, tests of

Table 10.   Comparison between Results of 1969 Study and Those Ob-
            tained by Larger and/or Representative Samples of
            Santiago's Peripheral Slum Population

Source	Relevant figure	Comparable figure from 1969 study N = 382
CELAP (I)	46.5% of respondents born in Santiago	42.0%
CELAP (I)	70.0% of respondents urban born (versus small-town and rural)	76.0%
CELAP (I)	22.8% of migrants arrived in or before 1939	23.9%
	22.7% of migrants arrived in or before 1949	20.7%
	28.2% of migrants arrived in or before 1959	35.1%
	19.4% of migrants arrived in or before 1964	15.0%
	3.5% of migrants arrived in 1965 or 1966	5.4% (1965 to 1968)
CELAP (I)	8.4% of respondents did not attend school	10.0%
	23.0% of respondents completed 1-3 years of elementary school	29.0%
	44.0% of respondents completed 4-6 years of elementary school	43.0%
	22.6% of respondents completed 1 or more years of high school	18.0%
CELAP (I)	84.0% of respondents report newspaper reading frequently or from time to time	87.0%
CELAP (I)	1.4% of working respondents employed in agriculture	1.6%
	30.4% of working respondents employed in industry	35.8%
	13.1% of working respondents employed in construction	13.1%
	14.2% of working respondents employed in commerce	16.8%
	8.0% of working respondents employed in skilled services (government and finance)	6.7%
	32.9% of working respondents employed in unskilled services	26.0%

CORHABIT   1.7% of working respondents employed in
                     primary occupations   1.6%
             49.0% of working respondents employed in
                     secondary occupations   48.9%
             49.3% of working respondents employed in
                     tertiary occupations   49.5%

CELAP (I)   27.0% of respondents are members of trade
                     unions   32.0%

CELAP (II)   76.1% of respondents above 19 are married,
                     legally or by common law   80.0%

Source: Portes (1972).

CELAP – Latin American Population Center, Survey of Family and Fertility
        in Marginal Areas of Greater Santiago 1966/67. Based on a two-
        stage area sample of slum settlements:

    I – Results for combined samples of male and female adult re-
        spondents (N = 1,231); inner-city tenements excluded.

   II – Results of first stage census from which the final sample
        was drawn (N = approximately 13,000); inner-city tenements
        excluded.

CORHABIT – National Corporation of Housing Services of Chile (Council
        of Popular Promotion), 1969 Census of Marginal Slum Settle-
        ments. Nonprobability sample based on interviews with all
        adult inhabitants in many peripheral slums of Santiago
        (N = 71,570).

significance in this special instance should be oriented
toward minimizing the chances of a Type I error (failing
to reject the null hypothesis when it is false) and not,
as is usually the case in hypothesis testing, the probability of a Type II error (rejecting the null hypothesis when
it is true). For this reason a much higher level of significance (at least .50) should be employed, which, with a
large number of cases, almost automatically will yield statistical significance. Because of excessive statistical
zeal, parallel results which are in fact substantially similar would thus be taken as evidence of nongeneralizability
of findings beyond the specific sample involved.

Conclusion

The discussion of procedures for evaluating reliability, validity, and representativeness has been aimed at
guiding the researcher's first steps in confronting an un-
familiar set of data. Obviously one should not plunge directly into analysis of a group of figures just because
they look interesting or relevant to one's topic. Doing
so entails the risk that final results will reflect error
and bias in the data, not actual empirical phenomena. Before carrying out substantive analyses on secondary information, it is necessary to evaluate its quality, a task in
which the techniques presented above should be helpful. A
good procedure is working in the same order as that outlined above: first, determining whether the information
is adequate for establishing reliability; then searching
for alternative means of validating relevant measures; and
finally checking the actual or potential generalizability
of results.

These steps omit procedures for establishing cross-
national validity or the conceptual equivalence of variables. While this is an interesting topic in itself, the
research strategy most frequently employed at present and

the one likely to yield the greatest results for theory-building in the social sciences is the use of survey data to test general hypotheses within specific settings.

It is not superfluous to add that survey analysis as a research tool has definite limitations. Studies conducted at this level must be complemented by research at the aggregate or macro-social level. While researchers have long been warned against the fallacy of inferring individual characteristics from aggregate correlations, it is no less true that survey analysts should not go beyond relationships at the individual level to attempt to predict or account for complex macro-societal processes. The fallacy of interpreting societal phenomena as mere additive results of individual characteristics should be avoided as much by users of secondary data as by those employing primary information.

NOTES

[1] For example, my own interviews and card decks on political attitudes in lower-class settlements of Santiago are deposited at the Center for Socio-Economic Studies, University of Chile.

[2] A sustained effort in this direction has been conducted in recent years by the *Latin American Research Review* and on a smaller scale by *Aportes* (France).

[3] Interested readers may find general treatments of measurement quality and representativeness in introductory research methods and attitude measurement texts. See Cronbach (1960), Selltiz *et al.* (1959), Festinger and Katz (1966), Miller (1970), Green (1954), and Campbell and Stanley (1963). Applications to cross-national primary data are found in Schnaiberg (1970), Smith and Inkeles (1966), Kahl (1968), and van Es and Wilkening (1970), among others.

[4] This technique is virtually identical to principal axes, except that unity (1.00) instead of communality estimates are inserted in the diagonal of the correlation matrix used for analysis in the factor analytic solution. Thus there is a possibility that the factor analysis would yield as many factors as items included in the original correlation matrix (Fruchter 1954).

REFERENCES

Amaro, Nelson
  1968   *Encuesta sobre el condicionamiento socio-cultural de la
          fecundidad en areas marginales urbanas-metropolitanas,
          ladino-rurales e indígenas tradicionales.* Guatemala:
          Ediciones ICAPF/IDESAC, Vol. 4.

Armer, Michael, and Youtz, Robert
  1971   Formal education and individual modernity in an African
          society. *American Journal of Sociology* 76:604-626.

_____, and Schnaiberg, Allan
  1972   Measuring individual modernity: a near myth. *American
          Sociological Review* 37:301-316.

Blair, Calvin P.
  1969   The nature of U.S. interest and involvement in Guatemala:
          an American view. In *Responsibilities of the foreign
          scholar to the local scholarly community.* Education and
          world affairs publication. Pp. 15-43.

Blalock, Hubert M.
  1960   *Social statistics.* New York.

Bohrnstedt, George W.
  1969   A quick method for determining the reliability and valid-
          ity of multiple-item scales. *American Sociological Re-
          view* 34:542-48.

Campbell, Donald T., and Fiske, Donald
  1959   Convergent and discriminant validation by the multitrait-
          multimethod matrix. *Psychological Bulletin* 56:81-105.

Campbell, Donald T., and Stanley, Julian C.
  1963   *Experimental and quasi-experimental designs for research.*
          Chicago.

Centers, Richard.
  1949   *The psychology of social classes.* Princeton, N.J.

Cronbach, Lee
  1960   *Essentials of psychological testing.* 2nd ed. New York.

Cutwright, Phillips
  1963   National political development: measurement and analysis.
          American Sociological Review 28:253-64.

Festinger, Leon, and Katz, Daniel
  1966   *Research methods in the behavioral sciences.* New York.

Form, William H.
1971   Field problems in comparative research: the politics
of distrust. Paper presented at the Conference on Methodological Problems in Comparative Sociological Research,
Institute for Comparative Sociology. Bloomington, Ind.

Fruchter, Benjamin
1954   *Introduction to factor analysis.* Princeton, N.J.

Graciarena, Jorge
1965   Algunas consideraciones sobre la cooperación internacional
y el desarrollo reciente de la investigación sociológica.
Revista Latino-Americana de Sociología 2:231-42.

Green, Bert F.
1954   Attitude measurement. In *Handbook of social psychology,*
I, Gardner Lindzey, ed. New York.

Haller, Archibald O.
1969   Stability of variables in a backward region. Mimeo MS, Department of Sociology, University of Wisconsin, Madison,
Wis.

Horowitz, Irving L.
1967   *The rise and fall of Project Camelot.* Cambridge, Mass.

Hyman, Herbert
1967   *Survey design and analysis.* New York.

Janowitz, Morris and Segal, David R.
1970   Social cleavage and party affiliation: Germany, Great
Britain, and the United States. In *Political conflict,*
M. Janowitz, ed. Chicago.

Kahl, Joseph A.
1968   *The measurement of modernism: a study of values in Brazil
and Mexico.* Austin, Tex.

Kish, Leslie
1967   *Survey sampling.* New York.

Lerner, Daniel
1958   *The passing of traditional society: modernizing the
Middle East.* Glencoe, Ill.

McClelland, David C.
1967   *The achieving society.* New York.

Middleton, Russell
1963   Alienation, race, and education. *American Sociological
Review* 28:973-77.

Miller, Delbert C.
    1970   *Handbook of research design and social measurement.*   2nd
            ed. New York.

Nagel, Ernst
    1970   *The structure of science.*   New York.

Portes, Alejandro
    1970a   Leftist radicalism in Chile: a test of three hypotheses.
            Comparative Politics 2:251-74.
    1970b   Radicalism in the slum: a study of political attitudes
            in Chilean lower-class settlements. Ph.D. dissertation,
            University of Wisconsin.
    1972a   Society's perception of the sociologist and its impact
            on cross-national research. *Rural Sociology* 37:27-42.
    1972b   Status inconsistency and lower-class leftist radicalism.
            Sociological Quarterly 13:361-82.
    1973   The factorial structure of modernity: empirical replications
            and a critique. *American Journal of Sociology* 79:15-44.

Russett, Bruce M., *et al.*
    1964   *World handbook of political and social indicators.*   New
            Haven, Conn.

Schmitter, Philippe C.
    1969   New strategies for the comparative analysis of Latin
            American politics. *Latin American Research Review* 4:83-
            110.

Schnaiberg, Allan
    1970   Measuring modernism: theoretical and empirical explora-
            tions. *American Journal of Sociology* 76:399-425.

Selltiz, Claire; Jahoda, Marie; Deutsch, Morton; and Cook, Stuart W.
    1959   *Research methods in social relations.*   New York.

Selser, Gregorio
    1966   *Espionaje en América Latina.*   Buenos Aires.

Smith, David H., and Inkeles, Alex
    1966   The OM scale: a comparative socio-psychological measure
            of individual modernity. *Sociometry* 29:353-77.

Srole, Leo F.
    1956   Social integration: certain corollaries. *American Socio-
            logical Review* 21:709-16.

Strauss, Murray A.
    1969   A phenomenal identity and conceptual equivalence of meas-
            urement in cross-national comparative research. *Journal
            of Marriage and the Family* 31:233-41.

van Es, John C., and Wilkening, Eugene A.
    1970   Response stability in survey research: a cross-cultural
            comparison. *Rural Sociology* 35:191–205.

Whyte, William F.
    1969   The role of the U.S. professor in developing countries.
            American Sociologist 4:19–28.

APPENDIX

Data Banks Containing Latin American Materials

Banks are ordered alphabetically. The editors have attempted to list and describe briefly all data banks currently containing Latin American materials. Some of the information was provided by archive directors in personal correspondence; information solicited from other banks, regrettably, was not supplied.

BUREAU OF APPLIED SOCIAL RESEARCH
Columbia University
605 West 115th Street
New York, New York 10025

Research is being conducted in Argentina, Brazil, and Colombia by the Bureau and the United Nations. In 1972 the Bureau collected sample survey data for these countries on the "brain drain." Future studies on the same topic may include Chile, Venezuela, Uruguay, Jamaica, Trinidad, and Tobago.

CENTER OF SOCIAL AND POLITICAL DATA
Departamento de Ciência Política
Universidade Federal de Minas Gerais
Belo Horizonte, Minas Gerais
Brazil

Bank contains aggregate data sets using the Brazilian *município* as the unit of data collection. Materials are useful for studies of political development, and they include socioeconomic information gleaned from various censuses, voting statistics, and policy process data at the local, state, and national levels.

The Center plans to expand its holdings to include material on other Latin American countries, other collection units, and sample survey data. Operations began in 1968, and currently available data are largely for the 1940–69 period. Some data sets include all Brazilian censuses from 1890 to 1960.

DATA AND PROGRAM LIBRARY SERVICE
Room 4451
Social Science Building
University of Wisconsin
Madison, Wisconsin 53706

Data holdings on Latin America contain both survey and aggregate
types. In addition to materials obtained from the Inter-University
Consortium for Political Research at Ann Arbor (see entry) and the
International Data Library and Reference Service at Berkeley (see
entry), Wisconsin's archive possesses unique data sets.

Aggregate data cover such topics as social, economic, and political development; demography; the diffusion of innovation; and
slave ship arrivals at Rio de Janeiro (1775-1811). Most Latin American countries are included in many of the aggregate data sets; specialized collections focus on Argentina, Brazil, and Mexico.

Survey material covers such areas as political and career expectations of medical students in Argentina; social stratification and
mobility in Argentina and Chile; migration patterns in Brazil;
career values of urban workers in Brazil and Mexico; aspirations
and fears of the citizenry in Brazil, Chile, the Dominican Republic,
and Panama; patterns of rural leadership in Brazil; Spanish language
training for Indian children in Peru. Most surveys were conducted
during the 1960's.

DIMENSIONALITY OF NATIONS PROJECT
University of Hawaii
2500 Campus Road
Honolulu, Hawaii 96822

Data from the Dimensionality of Nations (DON) project are dis-
tributed by the Inter-University Consortium for Political Research
at the University of Michigan (see entry). The data sets for the
DON project involve most nations of the world around 1955, and they
are primarily of an aggregate nature. Data cover a variety of attributes such as urbanization, economic characteristics, and political and cultural information.

ECONOMIC GROWTH CENTER
Department of Economics
Yale University
Box 1987, Yale Station
New Haven, Connecticut 06520

At present the Center does not have any systematic compilation
of Latin American data. Studies completed or in progress treat
Argentina, Chile, Colombia, Brazil, and Mexico.

HUMAN RELATIONS AREA FILES
Yale University
P.O. Box 2054, Yale Station
New Haven, Connecticut 06520

HRAF is concerned principally with reorganizing published (and
some unpublished) material on ethnic groups, social structure,
social organization, culture, and kinship patterns. Researchers
who wish to perform quantitative analyses can easily convert these
data to machine-readable form.

INTERNATIONAL DATA LIBRARY AND REFERENCE SERVICE
Survey Research Center
University of California
2220 Piedmont Avenue
Berkeley, California 94720

This excellent data bank has extensive sample survey holdings
for Latin America. Topics include attitudes toward family planning, career values, mental health, rural-urban migrations, social
mobility, agricultural development, aspirations of slum dwellers,
race relations, voting behavior, political ideology, urbanization,
education, communication, political culture, bureaucracy, labor,
youth, and international outlooks.

The following Latin American countries and areas are represented
in these data sets: Argentina, Brazil, Chile, Colombia, Costa
Rica, Cuba, Ecuador, El Salvador, Guatemala, Mexico, Panama, Paraguay, Peru, Puerto Rico, Uruguay, Venezuela, and the West Indies.

Data for the numerous sample survey studies were gathered from
the early 1950's to the late 1960's. The Library also contains
aggregate data sets for a few Latin American nations, notably Brazil.

INTERNATIONAL DEVELOPMENT DATA BANK
426 South Kedzie Hall
Michigan State University
East Lansing, Michigan 48823

This repository contains sample survey material from studies
conducted in Latin America. Materials relate to issues of modernization and development. (No other information supplied.)

INTERSOCIETAL INFORMATION CENTER
Northwestern University
1818 Sheridan Road
Evanston, Illinois 60201

The Center contains a variety of cross-national aggregate data
sets, including the Five-Nation Study of Almond and Verba (see
following entry). The archive also has microfilm texts on political parties in Argentina.

INTER-UNIVERSITY CONSORTIUM FOR POLITICAL RESEARCH
Institute for Social Research
P.O. Box 1248
Ann Arbor, Michigan 48106

The Survey Research Center of the ISR has several sample survey
studies dealing with Latin America, including Cantril's survey of
individual and collective fears and aspirations, which contains data
collected in the early 1960's. Other studies span a broad range of
topics, such as family planning, the values and attitudes of university students, social class and mobility, voting, political violence,
attitudes regarding work and education, political apathy, modernity,
and manager-worker relations. Data were gathered for most studies
between 1955 and 1965, and the following countries are represented:
Argentina, Brazil, Chile, Colombia, Cuba, the Dominican Republic,
Mexico, Panama, Paraguay, Puerto Rico, and Uruguay.

The International Relations Archive contains aggregate data sets
of worldwide scope on numerous subjects, and most data packages include material on Latin American countries. The archive has data
pertaining to such topics as political and economic development;
modernization; political stability/instability; center-periphery
relations; military alliances, expenditures, and equipment transfers;
conflict and violence; and the interactions of United Nations delegates.

The Center for Political Studies of the ISR is conducting surveys
in selected Latin American countries. Brazil is the focus of recent

work, and tentative plans involve surveys in Chile and Argentina. Data for these studies, however, will not be available for general distribution for several years.

LABORATORY FOR POLITICAL RESEARCH
Department of Political Science
University of Iowa
Iowa City, Iowa 52240

The Laboratory houses election statistics, roll-call data, and materials on the socioeconomic backgrounds and career patterns of politicians in Argentina.

Also included in the Laboratory's archive are survey materials on attitudes toward economic and political problems in Uruguay (1965-67) and Brazil (1968-69). Many of the public opinion survey data originate in the Roper Center (see entry).

LATIN AMERICAN DATA BANK
107 Peabody Hall
University of Florida
Gainesville, Florida 32601

This archive contains the first census data bank established in the United States for the storage of Latin American materials. It contains political, social, and economic data, plus census files on population, housing, agriculture, industry, and commerce. The Data Bank also includes voting statistics, time-sequence population data, budgetary information, and aggregate statistics on education and labor.

The following countries are represented in the archive: Argentina, Bolivia, Brazil, Chile, Colombia, Costa Rica, Cuba, the Dominican Republic, Ecuador, El Salvador, Guatemala, Haiti, Honduras, Mexico, Nicaragua, Panama, Paraguay, Peru, Uruguay, and Venezuela.

Time frames for the material vary from country to country and differ according to the kind of data collected.

MIT SOCIAL SCIENCE DATA BANK
Center for International Studies
E53-365, Hermann Building
Massachusetts Institute of Technology
Cambridge, Massachusetts 02139

The data bank has survey material on social and political behavior, public opinion, and urban affairs. Some of the surveys originate in the Roper Center (see entry below); others have been conducted by the Center for International Studies at MIT. Latin American countries are represented. All data available must be obtained through the Roper Center.

POLITICAL SCIENCE DATA ARCHIVE
Woodburn Hall, Room 248
Indiana University
Bloomington, Indiana 47401

The Archive houses the tapes for numerous studies on Latin American politics. Surveys include attitudes of the general population on the following topics: work and education, social stratification and social mobility, political violence, agrarian reform, family planning, and voting. More specialized surveys include the attitudes, values, and beliefs of students, union leaders, and union members.

Data were collected in the early and mid 1960's, and the following countries are represented: Argentina, Brazil, Chile, Colombia, Cuba, Mexico, Puerto Rico, Uruguay, and Venezuela. Aggregate data sets available from the Inter-University Consortium for Political Research (see entry) can also be found here.

ROPER PUBLIC OPINION RESEARCH CENTER
Williams College
P.O. Box 624
Williamstown, Massachusetts 01267

The Center has a wide assortment of sample survey data on such diverse topics as domestic and international politics, economics, education, commerce, public health and welfare, communications, employment, social organizations, community relations, religion, intergroup relations, urbanization, sports, entertainment, social classes, and population growth.

The following Latin American countries are represented in the Roper data: Argentina, Bolivia, Brazil, Chile, Colombia, the Dominican Republic, Ecuador, El Salvador, Guatemala, Honduras, Mexico,

Nicaragua, Panama, Peru, Puerto Rico, Uruguay, and Venezuela.

Surveys currently available were carried out in the middle 1950's through the late 1960's, for the most part.

SCHOOL OF PUBLIC HEALTH AND ADMINISTRATIVE MEDICINE:
RESEARCH ARCHIVE
Columbia University
630 West 168th Street
New York, New York 10032

This archive is limited to survey data on public health and administrative medicine. Puerto Rico is the only Latin American area currently represented.

Data Banks in the Formative Stage

Jorge I. Domínguez of the Center for International Affairs at Harvard University is currently organizing a data bank on Chile, Cuba, Mexico, and Venezuela. The materials will cover the whole period since independence.

The Consejo Latinoamericano de Ciencias Sociales (CLACSO) in 1972 abandoned its attempt to organize data archives.

At least two other Latin American institutions have considered organizing machine-readable data banks—the Fundación Bariloche and the Instituto Torcuato di Tella, both in Buenos Aires. As of August, 1972, neither of the projected banks was operational.

Notes on Contributors

ROBERT S. BYARS is assistant professor of political science and director of research for the Center for Latin American Studies, University of Illinois, Urbana. Two of his recent articles concerning styles of political leadership have appeared in *Comparative Political Studies*. His current research interests concern the urban poor and political change in Latin America, as reflected in his "Culture, Politics, and the Urban Factory Worker in Brazil," in *Latin American Modernization Problems* (1973), edited by Robert E. Scott.

JOSEPH L. LOVE is the author of *Rio Grande do Sul and Brazilian Regionalism, 1882-1930* (1971). He is associate professor of history at the University of Illinois, Urbana, and has also published various articles on Brazilian and Latin American history. He is interested in regional dimensions of the economic and political history of Brazil, and in messianic movements in Latin America.

PETER H. SMITH, professor of history at the University of Wisconsin, is currently a visiting member at the Institute for Advanced Study in Princeton. His research interests focus on political change in Latin America since the late nineteenth century, particularly in Argentina and Mexico. He is the author of *Politics and Beef in Argentina* (1969).

ROBERT C. HUNT is associate professor of anthropology, Brandeis University. His special interests include politics, economic exchanges, household organization, and the epistemology of the comparative method. He and his wife have coauthored "Irrigation, Conflict, and Politics: A Mexican Case," which will appear in *Irrigation's Impact on Society*, edited by Downing and Gibson.

GEORGE L. COWGILL is engaged in a large-scale study of the ancient city of Teotihuacán, Mexico, in association with René Millon of the University of Rochester. He is associate professor of anthropology at Brandeis University. His special interests include mathematical and computer methods in archaeology and anthropology, study of the origins and nature of early New and Old World civilizations, and archaeological method and theory.

HOWARD L. GAUTHIER is professor of geography at Ohio State University. He has served as a senior consultant to the Instituto Brasileiro de Geografia, Ministério de Planejamento. Recent publications include a book on transportation geography, articles on growth poles in regional planning, and a study of the Appalachian highway development program.

CLIFFORD KAUFMAN, associate professor of political science at Wayne State University, is especially interested in comparative urban politics. An article on political involvement of the poor in Mexico City has appeared in *Comparative Political Studies*, and the poor's mass support for national political institutions is examined in his contribution to the forthcoming *Studying Politics in Latin America*, edited by Coleman and Sindup.

ALEJANDRO PORTES is associate professor of sociology at the University of Texas. He was born in Cuba, and one of his research interests remains the study of assimilation of foreign minorities into U.S. society. He is presently a Fellow of the Council on Foreign Relations; his research subject is emigration of professionals to the United States from Argentina and Mexico.